More Praise for *Walking to Listen*

"In this moving and deeply introspective memoir, Forsthoefel writes about the uncertainties, melodramas, ambiguities, and loneliness of youth . . . Forsthoefel's walk becomes a meditation on vulnerability, trust, and the tragedy of suburban and rural alienation . . . [His] conversation with America is fascinating, terrifying, mundane, and at times heartbreaking, but ultimately transformative and wise."
—*Publishers Weekly*

"Whoever you are, wherever you're from, you need to read this book. You need to read it for its searing honesty, its hopefulness, and its grace. You need to read it because its story is your story, too. Andrew Forsthoefel walked across a continent to listen to strangers and learn from them. There is great wisdom in his footfalls, and you are holding it in your hands." —Sue Halpern, author of *A Dog Walks Into a Nursing Home*

"Forsthoefel offers moments of genuine kinship and transcendence . . . Millennial ennui turns into a search for meaning in an intriguing portrait of America." —*Kirkus Reviews*

"In a world of congestion and noise, Andrew Forsthoefel has written a book that opens up an ocean of sublime reflective space. As refreshing as it is timeless and endearing, Forsthoefel deftly shifts between his inner being and the people's lives that flow through him, mile by mile. His enduring determination to understand others is infectious, and like the many walks of life who embrace him into their homes and hearts, we cannot help but be disarmed of any lingering cynicism or distrust. Ultimately Forsthoefel inspires us to be more curious in life and less offended—a virtuous philosophy in what appears to be an age of increasing polarity in American society." —Tim Cope, award-winning author of *On the Trail of Genghis Khan*

"Soulful ... [Forsthoefel's] openness provides a window into the extraordinary lessons to be learned from ordinary people. This is a memorable and heartfelt exploration of what it takes to hike 4,000 miles across the country and how one young man learned to walk without fear into his future." —*Booklist*

"If you look at Andrew Forsthoefel's journey on a map, it's a tiny thread, an infinitesimal crack, yet it's enough to break loose America's stories: the open hearts and closed minds, the love and the fear, the beauty and danger, the wisdom." —Jay Allison, producer of *The Moth Radio Hour*

"[Forsthoefel's] observations are frank, sometimes humorous and always thoughtful. The metaphors he employs to illuminate his experiences are vivid and powerful. And the lessons he takes away from his interactions with people of all walks of life are extraordinary, reshaping his very existence. Reading about it will undoubtedly transform his audience as well." —*Shelf Awareness*

"With a name like Forsthoefel, it had better be good. And it is, combining the best humanistic aspects of Walt Whitman, Barry Lopez, John Steinbeck, William Least Heat-Moon, and Marco Polo." —Albert Podell, author of *Around the World in 50 Years*

ANDREW FORSTHOEFEL

WALKING
TO
LISTEN

4,000 MILES ACROSS AMERICA, ONE STORY AT A TIME

BLOOMSBURY PUBLISHING

NEW YORK · LONDON · OXFORD · NEW DELHI · SYDNEY

BLOOMSBURY PUBLISHING
Bloomsbury Publishing Inc.
1385 Broadway, New York, NY 10018, USA

BLOOMSBURY, BLOOMSBURY PUBLISHING, and the Diana logo are trademarks
of Bloomsbury Publishing Plc

First published in the United States 2017
This paperback edition published 2018

ISBN: HB: 978-1-63286-700-1; eBook: 978-1-63286-702-5; PB: 978-1-63286-701-8

LIBRARY OF CONGRESS CATALOGING-IN-PUBLICATION DATA

Names: Forsthoefel, Andrew, author.
Title: Walking to listen : 4,000 miles across America, one story at a time /
Andrew Forsthoefel.
Description: New York : Bloomsbury USA, an imprint of Bloomsbury Publishing, Plc,
[2017] | Includes bibliographical references and index.
Identifiers: LCCN 2016011678 (print) | LCCN 2016023810 (ebook) |
ISBN 9781632867001 (hardcover : alk. paper) | ISBN 9781632867025 (ePub) |
ISBN 9781632867025 (eBook)
Subjects: LCSH: Forsthoefel, Andrew—Travel—United States. | Hiking—United
States. | Hikers—United States—Biography. | Social psychology—United States. |
Interviews—United States. | United States—Description and travel.
Classification: LCC GV199.92.F675 A3 2017 (print) | LCC GV199.92.F675 (ebook) |
DDC 796.510973—dc23
LC record available at https://lccn.loc.gov/2016011678

2 4 6 8 10 9 7 5 3 1

Typeset by RefineCatch Limited, Bungay, Suffolk
Printed and bound in the U.S.A. by Berryville Graphics Inc., Berryville, Virginia

To find out more about our authors and books visit www.bloomsbury.com
and sign up for our newsletters.

Bloomsbury books may be purchased for business or promotional use.
For information on bulk purchases please contact Macmillan Corporate
and Premium Sales Department at specialmarkets@macmillan.com.

For my mother, Therese Jornlin.
Impossible to say what I owe you, but I do my
best with thank you.
I will hear your prayers forever.

I think I will do nothing for a long time but listen,
And accrue what I hear into myself . . . and let sounds contribute
toward me.
—*Walt Whitman*

You, yesterday's boy,
to whom confusion came:
Listen, lest you forget who you are.
—*Rainer Maria Rilke*

Was it I who spoke? Was I not also a listener?
—*Kahlil Gibran*

Author's Note

I recorded eighty-five hours of interviews while walking across the United States, which I've edited to create most of the dialogue in this book. However, there were many conversations that went unrecorded over the course of my year on the road, exchanges that happened too fast to catch or interactions that precluded the use of an audio recorder for various reasons. I've included several of these moments as scenes in this book, consulting the notes in my travel journal to recreate the conversations. For all dialogue, I've limited my own editing of these voices as much as possible, attempting to stay true to what people said and how they said it.

I used real names with a few exceptions, noted here. The following are pseudonyms: "Dan," "Frank," "Simon," "Don," "Mae," "Eric," "Manny," "Jay," "Maia," "Veronica," "Bea," "Mayor Rousseau," "Phil," and "Henry."

Prologue

"Remember me."

The hills of northeastern Georgia shimmered with dawn light, sea green, strung together by the black thread of the highway. I was on this highway again, walking alone through the winter, filthy and far from home, virtually clueless as to what lay ahead. But that actually seemed okay today. Familiar. It was a kind of home in its own way right now, this feeling of familiarity, the sense that I actually belonged here, wherever I happened to be. It was getting steadier, that feeling, and with each day on the road I believed it a little more. Maybe someday it'd be unshakeable, a kind of knowing that went beyond believing. I walked a mile in the unseasonable December warmth, and then another, and another, and it felt like I was being held between two great hands—the high sky above and the fertile ground all around. No effort this morning, just floating. *Who am I today?* I wondered silently. *Who do I want to be?* The answer could've been anything, with so much space all around me, so much unknown.

I'd only been walking for two months, but it seemed like there'd never been anything else but this. Everything that had come before was fading into my footsteps: my childhood, nothing but whispers and flashes; adolescence, a blurry wash marked by a single vivid streak, the divorce; memories of college that felt ancient, as those passed on by an ancestor, or someone else long dead; and then my doomed job on the lobster boat, like a story told so late at night it actually might've just been a dream. It all felt so far away, almost forgotten. Only the cars were close now, and the trucks, and if they got too close they would kill me. Their airstreams were monstrous invisible tongues, licking me good-bye over and over again all day long.

Around eight A.M. there was a handwritten love letter on the shoulder, highway trash. I picked it up and read. "Dear Caleb, Happy two months! I love you so much! It's been great like really. I know we're going to have more great times together."

It was something to think about. Not that I needed it. There's a lot to think about when you're walking alone on the highway all day. I tended to think about people—the people I'd met so far, the people I loved. And food. I thought a lot about food. Now, though, I thought about Caleb and his girl, and about how two months can seem like a lifetime when you're in love, or walking across a country, and how it all goes so fast until there's nothing left to go, and it's gone. "You are my absolute everything. Im sittin here missin you as usual. I hope your doing the same." What once had been a love letter was now litter, and this would soon disintegrate back into the earth. I wasn't that much different—destined to disintegrate someday. I placed the love letter back onto the grass. Didn't seem right to keep it.

I'd spent the night before in a barn owned by a chicken farmer named Diane. Her house was nestled in a stand of pines at the end of a long dirt driveway. A row of Christmas candy canes led me up to the front door. It was just before dark when I knocked, and as always, my breath turned shallow. *Who's going to answer?* This was the trickiest part, finding a safe place to sleep at night. *Are they going to scream at me? Bring out the dogs?* An older woman opened the door. I started talking before she could slam it.

"Hi, my name's Andrew. I'm walking across America listening to people's stories. I started two months ago in Pennsylvania and

I'm heading to California. Do you mind if I camp out in your yard?"

I always tried to pretend there was nothing unusual about a stranger knocking on someone's door at night—in 2011, no less. These days, that kind of thing happened online, safely scrubbed of all vulnerability. Interacting with strangers in the real world beyond the realm of superficial pleasantries, that was an endangered experience. Maybe it'd go extinct someday and we'd never have to feel the uncertainty I was feeling now, the nakedness. I was never as uncomfortable as I was when I knocked on a stranger's door, but at the same time, I never felt so alive, electrified by the unknown world on the other side, waiting to make itself known to me as soon as the door opened, any second now. *Just act normal. Smile.* This time it worked. Diane, still standing in the doorway, said I could camp on her front lawn.

The reds and whites of the electric candy canes bled like watercolors into my tent. The winter grass was soft beneath me, the night air almost warm. All my tension began to dissipate—the stress of walking on a highway all day, the muscle ache—but then I heard Diane's voice outside.

"Andrew? You in there? I'm so sorry, honey, but you can't stay here tonight."

I poked my head out of the tent, and Diane explained that she'd called her husband to let him know about me, and he hadn't taken the news well. He wanted me off the property immediately.

"He's not always like this," Diane said. "He's a veteran, and he got meaner when he came back from Vietnam. He would think you were going to break into the house at night and cut him up into little pieces."

I hated to be misunderstood like this, perceived as some kind of threat. All it would've taken was the slightest measure of openness, a single conversation, and her husband and I might've met each other somewhere beyond fear. It had already happened like that with so many strangers since I'd left home. Not this time, though, but I couldn't blame the guy. Knocking on a stranger's door isn't easy, but opening the door when a stranger knocks isn't easy, either. And then letting that stranger camp out on your lawn? Or sleep on your couch, with your kids in the other room and your beloved by your side, all of you soon to be made utterly defenseless by the unconsciousness of sleep? I'm not sure I would've taken me in. I couldn't believe so many people already had.

Diane felt bad. She offered to drive me to a family barn a mile back east from where I'd come. I was walking west, so it'd be an extra mile for the next day, but I didn't mind. I broke camp and tossed everything in Diane's car, expecting to see her husband barreling down the driveway at any second, but he never did come.

The barn was right next to the road. Diane dropped me off and drove away. I sat down in a mess of straw, hidden by the warm, dark night. All my anxiety loosed itself back into the black sky, and the cars flew by me like earthbound comets, one every minute or so. I'd walked all day, and now I could be still. I'd been exposed, and now I was invisible, protected. Suddenly, unexpectedly, everything felt simple and profoundly beautiful: the moon, the barn, the bananas for dinner. Somehow even my sweat and grime pleased me. I couldn't understand it. *Why this subtle peace? How to hold on?* "Satisfied," I wrote in my journal. "Can't explain why, but so satisfied." One of Walt Whitman's verses from *Leaves of Grass* came to mind: "I cannot define my satisfaction . . . yet it is so, / I cannot define my life . . . yet it is so."

My breath rose and fell, rose and fell. I wasn't doing any of it. It was all just happening, and I thought that maybe I didn't have to become anything more than what I already was. That it would all just happen, like my breath. That it was already happening. Sitting in the straw, it was spontaneously clear that there was nowhere else to be but here, and nothing else to do but this, breathe the air and witness the night, alone and yet not.

The feeling didn't last. I woke up the next morning anxious to get walking again, toward what, I didn't quite know. Whatever it was, it seemed far away.

After an hour or two I made it to the little town of Royston, where my friend Penn met me at a diner for breakfast. He was the first old friend I'd seen since leaving home, and I'd been looking forward to it. We laughed a lot in our booth, like we always used to in high school, and I caught a glimpse of what it might've been like to do this walk with somebody else, not just on my own. It was hard to watch him drive off.

Even still, the solitude felt important. It scared me, but that's exactly why I'd chosen it. I didn't want to be afraid of the very thing I'd be stuck with for the rest of my life: myself. I'd much rather enjoy it, and to enjoy it, it seemed I had to learn it and know it well. Solitude was the best place to do that work.

I was walking out of Royston when an old man stopped me on the sidewalk outside his antiques shop. His molars were filled with gold. A red polo shirt stretched tightly across his massive chest—I could tell he'd once been an ox—and he'd combed his white hair back neatly.

"Where are you going?" he asked me, nodding at my backpack.

I said I was just walking, east to west, probably all the way across the United States but I wasn't sure yet. I showed him the sign I wore on my backpack—WALKING TO LISTEN—and explained that

I was gathering stories and advice from the people I met along the way. The old man was intrigued, and we talked for a while on the sidewalk. The conversation was even better than breakfast, food for a soul that hungered for company, because Penn was gone and I was alone again and I wasn't ready for that yet. The solitude had been so satisfying the night before, but now it was sending me into a quiet panic. It happened that way sometimes, when all I wanted was to talk to somebody, or even just listen; anyone would do, anyone at all. That morning, it was the old man. We didn't talk about anything special, but that was fine because, for me, it wasn't really about what was being said. It was just about being together, that was all—two Americans in a little town in Georgia; two humans on a big, blue planet; two earthlings in a vast cosmos.

When I began my cross-country walkabout, I didn't know where I was going, how long I'd be gone, or what would happen along the way. I knew how I'd get there, though: I'd walk. And I knew why I was walking: I wanted to learn what it actually meant to come of age, to transform into the adult who would carry me through the rest of my life. I wanted to meet that man. Who was he? What did he know? How would he finally become himself, and where did he belong?

Sometimes, this search felt urgent. I was twenty-three years old. Soon, I'd be thirty-three, and then forty-three, and I had no idea how I was going to do it, though my life was already in motion. There was no turning back. I needed information and experience, some kind of rudder that would help me navigate whatever lay ahead.

I wore the WALKING TO LISTEN sign because I hoped people would help guide me through these questions, and others. Everyone was to be my teacher in some way, that's how I saw it. The walk would be like a graduate program in the human experience, an initiation into the adulthood I still felt wasn't mine. I'd brought along an audio recorder to capture whatever it was people had to say. Over and over again I asked, "What would you tell your twenty-three-year-old self?" I figured if I walked well and listened close, there was a chance I'd find out what I needed to know. I'd walked over a million footsteps to get to Royston, Georgia, and I'd walk millions more if I had to.

When I told the man I had to get going, he asked me to wait. He rushed into his shop and came out a few seconds later holding a polished cane the color of dark amber. "It's strong," he said. "Hickory wood. Good for hitting the dogs away." He held it out for me to take. "Remember me."

I imagined the old man waking up that morning in the glow of dawn, walking out to the front porch with his black coffee steaming. I could see him staring in silence at the winter hills. What thoughts greeted him when he awoke each day? Maybe he felt he'd been a young man just a few days before, and that it had all gone so quickly, and that there was so much forgotten. Maybe he thought he'd be forgotten, too.

His name was Ernest Jackson. Four years later, I do remember him, but he's fading fast. He's getting hazier and hazier in my mind, and soon I won't be able to recall anything at all about him. This forgetting disturbs me—the good-bye implied by hello, the inevitable letting go, the dying that makes living possible. Best to remember everything while I still can, especially them, all the people I met on this walk, and the ones who came before and after, too. In remembering them, I remember myself—how they've contributed to the making of me, and I to the making of them, and how we continue to make one another even now. I remember how impossible it is to be truly alone (though loneliness would have me believe otherwise), how nothing exists on its own. I remember that

I am nothing if not connected to all of these people, and to you, whoever you are, and that we're all walking together, like it or not, and that to deny this is just another form of forgetting. But maybe the forgetting is a part of the remembering. After all, how can I remember if I haven't forgotten first?

"Remember me," Ernest Jackson said, and that's what I want to do here. Remember.

KEVIN JORNLIN, *Wells Fargo area manager and one of my uncles*
CHADDS FORD, PENNSYLVANIA, *at the kitchen table in my mom's house*
OCTOBER, *right before I set out to walk*

"You can eat maggots out there on the road, you know. They have great protein. And drink your own urine. It'll keep you hydrated. I want urine and maggots or else you failed."

Chapter One

"Don't trust anybody."

I was walking on the train tracks outside Kennett Square, Pennsylvania, when I first saw them, four men in the distance sitting on the rails. I looked around: forest to the north, vacant industrial lots to the south, no one else in sight and no one in shouting distance. *Who hangs out on the train tracks outside of town?* Two hours into my walk, seven miles from home, and I was going to get robbed, shot, and left for dead. This seemed quite certain. *Maybe I should turn back*, I thought, but my feet kept moving.

The same set of train tracks ran right through my backyard, and the plan had been to follow them for twenty-five miles into Maryland. It was better than walking on the road. I wasn't ready for the road on day one. Too much exposure. Too much noise. The train tracks wended through a serene otherworld—forests and farmland and suburban backyards. Only an occasional freight train split the silence, and it ran safely slow, about as fast as I could run. It was a good place to start the walk. Even the industrial mess outside town had seemed peaceful, until now, with the four men ahead. One of them noticed me, and then the other three turned their heads my way. *Shit.*

Two hours earlier, my mom's landlord, Bob, had chased me down in his car to tell me I shouldn't be doing this. I didn't recognize him when he first pulled off the road. Whoever he was, I assumed he must've seen my WALKING TO LISTEN sign. Clearly he had something important to tell me because he had to bushwhack through dense underbrush to reach me.

Then I saw that it was Bob—rider of motorcycles, builder of houses, unsmiling veteran of the Philadelphia police force. He wore a sharp goatee and a grim look on his face. But then again he always wore that look. Bob kept an old trailer in our backyard—his backyard, technically—and he was often out there tinkering in his graveyard of derelict machinery, piling more branches on the brush pile to burn someday. We'd wave to each other, but didn't talk much, most of the time.

"Hi, Bob," I said as he joined me on the train tracks. "What a coincidence."

"It's not a coincidence," Bob said. He sounded, as usual, quite somber. "Your mom's a wreck back at the house. You don't have to do this."

I looked down at his feet, unsure of whether to thank him for coming or to apologize. Instead, I just said, "Yeah."

"This can be six months or it can be six hours," he said, still looking at me. Maybe he felt some sort of fatherly responsibility. My own dad wasn't there to stop me. He lived across the state of Pennsylvania, seven hours away. I only saw him a few times a year these days.

"I know," I said to Bob. "We'll see what happens."

"Do you have a knife?" he asked. Before I could tell him I did, he took out a folding-blade pocketknife, a heavy Winchester blade.

"Here, take this. You're on your own now. Don't trust anybody."

I didn't mention that that was kind of the whole point, to trust in people, to listen to them; closing myself off would be a contradiction of the entire endeavor. Instead, I just said thanks and told him I'd be thinking of him out there on the road.

"Don't think of me," he said, "think of your mother."

Six miles later, I could feel Bob's knife in my pocket as I walked toward the four men outside Kennett Square. Maybe I'd have to use it after all. I'd never been in a fight before. The closest I'd ever come was on the wrestling mat in high school, and although there was a kind of primal ferocity in the ring, there were also referees, and plus, the wrestlers all wore sparkly singlets that looked a lot like leotards. It's hard to take yourself seriously in a leotard, and you have to take yourself quite seriously to fight. This was different. It did feel serious. Would I really stab one of these guys if it came down to it?

My body felt fresh, ready to spring; I hadn't been walking long enough for it to hurt yet. Instead, everything just felt awkward. I'd loaded fifty pounds of stuff into my backpack that morning, and all of it lurched behind me now, an unraveling mess. A flaccid water bladder bowed out of a side pocket. My cooking pot swung madly with each step, clanging against my mug. My mandolin kept slipping out of position. An American flag poked me on the right side, and an Earth flag poked me on the left. I felt like a complete clown, a wannabe mountain man wading through the suburbs of Philly. I had no idea what I was doing. Surely the men could see that.

By the time I reached them they were all staring at me silently. One had a big potbelly and two had mustaches. They were Latino, and possibly homeless, and suddenly I was very aware of my whiteness, and how my freedom of movement was largely predicated on my skin color. My freedom of mind, too. How would it have been different walking out my back door into the American unknown, alone, if I were a person of color? A woman? Not that it would've been impossible. Arguably the most famous of all American transcontinental walkers was a woman—Mildred Norman, also known as "Peace Pilgrim"—and one of my own heroes was John Francis, "Planetwalker," a black environmentalist who spent twenty-two years walking, seventeen of them under a vow of silence. When I was a senior in college, I'd heard Dr. Francis give a lecture about his walk that became one of the inspirations for my own. Clearly, you didn't have to be a white male to walk across America in 2011, but to anyone even just halfway willing to look at the prejudice in this country, it was just as clear that being a white male certainly helped. Before I even left home, my walk had already been made easier by the unmerited social privilege of living in a white male's body: I hadn't had nightmares of getting raped or abducted on the road, and I wasn't utterly paralyzed by fear of the police, or by the hordes of Americans still waving their Confederate flags. I wouldn't be immune from violence while I walked, but the odds of survival and success were stacked in my favor, and at some level I knew that, and counted on it. That's what racism and sexism looked like today, that surreptitiously yet overwhelmingly lopsided distribution of privilege. What did that mean? It meant it might take generations before a young black man could walk out his back door as unconcerned as I had, or until a young woman could walk alone on the highway without dread, free in her mind and body. Where was *that* America? It wasn't the one I'd just begun to walk across, as much as I wished it were.

At the same time, though, my whiteness might also make me a target in some places. This could be one of those places, on the train tracks outside town coming up on the Latino guys. I wondered, in some wordless place, if perhaps these guys didn't like white boys like me. They were all looking my way. What were they thinking?

I nodded and said hello. The men appeared confused. I must have appeared confused, too. Possibly clinically confused. We all stood there for a second looking at one another, and then one of the men asked me in heavily accented English: "What are you doing?"

I said I was walking across America. It sounded ridiculous because I hadn't even walked ten miles yet, but they didn't know that.

"I'm listening to people's stories along the way," I said, "so, 'walking to listen.'" I showed them my homemade sign as if it gave me some sort of credibility.

They didn't seem convinced. The man who'd asked the question looked at the guy who was sitting on a pile of railroad ties. He said something in Spanish—my death sentence, no doubt—and the guy on the ties began looking for something in a big plastic bin at his side. Maybe it was time to go.

Before I could run away—or waddle, as running would have been impossible with my backpack—the guy pulled out an unopened package of cookies and a few apple juice boxes. He gestured for me to take them, and to come sit with him on the railroad ties. I did, and the other three joined us. Their names were Martín, Sergio, Pedro, and Gabriel. I played a song on my mandolin, then Martín took out a fifth of Nikolai vodka and passed it around.

"You got a credit card or something?" Martín asked at one point.

"Yeah," I said. "I'm not carrying much cash."

"Good, because we could just snatch it." He made a gun with his fingers. "But we're not that kind of people. Friends. Friends."

Everything took on a surreal sheen. I'd wanted to live this kind of story for as long as I could remember, a story in which a traveler casts off into the big unknown with nothing more than a loaded pack, and meets strangers on the road, and breaks bread with those strangers, learning the unique language of their lives before casting off into the big unknown again. It was an ancient kind of human experience, that of the pilgrim, the wayfarer, but as an American Millennial and a son of suburbia, it felt like a lost inheritance. Pilgrimages were something to study from a safe and scholarly distance, and wayfaring journeys were the hackneyed stuff of Hollywood, or best experienced in the isolation of your bedroom on the PS3, or in books not unlike this one. Journeys and pilgrimages; this was not common practice in the American middle class. Such things required a catalyst of existential urgency and curiosity that a lifestyle of constant comfort and consumption suppressed. I was comfortable, and secure enough. There was no reason I should want to set out and seek my fortune, because I already had the well-mapped path that would probably lead me to one.

But still, I felt something was missing on that path, and it had nothing to do with money or accumulation or achievement. It had something to do with the fact that I was a living mystery, and so were all of the neighbors I'd never met, and none of us were gathering together to discuss that astonishing phenomenon, the phenomenon of our existence and all the questions that came with it. No one seemed to care. No one even seemed to notice. Each of us was a cosmic improbability, brought into this life and sentenced to experience it, to suffer it when necessary, and there was precious little reflection about any of that, precious little support. And if you did need support, something wasn't quite right with you; you were weak or ill or just a little dense. Maybe, in my neighborhood, we were all too busy working to really be there for one another, too busy entertaining ourselves. Or maybe we desperately longed to connect, to share in the beauty and the sorrow of this fleeting life together, offline, face to face, but we just didn't know how, and so we stayed strangers and pretended that wasn't strange.

I couldn't live my life that way, but maybe I already was. When I finally graduated from college, I felt I had to do something drastic to ensure that I wasn't. I had to set off on a journey, go on a pilgrimage, *something*. It felt a little contrived, almost cliché, but it also felt necessary. A shock to the system was required, something to zap me out of the habit of forgetting, of believing that life could ever be unremarkable or mundane.

"Every one of us has an extraordinary story worth hearing, and I'm walking the country to listen." I wrote this on my travel blog a few weeks after I started walking. "There's no such thing as the Average Joe, no such thing as a boring, uninteresting, unexceptional life." I chose this as the premise for my walk, but the only problem was I didn't believe it about myself. Not really. Bob the landlord couldn't have said it much clearer: *You don't have to do this.* I dismissed him then, but now I think I understand him better. He was saying, "You don't have to do this to be enough." But I didn't hear that at the time, even though I was wearing a sign that said I was listening. So I kept walking.

I was still sitting on the railroad ties with the four men, playing mandolin and sipping vodka, when the sky darkened and thunderheads began to roll in from the west. A few minutes later we saw a misty gray wall rushing toward us.

"Hurry up!" Martín said. "It's coming! It's coming!" Pedro was already gone. Gabriel and Sergio were running through the field beside the tracks, heading for the trees. The thunderheads hemorrhaged above us and I was soaked in seconds.

"Come with us," Martín said. "We'll take you to our home."

Bob's knife was heavy in my pocket. But the cookies and the apple juice seemed like a good sign. And the vodka was a good sign, too, or maybe not, but before I could think about it anymore I followed Martín off the tracks, across the field, and into the forest. *I'm walking across America*, I thought. *What the hell, why not?*

It was a short walk to a clearing in the trees where the men had set up a camp. Each one of them had his own shelter. There were blue tarps for roofs and wood pallets for walls, and everything was reinforced by bungee cords and propped-up bicycles. We were right behind a strip mall I'd been to many times before. How often had I eaten lunch at the sandwich shop on the other side, clueless?

Martín invited me into his shelter. The two of us barely fit inside. "Sit, sit," he said, pointing to his mattress. He began sifting through several boxes until he found what he was looking for: a pair of sweatpants, dry and clean. He offered them to me. When I said I didn't need them, he stripped down to his underwear, his hairy potbelly exposed for a second, and then he put on the sweatpants himself, along with a new T-shirt.

We couldn't talk much because his English was terrible and my Spanish was far worse, but still, the connection was strangely intimate. Martín began showing me his stuff: photographs of his teenage daughter, a painting of Our Lady of Guadalupe, a poster of three half-naked Budweiser models. I showed him a picture of my family. "Your sister is beautiful," he said, "very beautiful." Then, we settled in to wait out the rain with more mandolin and vodka. The vodka burned.

"It's a storm outside and a storm inside," Martín said when I coughed.

The rain didn't last too long, and I hardly got drunk at all. Stepping outside again, a good-bye hung heavily in the air. None of us quite knew how to part from our brief and bizarre confluence. I wanted to hold on to it for just a little bit longer. Maybe they did, too.

"So, walking to listen," Martín said. "Okay, okay."

"What do you think?" I asked.

"It's your choice, man," he said, shrugging his shoulders.

"What do you think of Americans?" I said, even though Martín was American himself. He'd shown me his ID when I took out my recorder to interview him in his hut, perhaps thinking I might be an undercover cop.

"Some good, some bad," he said. "It's the same with Mexicans. It's the same with everybody."

Standing in the middle of the camp, I looked around me. Crushed beer cans littered the hard, wet earth, and the jury-rigged huts leaned. A grill slowly rusted on arthritic legs. It was a place of exile, and it couldn't have been more different from where I'd begun that morning: the suburban home-office of a single mother/ yoga teacher/massage therapist. But even still, it almost felt like home, a safe shelter when I needed it, at the beginning of a walk I didn't know how to walk yet.

Before I left, Martín gave me an orange pepper that set my tongue on fire and then sliced up a homegrown prickly pear. *Tuna*, he called it. It was sweet and it put out the burn.

"God bless you," Martín said, shaking my hand, "and be careful. Sleep with a knife, *o una pistola*." Once again, he made a gun with his fingers.

Back on the train tracks, I walked through an arching tunnel of sycamore and oak, maple and beech, all of it blazing with autumn. I passed stinking mushroom houses and fertilizer plants where plows worked the black, steaming stuff into head-high rows. I'd walked these tracks before, but never this far, and everything seemed different now, infused with a significance that was inexplicable but undeniable. Three horses turned to hold my gaze. A Mennonite man plowed his field with children in tow. An animal was dead on the tracks, split by the train and mashed beyond recognition. Fields of soybeans shivered in the wind.

By dusk, my pack had ravaged my shoulders, and I had two blisters that throbbed like they were alive. I hardly noticed. The light was a lustrous gold as the sun sank, and the tracks ahead were glowing.

I thought about my mom. She was not a wreck, like Bob had said. Far from it. Mom has described herself as a "Roman centurion" when it comes to her three children, and a "she-wolf." In other words, she doesn't wreck easily. But she couldn't fight for me now, and that was probably hard for her. Surely she knew I couldn't be walking without her, though. We were so close that there were times it seemed she could read my mind. I was the oldest of three, and she was like that with each one of us. After the divorce, we all just got closer. All of us except my dad. In an instant, he became a stranger. I was fifteen, old enough for a painful initiation into the human experience. Much of my wanderlust came from that pain, although I hardly ever thought about that connection. That was the trick: Don't think about it. Better to wander. Better to walk.

We left Dad in Erie, Pennsylvania, right after the split and moved across the state, landing in Bob's rental house outside Philadelphia. Dad would come to visit us whenever he could, bringing with him the pain I preferred to avoid. The scene was always the same: hours of arguing and squirming, and then the long silences when no one knew what else to say. Mom's cutting voice. Dad's bitter eyes. My sister, Caitlin, three years younger, doing most of my crying for me. Luke, nine years younger, hiding in his room. I would disappear for hours, afraid that I'd tear the house apart if I stayed, or tear Dad apart. So many families break up these days; you'd think you might be prepared for the shock when it happens to yours. But you can't prepare yourself for something like that, not really, especially if everything seems fine until the moment they tell you it's happening. I certainly wasn't prepared, and I didn't know how to handle it, so I didn't. Instead, I'd walk for miles on the train tracks, but it was never far enough. The trains ran so slowly that the temptation was excruciating, especially when Dad was around for a visit. It would've been so easy to catch one and ride off into something else, anything else.

The train tracks weren't just an escape from the pain, though. They were an escape from suburbia. It didn't feel like home to me. I didn't know where my home was anymore, and in this void my wanderlust blossomed. The word "wander," I discovered, was an anagram of my first name. *Wander.* My own name was a command. I didn't know what it meant to wander, but I liked the sound of it. It had something to do with a lightness of being, a receptive approach to each new moment that might take you anywhere. Obstacles didn't exist because there was nowhere in particular to get to. Each place was just as good as the next. The wanderer never lingered too long, always moving onward and yet always here. I wanted to live that way, the wander way, so I wandered the train tracks behind Mom's house. Or I tried to. I never fully let go, free of everything but the movement.

One summer, I found an abandoned camp on the train tracks under a culvert in dense woods. Strewn across the dirt floor were the remnants of someone's life: a filthy comforter, a fire-stained pot, a ratty oilskin jacket. It seemed a whole other world, and I wanted to be a part of it, if only for a moment. I wanted to know who had lived there, and where they'd come from, what they'd seen. It made me wonder: If a single square mile in suburban Pennsylvania contained two worlds as different as my home and the camp of this unknown vagabond, then how many different worlds did the continent contain? How many worlds did the Earth contain?

And then I discovered Walt Whitman in college: "Have you reckon'd a thousand acres much? Have you reckon'd the earth much?" After Whitman, there was no escaping this urge to go reckon the earth much. Jack Kerouac fanned the flames, too, but he was drunk all the time, reckless and crazed. I didn't trust him as a source of reliable guidance. Whitman was a bit crazed himself: "Ranting and frothing in my insane crisis," he wrote, ". . . I too am not a bit tamed, I too am untranslatable, / I sound my barbaric yawp over the roofs of the world." The poet was unhinged, no doubt, but he wasn't lost like Kerouac seemed to be, so I chose him as my guide.

Mom was there for all of this, watching and waiting. She wasn't surprised when I told her I was going to leave home and just walk for a while, but she wasn't thrilled, either.

"I'm mad at you," she'd said before I hugged her good-bye that morning. "It feels like I'm being blown open again, like when you were born."

We ate breakfast together in the living room, just the two of us. Caitlin and Luke were still sleeping. Mom had made surprises, one of her specialties: marshmallow-stuffed Pillsbury croissants. In the heat of the oven, the marshmallows transformed into a sweet syrup, a liquid heart. Surprises were one of the constants she brought with us wherever we moved—the apartments in Chicago, the rental houses outside Philly, the home she and my dad bought in Erie a few years before the divorce. We never really had our own place, so instead Mom brought home with us.

That morning she'd made our lattes, too. She'd never bothered to learn how to use the steam wand properly, so she always micro-waved them to get them hot enough. This used to annoy me, but at the table I realized I was going to miss this about her. I was going to miss her. I looked at her now. Her long hair was gray, almost white, and her face was furrowed. The past eight years had been hard on her. I could see it in her body. She'd lost so much weight she was almost frail. But even still, I felt safe around her. She taught yoga and meditation, and yet, she would've annihilated anyone who threatened her kids. The thought of never seeing her again was so unimaginable I couldn't think it, even if I tried.

She read me a poem over breakfast, one by the Sufi mystic Rumi. "So don't be timid," she read. "Load the ship and set out. No one knows for certain whether the vessel will sink or reach the harbor."

I wondered what it would look like, in my case, to sink. And the harbor. I wondered about that, too.

"Like it or not, Andrew, it *is* about breaking this hold that death has on us," Mom said. I had my recorder rolling—the first interview. "You might not be thinking that, but you're taking risks. You're working me hard. And I feel like I'm being blown up again. I really do. I'm living."

After breakfast, I hoisted on my backpack and the two of us walked out to the train tracks behind the house. Caitlin and Luke watched from the back porch, still in their pajamas. Mom insisted on taking my picture. One picture became a dozen, and I began to feel like a six-year-old on his first day of school—I had the backpack and everything.

"God, would you just hurry up and get on your journey?! Let's take as many pictures as possible, jeez!"

This was Luke, thirteen years old, shouting from the back porch, pissed off that he'd had to get up early for this. In an instant, the romance of my epic departure dissolved. I would've called him an asshole, but I was grateful for the excuse to just get going.

I hugged Mom good-bye. When I was a hundred yards down the tracks she shouted at me to lift up my arms for one last picture. I didn't stop, and I didn't turn around, but I did raise my arms, and it was only then that I cried, but I was laughing, too.

WOODY CURRY, *a Vietnam veteran and clinical therapist*
BALTIMORE, MARYLAND, *in his office before dinner at the*
Baltimore Station, a residential treatment center
OCTOBER, *one week into the walk*

"How do you think it feels to go and put your life on the line for two
and a half years and come back to find out everybody thinks you're
wrong? What do you think that does to all the shit you just went
through? When you come back and everybody thinks you're some
goddamn, crazy-ass, drug-addicted whatever? Shit. Made me pretty
angry. My whole foundation was gone. Nothing to latch on to. Not a
damn thing. I wound up in a mental institution for six or seven years
off and on, and drug detoxes, and jails, and the streets, and homeless,
and all of this trying to find out what was real. I needed to believe in
something, and I needed to own something, and I needed to control
something as an indication that I was real. So when I let go of that,
then all the shit that came with it went, too. And it came back that I am
whoever the fuck I feel like thinking, and that ain't got shit to do with
me. What's real is what I'm experiencing and feeling, that's what's
real, and my perception isn't real. That's my perception of what's real.
But who is it that's perceiving, right? Fact of it is, there's nothing
there."

   "What do you mean?"

   "No thing. I'm an activity. There's only one thing. I'm just a part
of that one thing, doing exactly what that thing does."

   "Doing that Woody Curry thing."

"That's what I call it, but it's no different from what everybody else does. I just got my own style. That's what makes it fun. I call the universe my playground. I say, 'This place is like Disneyland,' and I ain't bullshitting. I can get on a ride and scare the shit out of me, and then get off of that and relax, and then go climb on another one goddammit, and that's all it is. I'm the rider of the universe. But most people feel powerless because they see things outside of them being in control.

"I say, 'In control of what? They're not in control of your choices. They're not in control of what you accept or reject. You see your life as being at the whims of some power greater than you, but I want to know, what fucking power is there in the universe greater than you when you can accept or reject any damn thing coming at you? Now that is the ultimate power.' I ask people what they're afraid of and they don't even know. All they know is their fear. I say, 'Don't worry, that's called free-floating anxiety. You'll find some shit to hook it up on.'

"You feel the same way I felt at your age, that, 'I gotta know, and what I gotta know is why, and I also have to know what it all means.' Well, it means whatever the fuck you want it to mean. It's not out there, what you're looking for. It's in you. It's been there all along. It's just yours. Shakespeare said that shit a long time ago. It's been said for ages. It says so in Genesis: God created the heaven and the earth and everything in it, then created man in his own image. So if you're in his image, then it stands to reason that you create the heaven and the earth and everything that's in it. That's what you do. So you're the creator of this thing you're looking at, this thing you call the world.

"So what's the problem? Why are you looking for what's happening? You happening, goddammit. Nothing happening to you. You happening to it. You don't know who you are, and that's what your search is. You're gonna hear it. When you arrive at wherever you're

going, that's where you're gonna be, and you'll see, just like I did. You're gonna find the same shit going on everywhere. But you will be a much wiser person. And I think you'll have a whole lot less stress and questions when you get finished. Yeah, you'll know. You'll know who you are, because that's what you're looking for anyway. This is just the vehicle that you chose to find out."

Chapter Two

"You should start looking for another job."

A few months before I started walking, I was a senior at Middlebury College in the state of Vermont, where the rivers have been carving cliffs into the Green Mountains for millennia. My friends and I would often seek out those cliffs, climb them, and then leap off into the flowing water below. There was something irresistible to me about stepping out onto that brink where the rock ended and the air began. And then the launch. The letting go. It felt like the threshold between life and death, and once or twice it actually was. Those quick plummeting seconds connected me to the tremendous gravity of being fully alive, and to the forgettable fact that I often wasn't.

It might have been that I felt more alive falling through the air over a cold mountain river than I did sitting in most classrooms, or doing keg stands to a chorus of "Eight! Nine! Ten! Eleven! Eleven! Eleven! Eleven!" chanted by my rugby buddies. There was a lot to learn in college, certainly, and much of it had nothing to do with the course curriculum. It was a revelation, for example, when I realized that it was actually okay to spend a Friday night alone in the swaying crown of a pine tree, sailing the sky—that it didn't necessarily mean I was sad or sick or missing out. Quite the opposite, in fact. I didn't learn that one till I'd just about graduated, though. First, I had to learn how to shotgun beer, how to make apple pie cocktails directly inside my mouth, how many apple pie cocktails it took for me to throw up, and how interested I seemed to be in throwing up on the weekends, until I finally wasn't.

I learned a little bit about love, too. And then when she broke up with me after two years, I learned about heartbreak. That's when I took to the pine trees at night and realized that I liked it there, that being alone in the dark wasn't something to be afraid of.

One semester, I heard about a class on historiography that was taught by a beloved professor. It was rumored the class would change you forever. I wanted that, to be changed, enlightened in some lasting way. That kind of class was the reason I'd come to college; I wanted a teacher who'd show me how to do the work of being human. I'd found a few such teachers, and we did some of that work obliquely, through the middlemen of poetry, philosophy, and creative writing. But I wanted a full immersion without the degrees of separation afforded by theories and narratives, an apprenticeship to the craft of navigating life, not a seminar in how a bunch of dead people had done it. You could only get so far by reading the old poets, philosophers, and writers. You had to experience it, whatever it was they were talking about, know it for yourself. Maybe this historiography class would show me how. The class was in high demand, so every applicant had to write an entry essay. The only detail I remember from my essay is a metaphor I made about a pencil. I was a pencil, I said, but I was blunt. This class would sharpen me into the well-honed pencil I had always wanted to be. Needless to say, I never heard back from the professor.

Although the pencil metaphor fell a bit flat, it was made in earnest, and in my last semester at Middlebury I still had that feeling of bluntness. I was operating this incredibly complex biochemical, psycho-emotional machine that thought things and felt things, and wondered and worried, and just wanted to understand what the hell was going on. I was this machine, in fact, but I'd never read the owner's manual, and I still hadn't found the class that would show me how. If those classes existed, I was too dull to find them. Or maybe I had found them and just wasn't asking the right questions.

With just a few months before graduation, I set out to interview a long list of men about what it meant to come of age, for my senior essay. I interviewed men because I was supposed to be a man but I didn't feel like one. And I couldn't talk to my dad about it. I didn't trust him as a source of reliable guidance, not after some of the choices he'd made.

"Coming of age, to me, is trying to get a balance," Marc Lapin told me. He was one of my environmental studies professors. "It's about integrating parts of yourself that you feel alienated from, and I think it's recognizing, 'I don't have to do more to be who I am.' Why is there so much anxiety today? What makes people anxious? It's the idea that what they're doing isn't right or okay. There's no trust in self."

I sat down with Greg Sharrow, a folklorist in town. "My shtick now is about empathy," he said. "I want to be able to imaginatively enter into someone's experience, understand where they're coming from, and if they're doing something hurtful to me, I want to be able to love them for their pain. Pretty much everyone experiences some degree of damage as a kid growing up, and that damage makes it hard for people to know themselves. People become stuck, stuck in their own pain. So coming of age, it's the whole business of growing into yourself."

I met with Jonathan Miller-Lane, an aikido sensei and a professor of education. "At its best, I think coming of age is a way in which an individual is shown that a community cares for him or her. It's not only the community recognizing this young adolescent as being a member of us, but the child has to look up and realize, 'Oh, I'm a part of this. I didn't realize all these people cared about me.'"

As I gathered interviews, my urgency increased. Graduation loomed. I'd applied for a Watson fellowship to continue studying the process of growing up, but the college committee rejected my proposal in the first round. I'd wanted to visit indigenous communities around the world to see how they guided their young people into adulthood, and compare those traditions to some of the mainstream methodologies in the United States, which had left me with so many unanswered questions. In my experience, there wasn't a sustained and personal conversation about what it meant to come of age. There wasn't a ritual of any kind, something to catalyze the transformation and mark it. The freshman-year initiation into my all-male a cappella group might've been the closest thing I got. I had to dress up in a bra and skirt, submit to getting splattered with condiments and fish oil, sing a song in the student union to a very confused crowd, and then get hammered if I wanted to, which I did. It was a wild night, but perhaps not the best model for manhood. We were a tribe of boys. Lots of the full-grown alums were, too. A middle-aged tenor came to one of our parties my freshman year. We were both wasted. "Fuck anything that moves," he advised me, "while you still can," and then he slapped me in the face—it was a forehand, level five or six out of ten. Then he told me to give him a backhand eight, straight to the cheek. I obliged. It was the blind leading the blind.

Before graduation, I decided I'd do my fellowship project anyway, just without the fellowship. I'd made contact with Malidoma Somé, a shaman with a Brandeis Ph.D., from the Dagara tribe in Burkina Faso; I'd read one of his books and tracked him down in upstate New York. He said I could live and study with his uncle in the village where he had grown up. This sounded perfect. Surely I'd discover something important that far away from anything I'd ever known.

One of my last interviews for my senior essay was with Jeff Howarth, a geography professor.

"The whole process of coming of age has to do with developing the ability to shift your focus from yourself to other people," he said. "It seems to be opening yourself up to not being so self-involved. It's about being able to recognize other people's needs as you're able to recognize your own. There comes a point when you've come of age that you're no longer disappointed by people. You're just empathetic for people. One way to think of it is when a kid develops parental love for his parents. It's when you realize your authority figures have faults, and you're no longer rebelling against those faults."

Jeff told me I should turn the lens on myself for the project. What did I think about coming of age? Where did I fit into the story? I realized I should probably interview my dad. We'd never tried anything quite like that. I decided to wait until I was ready.

A couple days after graduation, I was on a lobster boat in Cape Cod Bay stuffing bait bags full of fish skins. The plan was to make a lot of money as quickly as possible and then fly to West Africa. There was no time to lose. I could only put off my tuition debt for so long.

I'd never worked on a fishing boat before. It was nothing like college, and I loved it. My captain, Dan, was a stout man who didn't talk much. He was good-humored mostly, but sometimes grim. When I first met him I asked if I should call him Captain Dan or just Captain.

"I'm far from a captain," he said, even though that wasn't true. "I'm just a guy with a boat. Call me Dan."

The two of us spent long hours out on the silver water. Sometimes we'd long-line for dogfish—small sand sharks. They ascended from the depths on the three-hundred-hook lines like murky ghosts, their white bellies flashing as they rose. My job was to gaff them if they slipped off, and then pile the writhing bodies into boxes in the stern. By the end of each day, my orange coveralls were smeared with blood and yellow embryonic fluid from the fetuses the mothers aborted as they died. At first, I tossed these fetuses over the gunwale, hoping they might survive somehow. The seagulls loved that.

"It's pretty gross," Dan said on my first day. "The whole fishery's pretty gross."

I got used to it. We hauled hundreds of lobster traps, and I banded thousands of crustaceans that summer, mesmerized by the rainbows that shined across their shells. Stuffing the bait bags, hauling the traps, banding the lobsters—after a few hours my mind would get lost in the work and the wind and the hungry, heaving sea.

We always went to the bar before going home. I was just a sternman, but Dan let me join the captains' club, the end of the bar where only the fishermen sat. He didn't have any kids, and my dad was far away, and we got kind of close, despite the fact that we both seemed to be speaking different languages sometimes. We'd hang at the bar for hours, trash talking each other, "zooing" the other captains, sipping Bud Lite.

A few weeks into the summer, I started a storytelling blog about my fishing experience, inspired by the newness of it. When I told Dan about it, though, he wasn't pleased. After that first conversation, we didn't talk about it. Neither of us seemed to know how. I wasn't invited to the bar anymore, but I still kept writing stories on the blog, foolishly, and then on the first day of September Dan went fishing without me. He didn't respond to any of my texts. I went to his house that night and found him in his living room, watching a boxing match.

"What's going on?" I asked him.

"Why don't you tell me?" he said.

"Well, you went fishing without me today."

He looked at me for a second, and then he said, "I think you should start looking for another job."

It must have been the blog, but he never told me outright. Had I insulted him? Did he feel betrayed? I should have been more aware of the clash of sensibilities that my blog had initiated. But I wasn't, and he didn't want to talk about it. If you're a fisherman and you set your traps in someone else's waters, there won't be a truth and reconciliation process. You'll just get your buoys cut. Don't come back. It was one version of American masculinity that I'd had little experience with.

I'd been planning on fishing until December. Now, I didn't have the money I needed to get to West Africa. I didn't have any job prospects. I didn't have a backup plan. I did have all the questions I was seeking to answer, though, and the wanderlust, and I couldn't just forget about the whole thing. And I couldn't stay at home, either. I was now a college graduate living at his mom's house, and as much as I loved my mother, that wasn't going to wash.

A week after I got fired, I hatched a desperate plan. I started wondering what it would be like to walk out my back door and just keep going. The more I thought about it, the more it made sense. It still does, five years later. Walking is deep in the dirt bones of this country. It's practically a religion. Each year, thousands of modern-day American pilgrims thru-hike the long-distance trails. They're always out there, the walkers, hauling around the great weight of their wondering. And why not? Walking is an ancestral itch, evolution's urge. North Americans have been doing it for centuries. The Plains tribes were perambulatory by tradition. Others walked because they were forced to: the Navajo and their

Long Walk, the Cherokee's Trail of Tears. And then there were the pioneers, the Mormon refugees, the runaway slaves, the civil rights marchers, the peace activists, the wandering vagabonds of the beat and hippie eras. Plenty of people had walked before me. Why not take my place among them? I'd be in good company, even if I were alone. And plus, walking was free. I couldn't afford much else.

I had six weeks to prepare from the day I was fired. It was early autumn. If I left any later than mid-October I might freeze.

I took one training hike—a three-mile walk with two twenty-pound barbells in my backpack cushioned by some pillows. I quickly realized this was idiocy. I was already pathetically underprepared, so why bother?

Two weeks before I left, I told my friend Andrew—a fellow baritone—what I was about to do. He worked as a gear tester for *Outside Magazine*. He called his boss, and a few days later she sent me everything I needed. It was like Christmas came early, with a vengeance. The boxes kept coming. All the gear was worth more than I'd made that entire summer: boots, socks, pants, shirts, coat, rain gear, tent, sleeping bag, sleeping pad, water filter, sunglasses, backpack. Everything. I paid for none of it. It seemed like an omen from God, or maybe Santa Claus.

Before I left, I gave myself some rules:

I wouldn't take any rides to make forward progress. Walking only.

I wouldn't listen to music while I walked. No earbuds.

I'd use maps on the road. No smartphone.

I'd sleep in my tent unless someone took me in, camping with permission if possible, trespassing if necessary.

I'd keep to the roads, because I wanted to meet a diverse cross-section of people and the trails might be too self-selecting.

I'd stay as presentable as possible, because I wanted people to feel comfortable approaching me.

I'd take three poets as my guides: Walt Whitman (*Leaves of Grass*), Rainer Maria Rilke (*Letters to a Young Poet*), and Kahlil Gibran (*The Prophet*). I'd turn to them whenever I needed a boost of inspiration.

I'd view everyone as a teacher of some sort, and I'd interview anyone who would let me.

And the last rule: I'd walk until it felt like I should stop; until I broke my budget of four thousand dollars; or until I hit the Pacific Ocean. Whichever came first.

CYNTHIA SHANK, *mother of a Green Beret serving in Afghanistan*
ROANOKE, VIRGINIA, *at the dining room table in her friend Tina
Cannon's house*
NOVEMBER, *almost a month into my walk*

*"When I write him I tell him, 'I'm so glad you're my son. I'm very
proud of you and I love you. I'm your mom.' We always talked about
how life is an adventure, something that you experience, you don't sit
and watch. At eighteen he wanted to do this very badly, and then he
came to us at twenty and said, 'It's a done deal. I am doing this.' That
was really hard. And it's still hard, knowing that your son is willing
to put himself in harm's way. So yeah, you can see the tears even now,
three years later. It's still hard to think of your son making a choice
that's a constant life threat.*

*"He's our quiet child, but he's our intense child. He's our silly
guy who can also be dead serious. So, one of my questions to his
recruiter, and still this is one of my biggest worries: I cannot see
Caleb killing somebody. And I'm really concerned, worried, stressed
about what that will do to his psyche if he comes face to face with
somebody and he has to pick up his gun and shoot that person. He is a
sensitive kid. He loves people and he would come home from school
and be angry with teachers who would ridicule a student because they
got the wrong answer. He does not like that. And so I think the hardest
part will be to actually shoot someone and know that he's killed
someone. I still worry about that. His recruiter was a really nice guy,
but I kept asking him, 'What will happen with him once this happens?*

Is the army going to prepare him for this? Is the army going to talk with him afterwards?' Obviously I'm still upset about it because all of my questions were not answered in a way that I would've liked.

"We don't know when he'll come home. It's sometime at the beginning of next year. Not hearing from him day to day, or having the ability to call him when you want, that's pretty hard. Just like your mom. I'm sure it's really hard for her to know that she can't necessarily touch you. And I told him, I said, 'I just need to touch you right now.' You're our children, and for a mom it's something that never stops. You're always being our babies. And I know you guys hate that, but our thirty-three-year-old to our twenty-three-year-old, you're always our little ones. It's hard to see you grow up."

Chapter Three

"I was in another world."

Around noon on day two, I hopped off the train tracks and got onto the road for the first time. The highway on foot, I quickly learned, was hellish. The cars shrieked like banshees and the trucks bellowed murder. It was a two-to-sixteen-lane bottleneck of death. The asphalt had no mercy on my knees, and there was nothing to cover me from the sun, nothing to shield me from the wind. I was an alien in this place. I felt extremely alone; everyone passing me in their cars had no idea what it was actually like out here. I myself had been oblivious, the countless times I'd driven on highways. By its very nature, the highway was home to nothing. I hadn't expected it to be so bleak.

For the first week, I walked like a dazed child across Maryland's state highways, and then farther south onto more frightening behemoths near Washington, D.C. My body felt so delicate whenever the cars screamed by me, which was all day, every day. And then somewhere in Virginia I came across the remains of a deer. It was fresh, splattered across fifty yards of road. First I saw its heart, attached to an apparatus of bound muscle, wet with blood. Then I passed its intestines, a hind leg, and finally its head, resting on a pile of scarlet meat. It gazed up at me through a single glazed eye. "You wouldn't have fared any better," it seemed to say. A pickup truck sped past, swerving slightly to avoid the mess. The airstream in its wake buffeted both of us. I took a few pictures before I left.

The roads were slower in the Virginian countryside. Quieter. They were like the train tracks behind Mom's house. I could breathe again. There was so much to see: the dandelion yellow of the traffic lines slashing the rich black asphalt of the road, a lush field of grass with blades so fat I could make them sing opera between my thumbs, a slate sky ready to weep, a scrap-metal rooster guarding someone's driveway, a squirrel leaping from a telephone line to a tree branch—an astonishing feat of athletic grace that I'd never really appreciated before.

There were the barns, too: the green one with the giant painting of a cow and a pig dancing a jig, the dying red one, collapsed like a brittle old man made to stand for too long. I was moving slowly—about three miles an hour—so I had long moments with everything I passed. One day I watched a fat spider lounging in its web, seeming to float in midair, and sometimes solitary strands of gossamer silk floated by. Once, I saw a butterfly piss.

I read the road signs hungrily:

ADOPT

A

HIGHWAY

ANGRY REDNECKS

AGAINST LITTER

BURKE'S STATION RAID

BURKE'S STATION, FOUR MILES

SOUTH, WAS RAIDED BY STUART'S

CAVALRY, DECEMBER, 1862.

STUART TELEGRAPHED TO WASH—

INGTON COMPLAINING OF THE

BAD QUALITY OF THE MULES HE

HAD CAPTURED—A FAMOUS JOKE.

Calverton
BAPTIST CHURCH
WHERE WILL YOU SPEND ETERNITY

HEAVEN OR HELL

It all poured into my eyes every day. I liked thinking about the transfer between the outside and the inside worlds, how the things that I saw changed the neural patterns in my brain. My mind was a shape-shifting cloud in the wind, transmogrifying as the walked world swept over it.

The binge observing also distracted me from the pain. At the end of each day I felt like an arthritic elderly person hobbling on a bed of flaming needles. "Old people walk funny because they hurt," Jeff Howarth, my geography professor, had said in our interview. That made much more sense now.

My hips bore the brunt of my backpack, and my shoulders, too, were flayed by nightfall. I would sing to forget about the pain— Handel, Marvin Gaye, an odd handful of Christmas carols. I'd make up songs, too. Once, I passed a road called Peggy Lane. It could've been the name of a beautiful woman. I could almost see her. Why hadn't I asked her to walk with me? It was dusk and I was dying, so I took out my harmonica and honked out a train rhythm, free-styling verses about my wild love for Peggy Lane.

Sometimes I would rap, badly, to the cadence of my footsteps, or I'd spit poetry, also to the rhythm of the movement. It was appalling stuff, and often I'd start giggling hysterically at the absurdity of the whole thing. I must've looked completely unhinged, there on the side of the road, but I didn't care because it took me out of the pain. If it got really bad, I'd split myself into an array of imaginary characters. This way, I could dissociate myself from my suffering. There was a vulgar old man who would swear in truly unprintable ways, and a whiny boy, and an opera singer. There was even a guru, an unflustered fellow with an Indian accent who always knew the right thing to say. I'd be on the verge of collapsing and the guru would say something wise, like: "Don't worry, my son, because when you worry, you reject the offering that this moment is asking you to receive. To freak out is to be distracted and to be distracted is to miss the great harvest of life." It was crazy, and perhaps offensive, and it worked.

The guru character probably stemmed from the year my family spent in India when I was seven. My parents moved us there so Dad could work on his Ph.D. and Mom could study yoga. They signed me up to learn the *mridangam*, an oblong, double-sided drum. My teacher, Govind, would sit across from me and tell me what to play, an impossibly long series of words indicating various strokes and slaps on the two opposing membranes. Somehow I never had a problem remembering the order and then playing it. I think my unnatural skill had something to do with the teacher himself—his confidence in me, his sense of calm. Without him, I couldn't have done it, and sure enough, after we moved back to Chicago I stopped playing. I was surprised, then, to meet the guru on the road after all these years. Perhaps he'd been inside me all along.

The guru character was my last resort against pain and despair. If the guru didn't save me, I'd surrender to the madness, sanity gone, imagining the pain as an entity of its own. I'd start screaming at it: "I'm going to walk you into the ground, you motherfucker! Is that all you got?! Is that all you fucking got?!"

Then, I'd take a break. Taking a break always worked better than rage.

* * *

Two days north of Charlottesville, Virginia, I had breakfast with two old men at Bailey's Store in Brandy Station, an old depot town on Highway 29. Inside, a spectrum of vibrant commercial color lined the shelves. Tinsel spiders dangled from tinsel webs tacked to the ceiling for Halloween. I was almost tempted by a huge vat of pickled eggs by the register. Instead, I got some pancakes and sat down with the two old men. They were regulars, and they said I could join them.

"You think seventy's old?" Herman was saying to me. Willy, the man next to him, was seventy. "Seventy's nothing," Herman continued. "He's just a teenager. I'll be eighty next week."

Herman had a hushed voice, and Willy had a deep, watery one. While Willy didn't look seventy, Herman definitely looked eighty. Willy was black, Herman was white, and they'd been friends for a long time, or as Willy put it: "I been knowing Herman, I guess about fifty years now"; or as Herman put it: "He been knowing me all my life." I wondered what that friendship had looked like over the decades.

"He's a lover boy. Ain't no doubt about it. He got so many women!" This was Herman.

"Willy here?"

"Oh, yeah!" Herman said this so that each word had its own U-like intonation and crescendo.

"I used to have quite a few of them." This was Willy.

"What happened?"

"Time. Now I have a couple of—" and he paused here, searching for the right word. "Associates. I'll tell you what: age is a number. If you turn twenty-four around, what do you have? Forty-two."

"You only say that 'cause you try and get with them younger girls." The woman behind the counter weighed in as she brewed coffee.

"I don't! I don't bother them! But I will be honest with you, I get quite a few advances. That's because I'm a good person. I try to be a good person. But I can't say the same thing for some people." Willy looked at Herman accusingly. Herman shot back.

"Trying and doing is two different things, right?"

"Herman, you may not want to be my friend, but I been knowing you so long, when you say something like that I just let it pass on. When you say jump what do I normally say?"

"How high."

"That's right. And I'm still able to jump, that's the good thing."

Before I left, Willy looked up the weather for me in the newspaper. The headline on the front page read: SCOOTER DRIVER DIES IN CRASH WITH PICKUP. There was also an article about a crazed man in Zanesville, Ohio, who'd released his private collection of rare, exotic animals before killing himself. Bengal tigers and lions, grizzly bears and black bears, cougars and wolves—they'd all taken to the suburbs and the highways, and law enforcement had slaughtered nearly fifty of the beasts. No humans died, besides the man who shot himself. Dipping back into the news after a few weeks off the grid, I was struck hard by the strangeness and tragedy of America, the dysfunction. It was all so easy to forget in my own little world on the highway.

The forecast for that night was snow, and there'd be a wintry mix the next day. Willy suggested I find a place to stay indoors that night.

"Wouldn't want a car sliding off the road and crashing into your tent."

I had a good walk that day. For one thing, I'd completely forgotten about the Blue Ridge Mountains. They took me by surprise when I crested a hill and saw them rising out of the earth in the distance. *For purple mountain majesties!* I gave an involuntary whoop and began cheering. Then, a few miles later, I stumbled into a winery and had a tasting, which floated me on for the next mile or two.

But by four o'clock the buzz was gone. I'd walked twenty miles and was approaching the little hamlet of Brightwood. It was the freak-out hour: dusk had fallen and I had no place to stay. Plus, it was going to snow that night. Thick forests of maple and oak surrounded me, and at one point I looked into the trees and saw a graveyard of cannibalized cars and dead yellow school buses. It was haunting on its own, but then I passed a sign:

STOP

Private Road!

NO TRESPASSING

VIOLATORS MAY BE SHOT

SURVIVORS PROSECUTED

I needed permission to camp somewhere. There were a few houses in Brightwood, and most people were probably home, but I didn't have it in me to go knocking. There was the fear of who might open the door: what if they had shotguns, or dogs, or worse? And even if they weren't dangerous, they still might be mean, and I didn't need that at the end of the day. Farther on down the road in South Carolina, I camped under a bridge, and I thought that maybe the troll in the fairy tale wasn't such a monster after all. Maybe he was just far away from home and actually kind of blue. He kept threatening to gobble up the Billy Goats Gruff, but maybe what he really wanted was their company and he just didn't know how to ask, or he was too afraid they'd say no. It was like what Rainer Maria Rilke wrote in *Letters to a Young Poet*: "Perhaps everything that frightens us is, in its deepest essence, something helpless that wants our love."

Knocking on doors also required a lot of humility. It was hard to ask strangers for help. I'd never really had to do it before.

I'd only knocked on doors twice at that point. The second time, an old woman with an oxygen tank and a barking dog had answered and said no. Actually, "Go" was all she'd said. The first time—and this was the first night of my walk—a middle-aged woman had answered the door and said yes. She then invited me in for pumpkin soup. After some conversation we were both astonished to discover that she knew of my mom; they were both local yoga teachers and they'd been trying to meet each other for years. Her name was Alison Donley, and when her daughter came home we all sat by the fire with a bottle of red wine and chatted like we'd known one another for years. It was magical, but I didn't expect my luck to continue.

The light was fading rapidly in Brightwood. I passed a church, but it looked empty. To the left, a family mingled over a grill in their front yard, but I didn't go over. The thought of introducing myself made me nauseous. And then I saw a barnlike building up ahead. BRIGHTWOOD GENERAL STORE, said the sign. There was another: LIVE MUSIC EVERY FRIDAY! It was Friday, and I had a mandolin.

I walked inside. A family was eating dinner at a big wooden table—a mother, a father, and two sons. Floor-to-ceiling shelves lined the walls, and a mural was painted on the crown molding with the words "Faith," "Peace," "Hope," "Love." Photographs plastered the place: smiling children, old men with banjos, proud hunters showing off their turkeys. The smells of barbeque and homemade pizza wafted from the open kitchen.

I said hi to a woman standing behind the counter. She smiled at me politely. I explained what I was doing and told her about my predicament with the incoming snow.

"Okay," she said. It was an amused and slightly concerned "okay."

"Let me go ask Dave. He's the owner."

I waited. The family at the big wooden table pretended not to notice me, or smell me. A minute later, Dave Peake stormed up from the back of the store. His long, sandy hair was pinned down by an American flag bandana. He wore camouflage cargo pants and a short, dark beard. He pumped my hand hello with great enthusiasm.

"What, we got Forrest Gump here?" he said. He had a gentle wildness in his laugh, something that might have been volatile years earlier, and I began to relax.

"You carrying any guns with you in that pack?" he said.

"No, but I have a couple pocketknives. And a can of pepper spray."

"Are you a psycho?"

I assured Dave I wasn't a psycho, trying to sound believable, but how do you convince a stranger you're not a psycho? A crazy man wouldn't admit his craziness. I waited for Dave's judgment.

"Well, I live upstairs, and there's an extra room you can stay in if you're not carrying a gun on you. There's no bed, but it'll be warmer than outside. There's a shower, too. And Ashley tells me you have a mandolin? Hang around and play with us tonight. We'll jam until midnight, probably. And if it snows tomorrow you can stay the day."

It felt miraculous. Sometimes a long day of walking took me back into a child's state of consciousness, in which I was easily delighted and easily devastated, just like peekaboo used to be hilarious and saying good night tragic.

Slowly, the store began to fill with people, mostly men. Some of them dragged on cigarettes inside and the air grew thick with smoke and murmuring. Many of the men seemed to have come as a group. One of them sat next to me, a young guy with curly black hair dressed in what might've been pajamas. He was excited for the music, he told me. When he left to get up on stage, Dave came over and explained that the group was from the local Agape House.

"They're all schizophrenics," he said. "They come here on Fridays for the music, and because no one calls them freaks. We're all love here. There's God in this place, and it's like a magnet. The happiness just attracts itself. It's sad. There aren't many places like this in America anymore."

The curly-haired young man was on the stage singing John Denver with three of his friends, and their chaperone was playing guitar.

"Almost heaven, West Virginia, Blue Ridge Mountains, Shenandoah River!"

They were all off-key, including the chaperone. The timing was wrong and the words weren't always right, but they were singing without a hint of self-consciousness.

"I hear her voice in the morning hour she calls me, radio reminds me of my home far away!"

Watching them, I realized they were the next set of teachers on my walk, showing me what it looked like to simply be yourself without fear of judgment, to let it loose, let it go. They showed no signs of holding back. The sound itself was dissonant and I had to be careful not to wince, but the singers would not silence themselves and I loved them for that: the curly-haired young guy, the portly man with the suspenders and corduroy newsboy cap, the bespectacled man hunching over to see the lyrics, the chaperone. Why not sing out anyway? I felt a little braver about the possibility of getting up there myself.

"Country roads, take me home, to the place, I belong!" They finished on a G chord and the man with the suspenders shouted, "Yee-haw!"

An old, frail man wearing a mechanic's jacket got up next and played a few tunes on his guitar. He was with the group. His voice quaked, like his body, but he, too, sang with a quiet confidence, though he seemed to be making up the words as he went.

"Heaven is the home and the only, only home where we all want to be living all the time."

He was missing a finger on one hand, his chord hand, and when he came offstage I asked him about it. He had a twin brother, he told me, and once, when they were little, they were hacking away at a tree stump. It was his turn, but his brother wouldn't share the ax, so he put his hand on the stump. "Betchya won't do it," he said. Neither twin gave in. It wasn't a clean sever, so when he lifted his hand the finger was dangling. He only started crying after his brother did. They were taken to a judge later, for a lesson, and the judge said they were both guilty.

I told him I liked his songs.

"I get nervous," he said, "but I do my best."

After the open mic, the house band got up to do a few rockabilly songs. They asked me to play bass for them, because they were missing their regular guy. I'd never played bass before in my life, but the songs weren't too complicated and the lead guitarist, a young kid, walked me through every song, mouthing the chords as we went.

"E . . . A . . . B . . ."

I was missing a lot of the notes, but I remembered the nine-fingered old man and the "Country Roads" crew and I kept playing. The bass harmonies thundered from the body of the instrument right into my belly. I felt like an instrument myself, like something was playing me. The room seemed to slip from its moorings and I was lost in the sway of the resonance. The kid was a genius on the guitar, and there were certain moments, certain alignments of the sound between us that made me shiver. I played all night, long after everyone had left except Dave, a trucker named Norm who played the drums, and a guy named Larry who had a suitcase full of harmonicas.

"I was playing in my sleep back there," Norm said at one point from behind the drum set. "I got lost. I just zoned out. I was in another world."

I woke up the next morning to the near-silent patter of slushy snow on the roof. I took a hot shower. Not twelve hours earlier, I'd assumed I'd be waking up cold, wet, and miserable. I never thought it would be this. "Thank you," I whispered aloud. "Thank you."

Dave fixed me eggs benedict for breakfast. "One piece of advice for life: don't ever watch the news," he said, and I spent the day there, recording interviews and taking pictures. I was snowbound.

In the afternoon, a little girl came to carve a pumpkin. She cut out the stem and scraped out the seeds, making mounds on the newspaper. Her father stood by quietly, watching her, and her mother came out at one point to make sure she was warm enough in her pink I LOVE HORSES T-shirt. The girl forgot the pumpkin for a moment and rested her head against her mom's belly. I thought of my own mom back home. I thought of my dad, standing off in the distance watching me.

They'd never fought in front of us before, not like that, unannounced and uncontrolled. There was a photograph in one of the family albums that captured how I thought things still were between them. It was taken at their engagement party. In it, they're both in their twenties, facing each other and leaning forward, hands on their knees, noses just an inch or two apart. They're both mirroring each other's smile, this open-mouthed, goofy grin full of wonder and recognition. So much is possible. "What are we going to do together?" they seem to be saying. "Where will we go? What will we find?" There's a poem on the back of it now that Dad wrote to Mom right after the split, before enough time had passed for the wounds to fester as they did in the following years. A few lines still stand out:

> I see. I remember.
> I grieve. I'm grateful.
> I'm sorry.
> I wish you joy
> I love you.
> I breathe.
> I set you free
> Love of my life
> Therese Marie.

Words I cannot understand. What was it like to look at a photograph of your beloved, your once beloved, and to know it was all broken beyond repair? What was it like to say that kind of good-bye?

As everything I'd once trusted fell apart, I realized I'd been living a fantasy my whole life. This was how the fantasy went: Mom came from Delaware, the funky black sheep of a conservative family, the fourth of six kids, state politicians for parents. Dad came from Michigan, a high school teacher for a father, a nurse for a mother, also the fourth of six. Both were raised Catholic and took their faith seriously. Both went to India in their twenties, Dad to work at a mission church, Mom to work with Mother Teresa at the Home for the Dying. When they met in Chicago, Dad was a Jesuit novice, training to join the order, and Mom was thinking about entering a monastery in France. They fell in love so hard they dropped everything to get married. Now, we were a family. We moved all the time, apartment to apartment, house to house, but we moved together so it didn't matter. Eventually we landed in Erie. Dad was teaching religious studies at a college in town, and Mom was growing her massage practice, and the yoga. We even had our own little house in the suburbs, finally—oak trees in the front, a sledding hill in the back, a tire swing. We lived on Loveland Avenue.

One night they went out for a date at a nearby Panera, and only Mom came back, late. I knew something was wrong when I heard her slamming all the windows shut. First thing the next morning, Dad showed up, and they told us. Luke was five years old at the time; he stayed in the living room and watched cartoons. Caitlin would be twelve in a few days. I'd just turned fifteen. We both sat in Mom's lap, and Dad sat across from us. We were in the chairs where Mom met with her massage clients, where they told her what hurt and what wasn't working right.

"Well, tell them what's going on, Tom," Mom said, and Dad told us he was in love with a different woman. She was one of his college students, I found out later. We'd had her over for dinner.

I shouted a lot that morning. The whole neighborhood must've heard me. Dad just sat there and received it for hours. Eventually he left, who knows where. Mom sawed the bedframe in half. We brought the mattress down to the living room, and instead of eating dinner that night the four of us lay on the mattress and wept. After a while I couldn't stand it anymore. I went out into the warm, suburban night and made woodchips out of a tree stump with an ax. I ran and ran so everything in me burned. I struck a metal garbage can with my fists until they bled. I'd never known any of this was in me, this vulnerability to pain, this capacity for violence, this breakable heart now broken. I'd never known I could hurt so much.

One month later, we were packing up the minivan to move across Pennsylvania for good, hundreds of miles away. Dad wasn't coming with us, but he helped us get ready. The humdrum logistics of heartbreak were baffling: our clothes had to go in suitcases, our toys into boxes, and these had to go in the van. The pain was both transcendent and banal; it ripped me out of my skin, firing me off to another planet, but the van still had to be packed.

"Good-bye, Andrew," he said when it was done. "I'll see you soon. I love you." He opened his arms, and I turned away.

We pulled out of the driveway, but before we could get to the road that would take us to the interstate and then across Pennsylvania for good, I told Mom to stop. I ran out to him, and he held me. It was the first time I'd seen him cry that summer, the first time we'd cried together.

Our neighbor Al stood in his driveway across the street, watching everything. His bald head was glistening with sweat from the summer sun and his shirt was off, as it always seemed to be. I remember his immense gut. I remember his protruding belly button. As we drove away, he waved good-bye. He was smiling, but his cheeks were wet and it wasn't sweat. That's the last memory I have of that summer.

It was such a shock that I didn't know what I could trust anymore, or who. Everything I'd once believed now seemed suspect. I had to understand how this could've happened, and I had to prepare, in case it ever happened again.

I knew other kids whose parents had divorced, and they all seemed to survive. But as I experienced it for myself and continued on with my life, I realized that most people probably thought I was surviving, too, even when it felt like I was falling apart inside. The years passed, but the questions remained. They began to proliferate and shape-shift, but their origins remained the same: most had roots in the painful void of that loss. Who could I trust to fill that void? Only a real teacher, a mountaintop sage or an old wizard, someone who'd been living in a cave for a few decades and really knew his shit. I wanted this imaginary wise man to grab me by the shoulders, look me in the eyes, and tell me everything I needed to know: how to grow up and get old, how to be a good man, a good father, a good human being, and how to suffer well—or better yet, to my adolescent mind: how to avoid suffering altogether.

My questioning began in earnest the summer my parents separated, and with it, the fear that someday I would break like my dad had, that I would create something beautiful with someone and then destroy it, and lose myself in the process.

I thought of all this as I watched the little girl carve her pumpkin, and as she held her mother, and as her father gazed on in silence. Maybe I'd just keep walking for the rest of my life, alone. It might be better that way. I couldn't grieve the loss of a family I never had.

GAIL HOBBS-PAGE, *goat farmer and cheese maker*
ESMONT, VIRGINIA, *in the pen with her goats at Caromont Farm*
NOVEMBER, *one month on the road*

"Unlike any other group of livestock, they get into your blood and they get into—this is going to sound really corny—but they get into your heart. Each one of them has a wacky personality and so you sort of learn to be accepting of different kinds of personalities that don't necessarily fit into the norm. They are so loyal. They are so unemotional. They don't react. They act. You can be having the worst day and you can be so stressed out, and you can have an animal you're trying to manage, and she's acting awful and you want to discipline her or you want to yell at her, and you can do all those things, but it's only going to make you unhappy, because she's going to look at you and go, 'What?' Because she's a goat. It's a great life lesson.

"Let's see, other life lessons that really strike me about goats? Sisters, they're so loyal to each other. Goat sisters, there's nothing like them. They never forget each other. The boys, there's something to be learned there, too. They're vile creatures that are self-serving in many ways. They have an amazing ability to pleasure themselves, which is good to know!

"But, living a seasonal life with animals that you care about, that nurture you and give you milk and make food for your community, it just makes them so important. Every minute. There's not a day they're not checked. There's not a night that we don't tuck them into bed and make sure they're safe. If you're a good farmer, that's your *life. You don't regret it. You don't feel like you're confined. It's not confinement. It's your responsibility. It's your contract with the animal. And that relationship with that animal is what makes it worth doing, for me anyway."*

Chapter Four

"You've got a lot to learn."

If you want to walk across a continent, I'd recommend working as a manual laborer first. I worked summers, starting at thirteen as a blueberry picker. For the next ten summers, I did almost everything an unskilled freelance grunt can do. I even vacuumed a ceiling once.

One repeat client, an old Greek taskmaster named Gus, wanted to build a giant set of steps one summer. He hired a few other guys and trucked in enough stone, sand, and gravel to build the pyramids. He loved this metaphor, the pyramids. He'd sit in a director's chair like a pharaoh, shouting at us all day.

"This is how the Egyptians built the pyramids, you know!"

He'd bring us cold watermelon, and sometimes he'd work with us, even though he was in his seventies. He'd get in the dirt and toss the capstones around like they were Frisbees. But he preferred playing Pharaoh.

"That stone, put it right here. Hurry up. And put that one right there. What, it's too heavy? I thought you said you were strong. I'm paying you good money. The Egyptians didn't get paid good money. What a lazy shit."

I would then call him senile, move the slab, and we'd start the next stair. It was a long summer.

Most of my clients hired me to weed their lawns and gardens. I hated it, but unfortunately I was a good weeder, and there were always weeds, little reminders of the tenacious wildness waiting for suburbia to drop its guard. I was the guard. No dandelions allowed, by God, not on my watch! One summer I weeded a small forest for Gus. He wanted everything out but the pachysandra and the trees. I spent much of that summer waddling around in the squat position.

On the road, I could almost hear Gus laughing at me. "I was just getting you ready for your big walk, can't you see? I was teaching you patience and discipline. And you were so mad at me. You were such a pathetic, angry little shit."

When I set out to walk, I knew I didn't want it to be like building the stone stairs, the end determined from the beginning, each little detail micromanaged. I didn't want the walk to be an immaculate lawn, either, weedless and tamed and worried about. It's why I didn't take a smartphone. I knew I'd just end up nose-down, following the blue dot across the entire continent. There was magic in not knowing, a transformation of the unremarkable into the sublime. For example, gas stations. They became these little oases where I could drink sweet tea and eat ice cream, and the surprise of finding one unexpectedly was almost blissful. If I'd known there was a gas station exactly 0.3 miles ahead, the knee-jerk joy would've been diluted, the magic suffocated. And then there was serendipity, that inexplicable cascade of just-so conditions that moves you right where you didn't know you wanted to be, to people you didn't know you were looking for; by its very nature, it cannot be controlled, so I didn't try to. Instead, I let go, as best I could, into a lived experience of the unknown.

"This is in the end the only kind of courage that is required of us," Rilke wrote, in his *Letters*. "The courage to face the strangest, most unusual, most inexplicable experiences that can meet us . . . But the fear of the inexplicable has not only impoverished the reality of the individual; it has also narrowed the relationship between one human being and another, which has as it were been lifted out of the riverbed of infinite possibilities and set down in a fallow place on the bank, where nothing happens." The inexplicable. The unknown. The serendipitous. *Best make room for them*, I thought, *so something will happen.*

I did have a laptop, in order to scout out the basics of each week's route whenever I found an Internet connection. I was puzzling together a string of state highways and county roads that would get me south, because winter was coming. Some days I knew exactly where I'd be sleeping that night. I called those the "landing days," when I had a plan—it felt like touching down on solid earth again. But most days I didn't know. Those were the "flying days," when I took off into the unknown.

Farther south in Virginia, I was lost in the middle of nowhere, flying. I'd decided to take the back roads from Charlottesville to avoid walking on Highway 29. It had seemed pretty straightforward on Google Maps a few days before, when I'd scribbled down the directions in my notebook. Now, I saw that the back roads wended through the mountains, branching off left and right just like the rivers they followed, and the signage wasn't always clear. Houses were a rare sight in the dense autumn forest. At one point I was supposed to take a left onto Harlow Lane. It was a tiny dirt road that disappeared up a mountain, almost a trail. This was when I knew I was lost, or about to be.

It was only a twenty-minute climb to the top where the forest thinned. A few houses lined the roadside and everything was silent until a pickup truck roared to life. I saw it up ahead, rolling down a driveway. It turned my way, slowly creeping forward, and stopped right next to me. There were two white men in the truck—the driver, a very large fellow, and his passenger, an old man who was smiling and missing eye contact with me by an inch. He didn't seem to blink. The driver rolled down the window.

"Where are you going?" he said, emphasizing the "you." I explained my WALKING TO LISTEN sign and the sketchy Google Maps directions.

"This road dead-ends in half a mile," the driver said. "Your computer probably thought an old logging trail was a state road. You could end up going around in circles for hours if you don't know this neck of the woods. Hop in, I'll give you a ride back to the highway. Or you could try the logging road, if you really want to. You might make it."

I'd broken the rules to take rides twice at that point: over a bridge in Maryland—no walkers allowed—and then a few miles at dusk to a friend's house near D.C. That was enough. I wanted to walk every step. But I didn't want to get lost in the woods, either. The driver was waiting for an answer, and the old man in the passenger seat was still staring just beyond me. I didn't know what to do. Then, I heard a voice.

"Is this young man lost, Jeff?"

An old woman with close-cropped white hair and oval-lensed spectacles was walking across the front yard toward us. She was tall and sturdy, and a little girl trailed behind her. Jeff, the driver, was the old woman's son. We both explained the situation to her.

"It sounds like you're a long way from where you're trying to get, honey," she said. "You want some food? Something to drink?"

I hadn't been sure about Jeff. He'd done nothing wrong, but still, I hadn't gotten my bearings yet. I was like a prey animal, lost, alone, and on foot—easy to spook, ready to run. Trying to short-circuit my instinctual fear was like doing battle with evolution, fighting against a survival tactic that probably kept lots of my caveman ancestors alive. With the old woman, though, I didn't worry. She'd called me "honey."

Her last name was Harlow, just like the dirt road. I could call her Nettie, she said, or Nanny, which is what her granddaughter Christina called her. Christina stayed hidden behind her grandmother, peeking out occasionally to flash a smile. We went inside the house. The kitchen was tidy, everything just so. The sunlight had turned bronze with the late afternoon and it melted in through the windows. From the living room, I could hear the Redskins playing on TV. Nettie ordered me to get off my feet and to sit down at the table.

"Now, how about a big salad, just like you have at home," she said, "and a ham sandwich. And we can get you some crackers and a tall glass of milk, or a Dr. Pepper. Whatever you like."

I said, "Yes, ma'am, thank you, ma'am," like you're supposed to say in Virginia. Christina sat at the table with me. I made funny faces at her when her grandma wasn't looking. She was an easy giggle.

"We're just so glad you came here," Nettie said at one point, "and so honored to fill you up on your big walk. It's simple country food and a simple country home, but it's something. We're glad you got lost, because if you didn't we wouldn't have met you."

Something in me collapsed when I heard this, the way some runners do at the end of a marathon. Because this walk wasn't like running a marathon at all. There weren't any cheering crowds to remind me that I wasn't a complete fool to be doing this. I was anonymous. When the loneliness came, it came hard. I'd cried more in a single month than I had in ten years. My body always hurt. Every sunset, I just wanted to lie down and dissolve into the earth. And then someone like Nettie would come along.

I'd already met a number of exceptionally kind people on my walk, so many that the kindness was ceasing to be exceptional. Outside Baltimore, Corey Moseley and Lyneé Michelle had taken me into their home, right off the street. Lyneé sang R&B, and we all drove downtown together for her band practice. No one in the room seemed to mind me, a stranger, a random white guy in a predominantly black neighborhood. We all went out to karaoke after practice. And then near D.C., a construction worker named Rob had given me some cash straight out of his pocket, though I hadn't asked for it. "My son's gotta do a walk like that," he told me. "What does he do now?" I asked. "Drugs. Looking at two years in jail."

It kept happening. And then there were the interviews, this chorus of human voices. I listened to them in my memory when I was alone on the highway. "I'm so proud of you," Eddie Holmes said in Rising Sun, Maryland. "I'll be praying for you every morning." In Bel Air, not far away, Peggy Cherry told me, "You have to let go, even though it's hard." And now here was Nettie: "Enjoy it. And it'll be a transformation, when you get from Pennsylvania to California, or wherever you're going. You've got a lot to learn. You've got an education and a degree, but you've still got a lot to learn."

She'd already stuffed me full of food when she placed a slice of chocolate cake on the table. I managed to finish it, and before she could bring me anything else I carried my dishes to the sink. I tried to clean them, but she wouldn't let me.

"Don't touch those dishes. Go on into the living room and watch the Redskins game. You need to rest."

"Yes, ma'am," I said.

After a while, Jeff came back with his brother, Chris, a six-foot-eight-inch giant. We took out my map and discovered that I was only a few miles off track. But it was four o'clock. The walking day was done. I asked if I could pitch my tent in the yard, just for the night.

"No, darlin'," Nettie said, "you can sleep in the guest room upstairs. It's gonna be cold out tonight. And this way, if you stay, we can go for a drive and I'll show you the roads you'll take tomorrow so you won't get lost again."

We drove through a maze of backcountry byways that hugged the Appalachians and snaked along slow-flowing brooks—"We call 'em 'runs' down here." The roads and tractor paths and farmers' routes wrote an elegant cursive into the land. We flew by horse pastures and pumpkin fields littered with the rejects of Halloween, over train tracks mirroring the pink sky, and onward to the best spot in the county to watch the sunset: an emerald meadow, cows, a ragged red farmhouse, and the hills behind rising into the mountains.

"Now that we're out here we might as well go to Colleen's," Nettie said on our way back home. "You like ice cream, don't you? Colleen's is famous. I used to go there with my husband, RD, before he passed away. We'd sneak trips there together when he was on dialysis."

Here's the little I learned about Nettie Harlow during our ride together: She'd been taking care of Christina five days a week for the past four years while her parents worked. Christina would be five years old soon, and kindergarten would begin. "We won't have that connection after that," Nettie had said.

She was sixty-seven years old. She'd lived in tiny Arrington, Virginia, her whole life, working at the town post office for much of it. When she was a young woman, she used to have "dances and parties and get-togethers" where they'd push all the furniture back, put on some music, and waltz.

She had her first child at twenty-two. "I felt like a kid until he came into this world."

She believed in God—"It wasn't a coincidence you ended up with us, and it wasn't Google that googled you up here, either"— and she thought that Jesus was coming back someday, and that she was never alone, that no one ever was.

She thought more and more about death these days. She had a friend who called her every evening around eight o'clock to make sure she was okay.

Only fragments. I knew her just as she was right then and there. Her past wasn't present between us, and neither was mine. And yet, that presence felt so intimate. It was like a friendship on fast-forward.

Nettie pulled into Colleen's and we both got chocolate-vanilla twists and stood under the big ice cream cone sign licking them. Later, back at her kitchen table, she took out her banjo and I got my mandolin. Our sounds blended, slipping from dissonance to harmony and back again.

"We had a good time, didn't we?" Nettie said. "And we had some ice cream, too. Not everyone can say that."

I kept saying thank you, but the words felt so insufficient. I had these little polished pebbles I was giving everyone who helped me. The stone was called vogesite. A guy back home had told me it had a meaning behind it: unity in diversity, the antidote to apartheid. I liked that. And I liked imagining a string of human beings across the continent, each with their own little stone, connected to one another without even knowing it. Every stone looked different, but they were all from the same source, swirls of peach and gold, pink and brown and white. I gave Nettie a pebble. I think she appreciated the gesture, but after everything she'd done for me it almost seemed rude.

"Well, what about breakfast tomorrow?" Nettie asked. "I'll make a big one that I like to do sometimes. I call it my Bob Evans breakfast. We'll have scrambled eggs, pancakes, and sausage patties. We can have oatmeal, too. And do you like hot chocolate? I'd make you coffee, but I don't drink it. I made it every morning for forty years when RD was alive, but I got rid of the machine after he died."

On my way up to bed, I grazed a set of wind chimes hanging from the kitchen door frame. The slender metal rods struck one another gently, each one tinkling its own note, and the notes sang together, a song created only by contact.

"Good night, Andrew," Nettie said. "I love you."

I said good night, and that I loved her, too. It was a strange kind of love, but there was no denying it. It didn't matter that we'd only just met that day. Time had nothing to do with it. She'd found me when I was lost, and that was enough.

MEGHAN PCSOLYAR and *LAUCK HARRIS*, *seniors at Sweet Briar College*
SWEET BRIAR, VIRGINIA, *in their dormitory common room after showing me around campus*
NOVEMBER, *right before Thanksgiving*

"*We have these things called tap clubs, and they're our sororities basically. One of our roommates, Laura, is in the QVs. They're supposed to be the nice people on campus. Lauck and I are Chung Mungs, which are supposed to be the 'friendly ghosts.' We're supposed to be the people who are involved on campus but don't really get recognized for it. There's Paints and Patches, which are like the theater people. The Aints and Asses, which are the funny people. There's Bam. I don't really know what they do. They, like, clean up campus. What else, Lauck?*"

"*Katie and I are Green People. Those are the ones that help the QVs out all freshman year. Each club has a rival club. The QVs' rival is the Bum Chums, and they hunt out the girls in the middle of the night when they do their drops. Each QV baby has to go around and drop gifts at all the sophomores' doors. All in secret. The Bum Chums, during the drops, all run around campus looking for these babies. It's really weird to witness if you have no idea what's going on.*"

"*So what does it look like?*"

"*If you go into the upper quad after all these drops, all the Bums are up there, and then all the QVs in their costumes are chalking up on the driveway about how much they hate the Bum Chums, and how much better they are. It's really weird.*"

Chapter Five

"You're in this for quite a while."

I was carrying far more than I needed on my back, but in some ways, it was important. The mandolin, for example. It was an extra three or four pounds, but it helped me connect with people in a way that conversation just didn't allow. My Olympus LS-10 audio recorder, too. It gave people an excuse to reflect, to extrapolate meaning from their experiences. The taped conversations often became so rich. It was as if some of these people had been waiting to be asked these questions, holding their breath for years, and now finally they could breathe, share what they'd learned from their lives. No way was I going to get rid of the LS-10. I had more clothes than necessary, too, but to me it was worth the extra weight. Slipping on the same moist and reeking T-shirt in the cold at dawn just sucked, so I had a few T-shirts. The only thing I did end up dropping was my coffee operation. I had a mug, a filter that fit into the mug, loads of coffee grounds, sugar, and powdered creamer. But this was not an expedition in the wilderness. I was passing gas stations at least once a day. There was coffee everywhere.

I kept a bag full of food that would feed me for a week. I didn't need to carry so much, but I didn't want to risk it. The food bag normally had some combination of the following: instant oatmeal, Pop-Tarts, granola bars, peanut butter, Nutella, squeezable jelly, pita bread, tuna fish, beef jerky, Uncle Ben's precooked rice dinners, dried apricots, apples, and Snickers bars. I'd buy food at the grocery stores, which soon began to feel more alien than the highways. Once, somewhere in Virginia, I was standing in the checkout line, my backpack clogging up the aisle, and the tabloids informed me that Ashton Kutcher was embroiled in a cheating scandal and that Demi Moore was suicidal. The stuff seeped into my consciousness like poison, and something inside me railed to get back out into the unplugged inner space of walking, the wind, the arrhythmic lull of the highway. That was another privilege I was cashing in on: the privilege of going dark, of removing myself from the psychic bombardment of media and advertising that saturates America, online and off. So much noise. Many have no recourse against it, or can't even know how loud it really is because they don't have access to the gift of silence, no means to escape the noise, no refuge. I hadn't realized how much my mind had emptied over the past month on the road until I was caught in that grocery store aisle, and how good that growing emptiness actually felt. That quiet sense of peace was deeply subversive; the fate of entire industries depended on my discomfort with the silent emptiness, counted on my inability to just be with it.

The walking itself was slowly becoming my home, or something like it. It was the only constant, the connective thread that tied everything together. Heaving on my backpack and falling into the rhythm—right, left, right, left—I had three or four hours before my body really began to hurt, and that was the sweet spot. I'd be walking, but it felt more like easing into an old recliner that fit me perfectly, enthroned in a house that I myself had built.

There were all different kinds of walking: high-walking and howl-walking, groove-walking and daze-walking. Like separate airstreams swirling together in the sky, one would lead into the next. I'd flow through these currents all day, bliss-walking into burn-walking into fury-walking. I had little control over them, but

I did learn how they worked, and how they felt, and how to identify them, and there was a kind of power in that naming.

People kept taking me in. Strangers were passing me to one another like I was a baton in a relay race. In the Blue Ridge Mountains south of Roanoke, Becki Compton and Dale Crittenden put me up. They were in their fifties or sixties and lived in a little ranch house with wood-paneled walls and low ceilings. It smelled faintly of cigarettes inside. Outside, a sea of mist swallowed the mountaintops. Where the forests had been cleared, the land was a patchwork quilt of pastures and farm fields. Highway 221 ran through towns that didn't show up on the map. The world up there was silent—just the occasional cow or pickup truck. I'd been expecting to camp out every night for the next 130 miles, but at lunchtime I'd met Becki. She worked at the gas station in Bent Mountain. When I said I wasn't sure where I'd be sleeping that night, she offered to put me up, almost on the spot.

"It pulled my mother heartstrings," she said later that night.

By the time I arrived at the house at dusk, Becki had already driven home from work. She was cooking fried chicken. Dale was home, too, and he met me on the front stoop with coffee in a Winnie the Pooh mug, which steamed in the cold. He was balding, bespectacled, and he had skin like rough, pale granite. He spoke matter-of-factly and he always seemed to be chuckling, even when he was quiet. He was a mechanic now, but in the past he'd loved traveling. He had worked construction all across the Southeast and up into Pennsylvania. At one point he had landed in Wyoming where he'd stayed to work on the drilling rigs.

"It was hard work, but I really liked that type of work. It was just something that clicked for me. It was a real challenge every day, and I liked doing something I never done before. It's kind of like going, oh, I don't know, going out and climbing up some rocks and taking a chance of falling. It can be dangerous, but you just have to keep focused on your job. There's so many moving things, so many ways you could get hurt, easy. And a lot of people think you just drill a hole in the ground and oil starts squirting out. That's not the case. You might drill and never find anything, or not enough to make it worthwhile, so you just cap it off." The risk, the exhaustion, the search for something hidden far below—sounded a bit like my walk.

Dale told me about the person they referred to as "the worm." "He was the new guy," Dale said. "He was learning. He pretty much just got the grease gun, and there was a lot of greasing to be done."

I'd been walking for a month, but it still felt like I was the worm on the road, the clueless new guy, the poor bastard who spent the whole day working the grease gun. On the rigs, Dale told me, the worm was at the bottom of the hierarchy, and above him stood the chain hand, the motor hand, the derrick man, and the driller.

"If somebody's beginning, you have to take them around and show them the ins and outs of 'Don't do this. Don't do that. You gotta watch for this. You gotta watch for that. You gotta just be careful or you could get hurt, quick.'"

They'd torment the worm, tell him to climb up to the crown and put some water on the water table. The water table, of course, was underground. The crown was 120 feet up on the rig. The worm would fill a five-gallon bucket of water and lug all forty pounds of it up to the tippy-top.

"They'd get way up there and come back down," Dale said. "'Where do I put it? I don't see no place to put it.'" It still made him laugh.

How long would it take to become a chain hand, I wondered. And a driller? Being the worm could be fun, but it was also exasperating, and confusing, and sometimes terrifying. A worm really is the perfect metaphor for a beginner—vulnerable and blind, helpless and slow. And I wasn't just the worm on the road. I was the worm in life. It wasn't easy being the worm. I wished there were a way to speed the whole thing up.

But at least I wasn't a worm on an oil rig. That much I could appreciate after hearing Dale's stories. It was seventy degrees below zero on the coldest day Dale ever worked. He was up on the derrick where there wasn't any heat. He wore every piece of clothing he had, and duck coveralls on top. Before he climbed up to the derrick, he had a guy spray him down with water, which froze as soon as it hit him. This way, he was wearing a shield of ice and the wind couldn't get in. It blew from below, though, right up his pant legs. And I thought Virginia in November was bad.

One winter, Dale slipped and broke his temple bone. It was seven thirty in the morning. He worked all day. "Had a heck of a headache," he said. "Doctor said I'd look kind of funny running around with a cast on my head. I didn't think that was too funny, seeing as I couldn't talk." He laughed. "Oh, that was great."

We finished our coffee and went inside. Becki's daughter, Shannon, lived in the house, too, along with her two little kids, Storm and Bri. Storm, seven or eight years old, had a budding country southern accent. He shook my hand solemnly, as if I were the president.

"Show him where the shower is, Storm," Becki said, and he led me to the bathroom with ceremonial seriousness. "He practiced before you got here," Becki whispered to me as I passed.

After dinner, Storm and I formed a band, he on my harmonica, I on the mandolin. We played at the kitchen table while his little sister danced. It was another one of those magical moments, like the one when Dave said I could spend the night in his general store. Suddenly, there was no such thing as loneliness. My fear, so alive on the highway, was nowhere to be found in the presence of these children. We were just playing, that was all; I knew they had no idea of the magnitude of their influence on my state of mind, of the gift they were giving me. Maybe they'd understand someday.

Before she went to bed, Bri showed me a drawing she'd done. A wobbly egg shape took up most of the page. It had a dot for a right eye and a big circle for a left eye. Its mouth was a straight line and its limbs were sticks.

"Who is it?" I asked.

She didn't say anything—I hadn't heard her speak all night—but she tapped me on the head with her pencil like it was a magic wand. I stared at myself on the page, a wobbly egghead man, feeling honored.

"Normally she doesn't interact with strangers," Becki said. "She's too shy, most of the time."

We didn't play for too long because the kids had school the next day. On top of that, their mother didn't trust me. Shannon posted on Facebook that her folks had taken in a serial killer for the night. Becki pointed this out to me on the computer as we were all going to bed. She thought it was funny.

Would I take me in, I often wondered, *a complete stranger on the road?* The amount of trust required to put me up for the night was staggering. When Becki and Dale fell asleep they'd be completely vulnerable. They didn't know me. There was simply no guarantee I wouldn't do something heinous in the dark of night. I was only putting myself at risk when we all went to bed, but for them everything hung in the balance: their child, their grandchildren, their home. Their greatest offering to me wasn't just a place to sleep that night; it was their trust. They believed in my goodness, even though they'd only known me for a few hours. They saw me as worthy. They treated me better than I probably would've treated myself. It was utterly humbling, and it made me want to be the best possible version of myself.

By the time I woke up the next morning, the kids had already left for school. Storm had written me a note: "Andrew i had a fun time last night. Hope you stop by when you are going back home."

Leaving Becki and Dale was the only way to continue the walk, to meet the next person down the road; only with good-bye could there be hello. But it meant I had to start all over again. It meant I had to go back into the aloneness. In my tattered copy of *Leaves of Grass*, Whitman had anticipated this dilemma:

> Sit a while wayfarer,
> Here are biscuits to eat and here is milk to drink,
> But as soon as you sleep and renew yourself in sweet clothes
> I will certainly kiss you with my goodbye kiss and open
> the gate for your egress hence.

That was the hard part: to wake up each morning, say good-bye, and just walk away. And keep walking. Most of the time I didn't want to take the leap into the unknown that came with every sunrise. Easier to dream the leap than to live it. Less painful, too, to just dream. But Whitman was stern:

> Long enough have you dreamed contemptible dreams,
> Now I wash the gum from your eyes,
> You must habit yourself to the dazzle of the light and of
> every moment of your life.

> Long have you timidly waded, holding a plank by the shore,
> Now I will you to be a bold swimmer,

To jump off in the midst of the sea, and rise again and nod
to me and shout, and laughingly dash with your hair.

I was never this jubilant in the mornings, never laughingly
dashed my hair. I was a much more pathetic sight, often heavy-
hearted, sometimes sniffling, discomfited to be on my own again.

Old wooden barns marked the miles in the mountains. They seemed
ancient. Bare tree branches, ink black, wove labyrinths against the
clouds. I saw a stream of bubbles rising from behind a house, and
then a little boy chasing after them. His mother trailed behind.
Farther on, a gruesome blue cloud raced across a glen. A man was
smoking a cigarette nearby, working on his truck. He looked at me
and then nodded at the cloud.

"Be careful out there," he said.

A few nights later I had to camp without permission. It was
called "stealth camping," I'd read online. For the whole trip, I'd
been anticipating stealth camping with some anxiety. That night, I
was caught in the middle of the forest at the end of the day and I
had no choice but to trespass. The cold was crushing and I fumbled
with my tent. I still wasn't familiar with the puzzle of poles because
I'd hardly camped out at all. My hands were useless blocks of ice. I
set up silently. There could be anyone out there.

An afterglow of twilight glimmered through the branches
above, a stained-glass ceiling. I heated up a packet of Uncle Ben's
Spanish rice over my pocket stove. It wouldn't fill me, so I pulled
out a sleeve of tuna from the food bag and mixed it in. They say
anything tastes good after a long hike. They're wrong.

The temperature steadily fell. I crawled into my tent, and then
into my sleeping bag. The cold seeped through. It was too early to

sleep and too cold to do anything but lie there and wait for it. The forest was still and silent. I was still and silent, too, and it made me uncomfortable tonight. I didn't quite know how to be alone without doing something, no miles to walk, no calls to make, no words to write. Just nothing. It disturbed me, and the fact that it disturbed me disturbed me even more.

The cold climaxed at daybreak. My nose was numb and my neck was stiff. My breath had frozen to a crystalline powder on the mesh ceiling above. I gave it an upward slap, expecting the ice to slough off the outside. Instead, it sprinkled down on my face. The last thing I wanted to do was get out of my sleeping bag because it was so cold, but at the same time I just wanted to get the morning over with, which meant I had to get out of the sleeping bag. I was paralyzed for a while, and I could feel the doubt sliding into me. *Why am I doing this again?* Before it could go too deep I got moving. *Don't think about it. Just do what you have to do. Make the oatmeal. Break camp. Pack up. Get on the road.* The doubt began to dissipate into the walking, and after a mile or two it was mostly gone.

It wasn't long before I came across a run-down gas station. I was running low on water and wanted to fill up, but the entrance to the place was unclear. The front door looked like it might lead to a janitor's closet. When I opened it and stepped inside, I found myself in the middle of a circle of men sitting in chairs. Each one of them was mountainous and unspeaking.

"I'm sorry," I said, "am I interrupting something?"

"No, no," one of the men said, "we just meet every morning to discuss."

"Oh, okay . . . What do you guys discuss?"

"You know, this and that. Mostly Mr. Pumpkin's jacket here."

All the men in the circle guffawed, except for Mr. Pumpkin.

He was wearing a Halloween orange snowmobile jacket. He didn't look amused.

"Do you mind if I fill up my water bottle?"

"Of course. Go on back."

Shoulder-high shelves ran all the way to the back, most of them empty. The few snacks and canned goods for sale looked like antiques. A film of dust covered everything. If it weren't for the men up front, I'd have thought the place was abandoned, a gas station of ghosts. I filled up my bottle from a tap and then made for the exit.

"What's that mean, walking to listen?" one of the men asked as I squeezed through the circle to get to the door. I explained.

"Well, why don't you sit for a while? You can hear about what it's like to be a jack-o'-lantern."

Mr. Pumpkin frowned silently in response to the laughter. I didn't need the rest, but I was eager for company so I took a seat in the circle. The discussion turned to black bears.

"They say they can run twenty-five miles an hour. Faster than a deer and bigger than a moose, that's what I've heard."

"You heard right. I killed one earlier this week. Took me two days to haul out."

"What are you supposed to do when you see one?" I asked.

"Well, the first thing I do is shit my pants. Then, when that's all done and cleaned up, I get the hell out of there."

"What's it taste like?"

"Dog."

Farther on down the road, the forest opened up into pasture-land. Black Angus cattle lounged on green beds of grass. A field of cut cornstalks to the east recalled another such field two hundred miles north near Charlottesville where an old grandmother had been selling produce: swollen tomatoes, mason jars of honey, pumpkins and peanuts and baskets of apples. She had given me an apple.

This memory reminded me of a billboard I'd seen not far from that produce stand—the image of a car's rearview mirror reflecting an angry God riding the clouds of the apocalypse. Etched at the bottom of the mirror were the words: OBJECTS IN MIRROR ARE CLOSER THAN YOU THINK.

This memory, in turn, made me think of a sign I'd seen outside a church just the day before: FALL IN LOVE WITH JESUS LEAVE SATAN BEHIND.

The littlest things triggered memories from hundreds of miles past, and so I drew the unlikeliest connections between the seemingly disconnected. Black Angus cattle took me straight to Satan by way of a harvested cornfield, a sweet old grandma, and a billboard of Judgment Day.

The walk that day turned out to be one of the hardest yet. The doubt. I couldn't shake the feeling that I was utterly alone, that I always had been and always would be. I called it hurt-walking. Everything ached with a heaviness that wasn't my backpack. My footsteps became a blind laboring, every breath a task. I could feel my hope bleeding out, carrying with it my ability to see anything as beautiful or worthwhile. It was the opposite of float-walking, when the road carried me like a river and I couldn't help but laugh. Float-walking never lasted as long as I would've liked. Hurt-walking always lasted longer.

Just as the sun began to set, I saw a fire station sign up ahead. Salvation. Firefighters always helped me out.

The station came into view, but it didn't look good. There were no cars in the parking lot, and it was dark inside. The department's name was written on the brick facade in bold letters: HORSEPASTURE DIST. VOL. FIRE DEPT. Volunteer departments weren't staffed 24/7 like the career departments. I knocked on the door anyway. Nothing. I shouted hello. My voice was shrill. Nothing. I was on my own again.

As I was walking away, I saw a big warehouse behind the fire station with dozens of cars parked out front, so I meandered over. When I pulled open the door, a riotous ocean of sound hit me hard. The voices of nearly a hundred people bounced off the high ceiling into magnified echoes. Bright fluorescent lights illuminated the massive space. Grandfathers conferred together over the dinner tables. Children ran wild across the slick cement floor while their mothers kept watch. In the center of the warehouse, people were tossing beanbags at holed plywood boards lying on the ground. After feeling so profoundly alone all day, it seemed like I'd just walked onto a movie set, or maybe into another dream.

In front of me at the door, a woman sat behind a table selling admission tickets. I introduced myself and asked where I might find a firefighter. She pointed to a big guy with a goatee not far away.

"That's my husband over there," she said. "You can go talk to him."

"Thanks," I said. "Oh, and what is all this?"

"Cornhole," was all she said. I assumed she was referring to the beanbag game, but she might've been calling me a derogatory name. I didn't ask. Jeff Painter was her husband, and he said I could pitch my tent behind the fire station, out of the wind. The event was a fund-raiser: the Winter Cornhole Showdown. Cornhole was a game in which opponents threw beanbags tit-for-tat, trying to land them on top of the plywood boards or drop them right into the hole. The cornhole. The tournament had about a dozen games going on at once, so the warehouse reverberated with the sound of beanbags hitting plywood, like muffled shotgun blasts.

There were more people than I could possibly meet. It was the starkest contrast from the way I'd spent my day, hurt-walking in a quagmire of solipsistic pity. With each conversation my loneliness faded, until I felt a sense of unexpected belonging.

"Here we go, baby!" a woman named Connie kept shouting. Her husband and her father were on a team together, and they were vying for first place. "Come on, Daddy!" They'd won second place the month before: fifty dollars. First place was two hundred dollars. She told me there was a pretty big cornhole scene in Horsepasture, and that her family had their own tournaments out in their barn. "We love it," she said. I devoured this kind of small talk all night. For me, it wasn't small at all. It was so much better than stealth camping again.

People were starting to leave, and Jeff came over to me, arms folded across his chest. "When you first came in here I was worried," he said, his voice a rolling bass. "I thought you were Occupy, or someone here to make trouble. Just assumed, and I'm not proud of that. If you had to call me something, I'm a conservative. A conservative Republican. But I'm a thoughtful person and I want to hear what the other person has to say. And that's what you're doing. I'm envious, man. You're going to meet so many different people with so many different ways of thinking." He told me he'd arranged it with the fire chief so that I could spend the night inside the warehouse.

"If he said no, Ginger and I would have taken you back to our house," he said. "The more I got to thinking of you outside in your tent, the more I kept thinking, 'Oh, hell no.'"

Jeff began to fuss over me, almost pamper me. He showed me the bathroom and the shower. He made sure I knew about the leftover nachos and pizza. He pulled a thick carpet to the center of the warehouse so I wouldn't have to sleep on the cement. He explained how to use the big-screen TV hanging from the ceiling, in case I got bored. Ginger left for a few minutes and returned with a bag: shampoo and a towel, chocolates, a twenty-dollar bill. She insisted I hand over my dirty clothes so she could wash them.

"You sure you'll be all right in here?" Jeff said on his way out. "Lock all these doors so nobody can get you. I don't know what it is, but I feel like your damn mama."

The next morning, Jeff came by with my clean clothes and breakfast sandwiches from Ginger—homemade biscuits, fried eggs, country ham. As I was packing up, I asked him about firefighting, some questions I'd been wondering the night before. His voice was even deeper this morning, possibly from a slight hangover.

"It's pretty tough, sometimes it is," he said. "Especially when you lose somebody. But overall it's a waiting game. Ninety percent of the time you're doing nothing but cleaning trucks. And then when there's a fire? The adrenaline is what keeps you going. It's pretty interesting how you can go from a dead sleep at three in the morning to: you're in the vehicles and it's loud and there's a lot of light and a lot of action and you'd think you'd been awake for three days. It's good. It's better than sitting at home and watching football on TV."

I asked him about the worst fire he ever saw. He said it was a three-alarm fire. "Lost two babies and a daddy." He didn't say anything more, and I didn't press him. We were quiet for a few seconds, but it felt much longer.

"Do you ever feel fear?" I asked.

"You feel fear a lot of times, especially in a house fire, because you don't know what's going to happen next. But you just don't think about it."

I mentioned that I felt fear almost every day on the road, and that maybe walking and firefighting weren't as different as they seemed.

"I don't know," he said. "I think, for me, it's totally different. Because it's other folks could cause you to be fearful of something. And what we have here is fire, an inanimate object. That object can take you and it can kill you. But to me, it's a lot easier to take care of that object than what you might come upon on the road. People can be mean. Fire's mean all the time, but you know it up front. People can surprise you. They can fool you. And mine's over real quick. Yours will last for quite a while. Yeah, you're in this for quite a while."

All the unwalked miles ahead of me seemed to project themselves across the ceiling of the warehouse, a continent stretching out for thousands and thousands of miles. It was a preposterous number of footsteps. Dizzying. I tried not to think about it. Just fight the fire. Just weed the forest. Just walk.

I played a song for Jeff on my mandolin before I left, a kind of thank you. I didn't have much else to give, except for a polished vogesite pebble.

"This is for your tip jar," he said when I finished, handing me one hundred dollars. A few days after I made it to Greensboro, he posted a comment on my blog:

> Sunday am when you were walking out of sight from the fire dept I had the same feeling as if you were one of my children or a brother leaving for an extended time already wondering when you would be back but realizing that I would probably never see you again, in person, in this life. I felt this nagging sense of guilt, did I do enough? I should have done more!!!!! I can't imagine what your family is

going thru, I know we will be praying for you daily and looking forward to hearing about your adventures and SAFE travels. I am going to email everyone I know on your path and tell them to adopt you for an evening. Be safe and get back home to your family. Ginger says hello. If you see a cornhole game going on stop and play. Jeff.

We'd spent just a few hours together in the same warehouse, and just a couple moments in conversation, and yet there was this strange kind of love between us, the same thing I felt with Nettie Harlow and Dale and Becki. I'd never experienced that kind of instantaneous connection with strangers before this walk. It made me wonder why not, and if it was even possible without doing something outlandish like walking across a continent.

HACKY PITTS, Renaissance woman
HIGH POINT, NORTH CAROLINA, on the couch in her living
room over dinner
NOVEMBER, after Thanksgiving with my friends Jim and Nancy
Bryan in Greensboro

"I've been a widow for thirty years, so I'm used to being alone. I ought to be used to it by now. And I like it. I like not having to be on a schedule except my own schedule. And I don't like to have to explain things to people because I know in my head, so why do I have to tell you? Go find out yourself! And growing old, it's not bad at all. I'll tell you one thing, though: I don't mind being seventy-seven, but in three years, eighty! Oh God. I'll have to start acting like an old lady."

"If you could go back, and taking all of what you've learned in your life, tell your twenty-three-year-old self something, what might you say?"

"I wouldn't worry so much. I used to worry myself to death, and now I realize, the things you worry about, how many of them come true? Very seldom. I'd go barefoot more. And I wouldn't be nice. I wouldn't be the nice little southern girl. I'd be a bitch. A man got on the plane, six hundred pounds, 'You don't mind if I put this armrest up?' and I said, 'I certainly do!' But you know, years ago I would've said, 'Oh, that's quite all right. Please do. Crush me! I don't care.' I wasn't passive aggressive, I was just passive."

Chapter Six

"What are you really listening for?"

The autumn boomed in North Carolina. *North Carolina.* I couldn't believe I'd walked that far. The state sign welcomed me on a back road just north of Greensboro. There were no cars, and the forest was quiet. I put my backpack down and just stared at the sign for a while. The continent was slowly sliding away beneath me. I ate a few Snickers bars before I started walking again. They'd gotten me this far.

I'd been walking for over a month now, and I wasn't asking people about "transformation" or "coming of age" anymore. It came off too contrived, like I was trying to force my own agenda on the conversations. Instead, I just started talking to people about their lives and, sometimes, what their lives had taught them. The more authentically interested I was, the better I listened, the more it seemed people opened up. A few days into North Carolina, one woman pulled over in her minivan, her two daughters in the backseat, and after just a couple minutes she told me all about her hysterectomy and how it had changed her life, just like that. It was not an unusual interaction. Often people would go straight to the heart of things, to the alchemical life moments that made them. They told me about motherhood and fatherhood, abandonment and abuse, drug addiction and death, conversion experiences and war trauma. There was the lighter stuff, too—raccoon hunting and biscuit baking and the finer points of mudding (where you get your friends in the back of your pickup truck and spin donuts until everyone's filthy or the truck gets stuck). After walking alone on the highway all day, I could listen for hours, and sometimes I did. Mostly, it was a delight. An honor. Sometimes, though, I met people who said hateful things, and I didn't know how to listen to them.

Somewhere outside Thomasville, North Carolina, I met a big bald guy who wanted to walk with me for a while. We met in the middle of a crosswalk. He was coming right toward me. "Are you walking to listen?" he said, changing directions so we were now striding side by side. I explained my sign.

"That's great, brother. Mind if I join you?"

A rural swath of the North Carolina Piedmont lay ahead. It looked pretty remote on the map, so I was glad to have a companion. The guy didn't seem prepared for a long walk, though. He was wearing a blue button-down shirt with a tie and shiny black shoes. He was quite pale and he didn't have a hat, so his bald scalp would surely get sunburnt.

We crossed an overpass, stopping to watch I-85 rush below us. "Can I ask you something?" the guy said. "What are you *really* listening for?"

"What do you mean?" I asked, although I knew what was coming.

"What do you believe happens after you die, brother?" he said, clasping his hands together. And then he started "witnessing," as the evangelists call it. Proselytizing. He believed that babies were all born "sick with sin." He included homosexuality in a list of evils that also included rape, murder, and incest. He said we'd all broken the Ten Commandments and that Jesus was the only way to eternal life in heaven.

"I receive you," the true listener says with her eyes. "I see you, no matter what you say, and I accept you, just as you are." There's a deeper kind of listening that's mutually exclusive with judgment and the desire to control or convert. Oddly enough, this type of listening is often the most subversively transformative; as soon as you don't need someone to change their mind, they're much more inclined to do so, because it's not a fight. There's no need to defend, and so it's safe to explore something new. But that kind of listening isn't easy, especially when what's being heard is abhorrent to you, when you know it's causing harm. I didn't want to receive the evangelist, or see him, or accept him. I tried to shut down, but he wouldn't shut up.

"We were brought together by the hand of God, brother," the evangelist said. "We normally don't come to church out here, but we did today, and just as we were driving out we saw you and your sign. Walking to listen. I thought, 'God is sending me a signal here.' So I had to come back and catch you, because I believe you're listening for the good news, my friend, and I'm here to share it with you."

"The good news is you're wrong," I wanted to say, but I didn't. And I wasn't quick enough to quote Whitman, either, but I should have:

Divine am I inside and out, and I make holy whatever I
    touch or am touched from;
The scent of these arm-pits is aroma finer than prayer,
This head is more than churches or bibles or creeds.

I hadn't showered in several days, so the evangelist could've smelled how divine I was, if only I'd waxed poetic on Whitman. But instead, I froze. I just stayed quiet, nodding, itching with shame at my own silence.

He was a martial arts teacher in Denton, a few towns south, but evangelism was his real passion, he told me; he tied it into his karate lessons, somehow. The guy continued witnessing to me as we left the overpass, but before we could reach the state highway that would take us into the countryside, a woman pulled up in a minivan—his wife, I assumed.

"That's my ride, brother," he said, cutting off his sermon as abruptly as he'd begun it. "Thanks for the fellowship. I love you."

I wanted to call him an ignorant bastard, but instead I said, "I love you, too," and that made me feel even sicker. Because I didn't love him. I hated him. And I hated myself for not speaking up. Martin Luther King Jr. had always been one of my heroes, and he had a line about the "appalling silence of the good people." I didn't understand the allure of that silence until I started encountering prejudice on my walk. It was so much easier than speaking up. One old woman in Virginia said she "disagreed" with homosexuality. I said nothing. Not long after that, a young white guy told me he was "racial," which I took to mean "racist." He said it like it was his blood type or something. I responded: "Oh."

I was afraid of confrontation. I wanted people to like me. My logic was flawed: if I pretended like everything was fine, then surely it would be. I got quite familiar with my cowardice because the prejudice was everywhere, in all forms. It would pop up in conversation, or quietly on the road.

PARKING FOR
CONFEDERATES
ONLY
ALL OTHERS
GO BACK NORTH

Often it came from the very same people who took me in and cooked me dinner. Down the road in Georgia, a woman warned me about walking through the next town. "All the whites left," she said, "and the help stayed, and the southern black is a whole different animal than the northern black." This woman also put me up for the night, and took me out for dinner, and made me breakfast the next morning. It was extremely disconcerting to feel so grateful and repulsed at the same time.

I called my friend Rhiya when I made it to North Carolina and told her about all this, about not knowing how to speak up or what to say. She suggested I simply ask why. *Why do you believe that?* Let them work out the absurdity of it for themselves.

I didn't get that far with the evangelist. He got into the car and waved good-bye. There was a good chance I'd see him again, though, because I'd be passing through his town a few days later.

"Maybe I'll see you in Denton," I said as the car was rolling away.

"Maybe I'll see you in heaven," he shouted out the window.

That night, I slept in a Baptist church, in a prayer room littered with cricket carcasses. The pastor had come to my rescue when I stumbled into the church's community hall asking permission to camp out. It was Sunday, and that meant breakfast-for-dinner for the congregation. A bulbous, mustachioed man dressed in Carolina blue fried dozens of sausage patties and pancakes on a flattop grill. There was coffee. There were people. There was a roof over my head. This, to me, was heaven.

After dinner, the congregants went to the church, and the pastor invited me to join them. A missionary had come to give a guest lecture about his work in Brazil. It was part of a series they called "Missionary Extravaganza." Inside, the church was decorated for Christmas. Only a few of the front pews were filled. I sidled into one of them, taking my seat next to a potbellied guy with veiny cheeks. The piano sang and we accompanied: "Silent night, holy night, all is calm, all is bright." The carols carried me back home. I'd never missed Christmas before, and I was going to this year.

A very tall, gaunt man in a three-piece suit approached the altar: the missionary. He began his presentation, speaking in an unfamiliar language about "church planting" and the recruiting of "mature disciples," about all the "unreached people groups" in the Amazon, and about our role as officers on crusade in the army of God. He had a PowerPoint that explained everything.

At the end there was some time for questions. No one raised a hand. After several long seconds I finally raised mine, just to get the conversation going. It was like one of those awkward silences after a lecture in college. Somebody had to ask *something*, and no one else was volunteering.

"So, when you're trying to convert someone who doesn't know the first thing about Christianity, where do you even begin?" I asked. I was talking about the indigenous people he targeted in Brazil. However, the missionary thought I was referring to myself, and he took it as an invitation to witness, not unlike the big bald evangelist.

The missionary locked eyes with mine and began preaching the story of Jesus—the teachings, the miracles. He sped forward to the crucifixion, spreading his arms wide as if on a cross of his own, his voice trembling. It seemed he was seeing it happen right there in front of him—the forty lashes, the crown of thorns, the nails and the hammering and the cross. He was choking up. His eyes were glistening. He began walking toward me.

"Why did he have to die?" he said, his arms reaching for the walls. "Why, oh, why did he have to die?"

A woman sitting in the pew in front of me was crying quietly. Next to me, the potbellied guy with the veiny cheeks was smiling. The missionary was standing above me now.

"He died for you," he said, looking down at me. "That's why."

I hadn't broken eye contact with the missionary since he began. It was out of respect, at first, and then it became a weird sort of staring contest. My vision pulsed gently in the gaze. The missionary broke the spell and turned to the pastor.

"Brother, I want to ask you to come put your hands on this young man. We're all gonna pray that he'll be born again to God right here on this very night."

The pastor put his hands on my shoulders and prayed, and the missionary murmured, "Amen," and "Oh, yes," and "Oh, Lord." I closed my eyes, leaving to go float with the darkness inside.

I almost wanted something to happen. I was curious about God, and I wanted that curiosity to be more than just a wondering. I wanted it to be a knowing reinforced by experience, by visions that I myself had seen. I was looking for God the same way I had looked for Santa Claus as a nine-year-old, and so far with the same result. I'd planned it so well that Christmas. I kept the door to my room cracked so I had a clear line of sight into the living room. I set my alarm clock to go off in an hour—it'd wake me up if I fell asleep. Then, I sat, and waited, and watched. It wasn't long before I fell asleep, and the alarm clock didn't work. Missed him again.

When I left home, I didn't expect God to become such a constant question on my walk. To many, the WALKING TO LISTEN sign was highly suggestive of a spiritual quest, especially in the Bible Belt. Lots of people thought I was listening for God. They gave me Bibles and pamphlets—"Have you been naughty or nice?" They shared their "testimonies," extemporaneous soliloquies that were part personal story and part sales pitch. Jan, an old woman at a diner in Clover, South Carolina, told me hers:

"I would just like to say that we have a free choice. What you do with your life, what you do with Christ, is what determines whether you go to heaven or hell. He says, 'Come and accept me and I will give you peace and joy.' Now, you gonna have troubles. You gonna have trials. I lost a son over five years ago, and that was so hurtful. But God gave his son, so what is it? That I should just say, 'Oh, I can't do that?' Jesus Christ is my personal savior. And that way I have been able to go through life and walk with him and walk with people. I don't knock people's religion, because I love all of them. I love you. I love her. And why can't I love everybody? Because Jesus loves everybody. So, I love you."

Sometimes these testimonies offered raw glimpses into a person's past, and I was moved. Other times their contradictions and judgments rankled me. Either way I couldn't escape it, the question of God. People asked me over and over again: "Do you believe in God?" I'd never had to confront that in myself so directly before. *Do I? Don't I? What do I say?* Most people were looking for a yes or no answer. There didn't seem to be much of an interest in the question: What or who is God, anyway?

But maybe that was never the task at all, to answer the question. Sometimes just asking the question seemed to be enough. Maybe the answers would appear once I actually understood the questions. I'd recently turned to Rainer Maria Rilke about this, in *Letters to a Young Poet*: "Be patient toward all that is unsolved in your heart and try to love the questions themselves," he wrote. "Do not now seek the answers, which cannot be given you because you would not be able to live them. And the point is, to live everything. Live the questions now. Perhaps you will then gradually, without noticing it, live along some distant day into the answer." I'd come back to this passage often, especially when the questions felt unbearable.

In the Baptist church, with the pastor's hands on my shoulders, there was clearly some kind of spirit moving the people around me. The missionary was heaving with emotion. The woman in front of me was crying. But I just couldn't get there, not like that. I preferred my question to their answer.

The pastor finished praying over me. Opening my eyes, I thanked him, and I nodded at the missionary. Were they disappointed I didn't start convulsing or speaking in tongues? It was all a bit anticlimactic, and they probably thought it was my fault.

Back in the prayer room, the man who'd cooked breakfast for dinner had left me a box of leftover pancakes and sausage patties with a little container of syrup. This, perhaps, was God. I lay down on the floor in my sleeping bag among the cricket carcasses, under the giant wooden cross on the wall, dipping the pancakes into the sweet syrup, illuminated by moonlight.

The next morning, I entered the heart of the North Carolina Piedmont. Evergreen forests grew thick on the hills, and tobacco fields covered the earth like patches on a coat. Left foot, right foot, left foot, right foot. The strangeness of the previous night faded into the new day's light, the hum of the highway, this present moment.

A couple hours in, I saw a sign about a half-mile away. It shone neon orange against the tunnel of pines swallowing Highway 109, a quiet country road. I didn't think twice about it. Construction wasn't unusual in the eastern states, and it never bothered me—no such thing as traffic for a walker. Getting closer to the sign, though, something looked different, but it was still too far to read.

By North Carolina, I'd seen so many road signs that, before I could actually read them, I could guess what most of them said judging by the length and juxtaposition of each blurry word. It was a good way to interrupt the monotony, guessing signs. The green signs indicating how many miles to the next town were the best for this game because the stakes were high. If I overestimated, I'd get there sooner than expected and that could mean only good things: a cold sweet tea instead of stale water, a bathroom instead of a bush. Underestimates were devastating. It took about twenty minutes to walk one mile, so guessing a couple miles short could mean an extra hour or two before town. It wasn't the end of the world, but sometimes it felt pretty close, especially if I was jonesing for a toilet.

Before I could guess the sign, the two words crystallized in front of me: INMATES WORKING.

As usual, my mind jumped. I imagined a chain gang of tattooed men, all of them twice my size. They'd probably throw a riot just as I was passing. Assessing the armory in my backpack didn't help: I had a couple pocketknives and pepper spray, and a guy had just stopped to give me two cans of Mountain Dew. At least I could get the inmates annoyingly sticky before they murdered me. My breath grew shallow. I tried to relax, just keep walking. Each day on the road was a kind of dance with fear—learning how it worked and trying to let it go. But it was hard to let go, especially with a group of convicts waiting up ahead.

I hadn't had to do much of that before I started walking, feel fear, real fear. After my parents split, I went to a boarding school in Delaware called St. Andrew's surrounded by miles of farm fields and forests. The school gave me nearly a full ride last minute, taking me in while my family was still falling apart. I spent the next four years in a safe, magical bubble where the biggest thing I had to fear was getting caught exploring the castle of Founder's

Hall after lights out. It was like Hogwarts without Voldemort. Then, I was in the gentle forests of Vermont at a liberal arts college. Throughout all this, my home base was suburbia. It was a tremendously privileged hand of cards to be dealt, but it meant I was a stranger to certain parts of myself, the parts revealed only in crisis— fear, desperation, fury. I'd hardly ever had to meet those things in me before.

The shoulder was dotted with orange garbage bags, stretched tight and torn. I guessed the inmates were picking up trash, though I still didn't see them. Then I did, in the distance: little dots stippling the two grassy shoulders ahead, their reflective vests shining under the gray pallor of the sky. The only official presence was a white van pulling a trailer with a Porta Potty strapped to it. There were no wardens on horseback. There were no German shepherds. There wasn't even a police car.

When I was close enough to be noticed, I saw that the inmates were women. Before I could get closer, though, the guard driving the white van waved me over.

"Just walking through," I said.

"That's fine, but you can't tape anything here, and no pictures."

He was wearing sunglasses, so all I could see was my walleyed reflection. We shook hands, and he congratulated me for what I was doing, which surprised me. I'd expected him to be more confrontational.

"Do I need to, you know, worry about anything?"

"No," he said. "Men are more hands on. We don't have problems with the women. If you respect them, they respect you. But be careful down the road, walking and all. And good luck."

I entered the throng of inmates. The first woman I came across was holding a rod-and-reel fishing pole. It didn't stand a chance of fitting into the garbage bag. My walking stick would hold up well against it in a swordfight, if it came to that, although she'd have much better reach. I nodded hello.

"You like fishing, honey?" she said, offering me the pole. She was in her sixties, or maybe life had been hard. She addressed me confidently, without the slightest regard for what I might think of her.

"No, thanks," I said. "I'm not doing much fishing these days."

"What *are* you doing?" she asked. We were walking together, and we'd caught up to a few of the other women. There were about a dozen of them. Some looked younger than I, and there were some who looked nearly as old as my grandmother, a mix of white and black people. I explained what I was doing.

"That's so cool," one of them said. "I'd love to do that."

I said I was glad for the company, and that I'd be interested in hearing some of their stories. The woman with the fishing pole smiled and then pointed with her chin to the guard in the white van.

"That would've been nice under different circumstances."

We continued to walk together, and I mostly just listened to the women as they spoke.

"I'm getting out soon. Only three more years."

"I get out in a week. First thing I'm going to do is see my kids."

"First thing I'm going to do is just be alone. There's fifty people to a room in prison. Everyone's on top of each other. Ain't no business of yours nobody doesn't know."

"People throw things at us out here, dirty underwear and bottles of piss. But I don't give a shit because they don't know me. They can judge me all day and I don't care. I really don't."

The thick wall of pines next to us began to dwindle, fading into the parking lot of a small supermarket. We were entering the town of Denton, the home of the black belt evangelist. There was a woman loading groceries into her minivan at the far end of the lot close to the highway. Close to us. Catching movement in the corner of her eye, she looked over in our direction, only to return, rather quickly, to the task of loading the minivan.

Soon there was another orange INMATES WORKING sign ahead—the end of the road for the women. A white school bus with metal grated windows pulled up on the other side of the highway, waiting for them to board. I shook hands with each of them before they left.

"Be careful out there," one of them said, "not everybody's as nice as us."

They all lined up outside the white school bus, ascending one by one. I stood on the road watching them, acutely aware that I was imprisoned by nothing, free to walk as far as my body could take me. Though I couldn't see any of the women through the metal grated windows, I stood still and watched as the bus pulled off the shoulder and drove away into the dying autumn brown.

NICK HARRISON, *firefighter and emergency medical technician*
MOUNT PLEASANT, NORTH CAROLINA, in the lounge of the
Northeast Cabarrus Volunteer Fire Department, out of the rain
NOVEMBER

"You're walking on the road and you're walking in your mind. You're walking through everything that was and everything that is. Everything that will be. Everything that might have been. The hardest part for you must be leaving in the mornings. It's moving on. Every week I see one or two dead people. You have to move on. If I had a soft heart I wouldn't be able to do this job. It hurts for a moment. It really does. It literally hurts. Your chest starts to hurt. You get choked up. But you've moved on to where you can put it behind you. But that doesn't mean you forget. Moving on is not forgetting."

Chapter Seven

"You don't have any control of whether you're going to live or die."

Walking into Blacksburg, South Carolina, on a misty morning in early December, I was praying for a diner. I needed it. I'd spent the night before camped out behind the trailer of a red-eyed young man and his two chained pit bulls. I'd woken up soggy. I'd eaten a packet of tasteless oatmeal, and the dogs lunged at me as I was leaving. Finally, hopping on the highway—the blatting semis and the screaming cars and the loneliness—I'd surrendered to the misery.

This was hate-walking, not to be confused with hurt-walking, which was more of an aggrieved hopelessness. Hate-walking was something much more vile: disgust for self and road and everything. Clawing myself out of it was a task, nearly impossible without outside help. There were three ways of escape, as far as I could tell: I could throw a tantrum on the side of the road and scream it all out. I could sit down and just hope it would pass, running the risk of sinking even deeper into it. Or I could hold out for a big Southern breakfast.

A big Southern breakfast could fix just about anything, especially if I'd walked a long way to get it. Homemade was best, but anything from a diner would do, too. I'd learned to look for the run-down joints, the camouflaged kitchens so faded that only the locals could see them right away. If the words "Mama's" or "Country" or "Kitchen" were on the sign outside, I knew that

I'd probably found one. If they called me "Honey," or "Sugar," or "Baby," I was golden.

Hobbling into Blacksburg, the odds weren't looking good. The town was depressed. I saw closed storefronts with shattered windows like broken teeth, and a faint DRINK COCA-COLA mural on a crumbling brick edifice. A railroad paralleled the main street. In the boom days, when they'd found iron in the hills at the end of the nineteenth century, the trains must have rolled into a bustling platform every day heavy with ore, the factories pumping and belching and grinding away, dirty and alive. It wasn't alive anymore, though. Just dirty.

And then there it was, thank God, tucked away off the main thoroughfare in the heart of town: Yesterday's Diner. I made a beeline for it.

Inside, walls of white pine bead board conjured a cozy cabin vibe. Blinking Christmas trees hung on the walls, flat like flowers pressed in a dictionary. Nosefuls of fried-oil air billowed from the kitchen. Two gray-haired men sat at a table underneath one of the Christmas trees, one in hunter's orange, one in beige plaid. The scene was almost perfect, but not quite. People were screaming at one another on a TV in the back corner—*Dr. Phil.*

I took a booth not far from Hunter's Orange and Beige Plaid, dropping my backpack on the opposite seat. A waitress gave me a menu, raising an eyebrow at the sad, stinking sight of me, and a few minutes later it was all laid out on the table in full glory: two plate-size pancakes, two eggs over easy, a great lake of grits, country ham, and coffee. To me, this wasn't just food. The packet of tasteless oatmeal was food. This was miraculous, life-giving. Sometimes, it was nothing more than the hope for a breakfast like this that kept me going.

Not long after I began shoveling it down, Hunter's Orange asked me what I was doing with such a big backpack.

"Walking across America, huh?" he said. "The craziest people pass through here. But hell, I wish I had the time to do that."

"It takes more than just time," Beige Plaid said. "It takes inclination. It takes time and inclination, and you don't got either."

Hunter's Orange shook his head, his brow wrinkled with hurt. "I don't get treated with respect anymore," he said, looking at me to make sure I'd witnessed the impudence. It was an act, of course, one the two of them probably played out together every day at that same table. I could tell Hunter's Orange was tickled by his friend. It was the kind of routine that was smoothed by years of daily repetition, countless cups of coffee. It was as reliable as anything in the world, something to count on, and it was theirs, the regulars', so I was grateful to be included.

I finished the breakfast, all of it, and the waitress was bringing over my tab when Hunter's Orange called her over and seized it.

"I appreciate it," I said, "but you don't have to do that."

It had happened before, and it would continue all the way across the country. A waitress in North Carolina. A shrimper in Mississippi. Some elderly folks in Louisiana.

"I know I don't have to," Hunter's Orange said. "But it's something good I can do for you. And it comes with a condition. You gotta try the liver mush here. Best liver mush in South Carolina."

The waitress brought it out before I could escape: a brown brick of fried processed meat, genesis unknown and presumably disturbing. It had an experimental look about it, the Frankensteinian spawn of scrapple and Spam. I took a bite. Not half bad, actually. I finished it, not wanting to be rude—and plus, calories are calories when you're walking more than twenty miles a day with a fifty-pound backpack.

On the road again, the hate-walking was no more; the big Southern breakfast had worked. It always did. And I also had a place to sleep that night in Gaffney, the town ten miles ahead. The owner of Yesterday's had called a homeless shelter there and they said I'd be welcome to stay. I figured it was better than camping in the rain.

Blacksburg disintegrated into the countryside, a slow-motion ramshackle collapse. The houses on the main thoroughfare sagged with a great heaviness, swaybacked like old horses. Naked trees lined the boulevard. A supply store halfheartedly advertised two exhausted recliners out front. Dead plants spilled out of their plastic pots on a peeling porch. Everything was pallid. Everything was fading to gray.

There was beauty in the lack of pretense. The place was what it was—no glitz or gloss, no makeup. Passing a movie rental shop (a converted gas station), the garish faces of Nicole Kidman and Nicolas Cage gazed out at me. They looked utterly absurd, like mannequins pretending to be real humans.

A short, wiry man zoomed by on a lime green scooter with a tall woman balancing on the backseat. The man flashed a big smile—he was missing a tooth or two—and slammed on the brakes to pull a U-turn into the parking lot I'd just passed. The scooter was impossibly small for the two of them, but he was a dexterous driver and she a trusting passenger. They were both white, and had respectable crow's feet branching out from their eyes, faces carved deep with troughs and hollows. The man zipped the scooter up to me and stopped.

"What are you doing, man?" he asked, scratching his silver goatee. He was jumpy, like he'd just touched a live wire. I told him about my walk.

"You're not even getting paid? You're just walking?"

"Pretty much."

"Nothing more to it? Just walking around and listening to people?"

"That's it."

"I love that," he said. "I love you. Here, I got some money. Take some money for a juice or something."

I refused. The guy looked like he needed it more than I did.

"You sure? Shit, I just love what you're doing, man, because people are like cows. They keep walking in the same line until someone tells them not to. That's why we need flaggers at each end for roadwork, telling people where to go. They'll just keep driving until they hit something and then they sue your ass."

He introduced himself as Ken. His drawl was so thick I had to ask him to repeat his name twice.

"Cam?"

"Ken."

"Kim?"

"KEN. K-E-N. It's all right. You're a Yankee. Y'all think we talk funny."

Ken was a Sheetrock installer and his work had taken him just about everywhere.

"Where all I been?" he said, turning back to the woman sitting behind him, Gloria. She was wearing a red flannel coat. A bottle of Mountain Dew bulged from the front pocket. She reminded him of where all he'd been, about as many states as you can count on two hands.

"You can stay in my RV tonight and I will take care of your ass," Ken said. "I can feed you dinner. And I got beer if you drink, because I love drinking. Don't worry, I'm not drunk now, though."

I told him I had to keep walking, and that the homeless shelter in Gaffney was putting me up for the night.

"That's a nice shelter they got down there," Ken said. "It's all men, and they're good fellas. Just watch your stuff so it doesn't disappear while you're sleeping."

We shook hands, and he started up the scooter. Gloria wrapped her arms around him, tightly.

"She doesn't like my driving," Ken said, smiling. Before they sped away, he reached into his pocket and pulled out three crumpled one-dollar bills.

"You sure I can't give you something? No, that ain't right. Here, take it."

I float-walked the rest of the way to Gaffney, hardly noticing my own stench from the past few days of walking, the second skin of grime and salt all over my body. I passed kudzu-choked forests and quiet country homes, weightless and unbound in the warm winter of South Carolina.

It was twilight by the time I got to Gaffney. Like Blacksburg, the town was withering, with the exception of the main drag, dolled up for Christmas like a snow-globe village. Cash loan joints lined all the other streets, pawnshops and consignment stores, barbershops and beat-up delis. The houses wore crowns of corrugated tin, and exposed insulation protruded like unseemly flesh. Incandescent light spilled out the windows, yellow, illuminating the insides: an old couple eating at their table, a man on a couch watching TV, a little girl running into the open arms of her mother.

I got to the homeless shelter just as the rain began again, but I balked at the door. A woman at the visitors' center in town had told me that Gaffney was famous for two things: its giant peach water tower and the Gaffney Strangler of the 1960s. There were pamphlets on both. The woman also said there'd been another killer on the loose recently, an out-of-towner who had walked into a peach farmer's house, shot the farmer, and then driven through town on a rampage. The woman advised I carry a gun.

"You never do know," she'd said. "You gotta be careful around here, especially at this time of night. It's Satan's time."

Standing in front of the shelter while the soft rain fell, I wondered if I was about to get robbed in my sleep, or assaulted. Was I even allowed to stay at a homeless shelter? I wasn't homeless, not technically. But I was getting wetter and wetter, so I walked inside. A big, bearded man shaped like a pear sat behind a check-in desk. He waved at me and smiled. He was missing a front tooth.

"You must be Andrew," he said. The owner of Yesterday's Diner had mentioned my name. "I'm Frank. Come on in and let me get you signed up here."

To my surprise, Frank had an unmistakable Boston accent, which reminded me of my short-lived career as a lobster boat sternman on the coast of Massachusetts. *At least I'm not the only Yankee in the place*, I thought. Not that it really mattered, but it reminded me of home, or something like it.

After taking my information, Frank asked me to turn over everything that might be considered a weapon and then he took me to the room where I'd sleep, the place for one-night stays. It was generic and sterile, like the waiting room of a doctor's office, and there were a few mats spread out on the floor. I could choose whichever one I liked, except the one in the back left corner.

"There'll be another guy in here with you tonight," Frank said. "The preacher. He stays with us every night, but he won't take a bed like the rest of the long-term stays. Just a mat. He lost his wife a few years ago, and then he lost his mind. He used to be the best preacher in town, but now he just roams the streets. He'll still preach to you, but it ain't all, you know, there. I get it, though, where he's coming from. I've been where these guys have been. Maybe not where the preacher's been, but I get it."

I must have looked concerned, because Frank cracked a smile and patted me on the back. "You'll be all right. He won't bother you."

I dropped off my backpack by one of the mats, and Frank walked me to the cafeteria where the men were having dinner. We passed the front door on our way, and I saw a man pacing outside, bearded and portly. I wondered if he'd been there while I was standing in the rain, watching me from somewhere out of sight.

"That's him," Frank said. "The preacher. But he'll stay outside until it's late. He doesn't like to come in until he has to."

In the cafeteria, Frank introduced me in his booming Bostonian baritone and then left to resume his post at the check-in desk. I had flashbacks of third grade when I was the new kid, abandoned and dropped into the mix. Nodding to a few of the guys, I picked up a plastic tray and got in line for food.

Most of the men were between forty and sixty. Some looked homeless. Some didn't. Two of the shelter's residents were serving the dinner: mac 'n' cheese, pork 'n' gravy, baked beans, sweet corn, sweet potatoes, and sweet tea. I was fed generously and without question. I sat at a table with a big blond guy who said, "Walking across America, huh? That's a spiritual journey, my friend." He told me to have faith in the good Lord, to keep an eye out for that old-fashioned country friendliness, and to not get held up by any Georgia peaches.

After dinner, most of the men went to the rec room where *The Polar Express* was playing on TV. I sat on the couch next to a boulder of a man with electric blue eyes and a crew cut. His name was Simon. He'd thru-hiked the Appalachian Trail after he got out of the Marine Corps, "So I know what you're doing," he said. Simon told me about the AT thru-hike and the long training treks he'd done in the Marines. His triumph had been a sixty-eight-miler in the service. He'd carried a one-hundred-pound pack the whole way.

"It taught me that I can do more than my physical body tells me I can do," he said. "When it starts to hurt, think about how far you've already come. Think about how you'll get to rest at the end when you make it. And then just keep going."

Simon had served in the Marine Corps during Desert Shield and Desert Storm, and he'd done two tours of duty in Saudi Arabia and Afghanistan, too. I asked him about it. I had my recorder out and I could tell it made him nervous, robotic, but he opened up anyway. He spoke frankly, his voice wavering slightly, almost winded. I listened with the horrified fascination of a rubbernecker.

"I saw many children dead. It gave me compassion for other people, other than just Americans, other than just my family and friends. It gave me compassion for people as a whole. It also gave me insight on how cruel people really can be, and how cruel the world really is to its own people. The worst, inhumane thing was a woman killing her child in front of Iraqi soldiers because she was scared of the Iraqi soldiers. I understand that she was doing it to save her child from grief later on."

As he continued to talk, I wondered about the things he'd done. Maybe he'd killed someone, or lots of people, and maybe there were others who'd seen it, as he'd seen the mother kill her child, and maybe those witnesses were still haunted by it somewhere halfway around the world, as Simon was haunted here by the scene of that murder.

"Soldiers were really scared, as they are today. They don't show it on TV, but they're scared. They're scared every minute they're there, because you don't have any control. You don't have any control of whether you're going to live or die. You have all the training, but you don't have control.

"And the way we here in America treat our own people is no better than what I saw over in Iraq. I mean, there's compassion in spurts. But overall there's not compassion for each other. It's like over there. You're just a thing."

I thanked him and turned off the recorder, but Simon kept talking for a long time. As soon as he finished, I rushed into the bathroom to write it all down in my notebook. Simon had seen things that I couldn't even imagine in my nightmares, and I didn't want to forget any of it, get lost in a sugarcoated reality.

"They say you get used to it, but you don't. You never get used to seeing a decaying body they tried to bury. You never get used to seeing body parts. Legs and arms and hands. Not torn clean like you see in the movies, but tendons and nerve endings and skin hanging off. You can tell it was just ripped from a body. You don't forget it, either. The smell of gunpowder on skin, like burnt lemon. The smell of blood. It smells like metals and iron. It's a sweet smell if they had adrenaline running through their body right before they died, or estrogen or testosterone. You never forget that sweet smell.

"These boys coming home, every one of them is going to be lost, because all they know is how to shoot and kill. They don't know how to deal with a wife and kids. They're changed when they come back. And you'll be changed when you finish your journey, too. Some people might not even recognize you. Most of them didn't recognize me."

Of course they didn't recognize him, not after surviving that hell. I didn't doubt that I would change, too, after my walk, but it wouldn't be anything like that. It couldn't be. Simon reminded me of Jeff Painter, the firefighter in Virginia who had been so quick to downplay the risks of his own work in comparison to my trek, which, in my mind, paled in comparison. These people weren't giving themselves enough credit. Walking across America was nothing compared to fighting fires, or fighting wars, or a million other things—raising children, running a farm, caregiving for an elderly mother in her final years. Compared to the lives that most people were living, in fact, traveling across America on foot was actually kind of a cakewalk. All I had to do was put one foot in front of the other.

The night was late, and the men were slowly turning in. There was a six A.M. wake-up call at the shelter—all residents had to be out by seven. Facing another twenty miles to Spartanburg the next day, I figured I'd better get some sleep. I wished Simon and the rest of the men good night and headed for my mat in the one-night-stay room.

A sweet stink hit me at the door, and I thought of Simon—the smell of adrenaline-pumped blood at the moment of death. The lights were still on. In the back left corner a man was asleep and snoring under the white glare, fully dressed, shoes and all: the preacher. He was on his stomach, his face buried in the crook of his elbow. Quickly and quietly, I took out my sleeping bag, turned off the lights, and lay down. The preacher's breathing was labored, the inhalation a heaving gasp and the exhalation a raspy wheeze. It sounded close in the dark. I thought, once, that I felt it on my neck, but it couldn't have been.

My sleep was strange. I dreamt of burnt lemons and the sweet surrounding stink. I heard Simon. *And you'll be changed when you finish your journey, too. Some people might not even recognize you.* I woke up every couple hours dazed in the dark, disoriented on the hard floor, listening to the preacher mutter his nightmares. The next morning I could only remember a few words of what he'd said, and I wrote them down in my journal: "Jesus . . . preach . . . even a nigger." He was gone when my alarm went off at six.

The rain was still falling outside, lightly. After breakfast, I packed my backpack. I had it down at this point: first the tent and the clothes bag, then the sleeping bag and the deflated sleeping pad, then my laptop and the med kit, and finally the food bag. Everything had its place, and I found comfort in that. Frank was waiting for me at the door. He asked if he could say a prayer for me.

"Oh, Lord," he began, bowing his head, "protect this young man as he walks to Spartanburg today, and across our country. We thank you for bringing him here, and that we could help him on his way. And thank you that there is someone interested in listening no matter what situation we're in in our lives."

I didn't get this blessing on tape, but that last sentence is just about verbatim. In that moment, I felt that my decision to walk wasn't a totally selfish one, that it really wasn't just for me. I didn't always feel this way. Sometimes it seemed I was taking so much and never giving enough back—a meager vogesite pebble in exchange for shelter, a quick song on the mandolin for dinner. But, for some people, my willingness to listen was a profound offering. At least that's what Frank's prayer made me think. I was feeling quite magnanimous that morning until the sky opened up and began to piss all over me, a torrential downpour that would last for eight hours, tearing me out of my thoughts about the walk and back into the walk itself, which was, that day, nothing but wet and cold.

LEE TAYLOR, master stylist
CONCORD, NORTH CAROLINA, in his living room after giving
me a haircut at his salon
DECEMBER, and still no sign of the deep cold, thank God

"*The way this whole thing got started was actually my mother. I saw her putting on lipstick and I thought it was candy, so when she left I ate every tube of lipstick she had, thinking that the next one was going to taste better, but it didn't. And rather than my mother getting angry, she got home, got a piece of paper, drew a face, gave me makeup, and said, 'This goes here. Now put it where you think it needs to go.'*

"*Then, I would go to church and I would see these women and I would think, 'That just isn't right.' I was very critical of what was pretty at an early age.*

"*Then, the movie* Grease *came out, and Olivia Newton-John made this incredible transformation from Little Miss Pure Innocent to Sexy Hot Spandex Mama, and I had a blonde-headed sister so I sat her down and duplicated that exact look. My sisters started me doing their hair when I was nine. I did my sister's wedding at eleven. From there, I went to school for hair.*

"*You're trying to educate people to what's rare about them— what's your facial shape, what's the weaker side, what's the stronger side—so that you help them understand the fundamentals of who they are, so that then they know how to take hair and apply it to them. Trends are always out there. We always want to become the trend, when the trend is just out there as someone's idea of what should be. It's just an idea. You take what you need, because if you try to become the trend then you've lost your original self, because there's not another one like you. And I think that's one of the reasons why I'm so good at what I do, because I don't take a person and try to make them into something they're not. I try to cash in on all the assets they have, bring all of those out. Everybody wants to be perceived looking good. Well, you cross out your liabilities and cash in on your assets, but you can't do that if you're not aware of it. So you've got to know that your right eye is your weaker eye. You've got to know that you have a long neck, or a short neck, and what balances that out? You've got broad shoulders, or you've got petite shoulders, you know, what's going to work with those shoulders? How big is too big, of hair? How small is too small? It's all about helping people to come across as balanced. I guess it's really all about being balanced, more than anything else."*

Chapter Eight

"You can only get so high."

I was right on the edge of breaking down during my final days in South Carolina. SMILING FACES. BEAUTIFUL PLACES. it said on the license plates, but the Palmetto State had just about depleted me. It had rained almost every day, and the suburban sprawl oozed all the way from Gaffney to Greenville, a one-hundred-mile stretch of suspicious glances. I felt like a freak on the highway. And then there was the knockout blow: a bad stick of pepperoni. The nausea hit me at four thirty in the afternoon. With nowhere else to go, I snuck into the woods and set up my tent behind a fallen tree. Quickly. I pounded in the last stake, walked a few yards away, knelt down, and threw up all over the forest floor. It was raining lightly, and cold. I was in and out of the tent all night long. Lights from a house glimmered not far away. I hoped they couldn't hear me. I dazed in and out of sleep, a nightmarish soundscape swallowing me: my own demonic retching, a hooting owl, the distant lowing of a cow slowly rising to a scream. I took out my recorder in the middle of the night, just to talk out loud, hoping that documenting the struggle would make it a little less miserable; it sometimes worked.

"I'm in a weird twilight zone here. All the doubts: 'Man, you gonna keep doing this? You're cold. You're sick. You're in the middle of nowhere. You're trespassing.'"

I turned off the recorder after a few minutes. It wasn't helping, and I had to go vomit again. Above me, the tree branches interlaced, like that game where you make a church and steeple with your fingers, and the moonlight couldn't get through to me. I wasn't wearing my glasses. It was all a dark blur.

But then came Georgia. Sweet, sweet Georgia. I couldn't stop saying the name at first, pronouncing it as if it were spelled J-O-W-J-U-H, an octave deeper than my normal voice. I sang the sound like the state's undulant hills. *I said Georgia, oh Georgia, no peace I find, just an old sweet song keeps Georgia on my mind.* Everything seemed to sing on that first country road in Georgia. Dewy green pastures refracted the morning sunlight. Round bales of hay sat just so behind a barbed wire fence. A farmer freed his greens of their plastic blankets. I wanted that road to go on forever. The fact that it wouldn't only made it more beautiful, almost unbearably so.

The next morning, I passed through the little town of Royston, where I met up with my friend Penn and then Ernest Jackson, the old man with the gold fillings in his molars.

"Remember me," he said, handing me the hickory cane.

The walk seemed endless that day. I was still on the narrow country byway when night fell—full-on, dark-as-hell night. The cars were still on the road, too, flying by right next to me. I strapped on my headlamp and shifted gears to top speed—about five miles an hour. There was shelter ahead and I just wanted to get there.

A few miles back east in the little hamlet of Danielsville, a guy had offered to put me up for the night. Coming into town, I'd seen him in the parking lot of the gas station, leaning up against a car. A woman was sitting next to him on the hood, checking her phone. Don and Mae. I went over to ask where I might camp out, and in about ten seconds Mae was fretting over me like a worried auntie.

"You're a cutie pie, baby," she said, "and I'd hate to see something happen to you, even though I don't know you from a can of beans." Her fingernails were painted talons. She wore golden hoop earrings, and the perimeter of her red lipstick was traced with a thin black line.

"You can't trust everybody, baby. You got good people around here and you got some bad folks. Some folks will tell you, 'Oh, yeah, I can do this for you, I can do that,' and then they'll take you and go rob you. So the best thing for you to do is: If they can't look you in your face, don't you jump your ass in that damn car. Okay? You just say, 'No, thank you,' and you keep walking. You hear me?"

"Yes, ma'am," I said. A rooster crowed from somewhere behind the gas station. Pickup trucks rolled in and out of the parking lot.

"But this is a good man right here," Mae said, putting her hand on Don's shoulder. Don hadn't said a whole lot. He mostly just smiled. When he did talk, it was slow and a little stuttered. Subtle tremors ran through his fingers up to his neck—the beginning of Parkinson's, maybe, or the echoes of a hard life. He was white, Mae was black, and he was probably a decade or two older than she.

"Just make sure you don't go to that damn park," Mae continued. "I'm dead serious. Because there's already one man that stays up there, homeless. And you got lots of deers. You feeling what I'm saying? Deers and stuff. And, what they call them? Hyenees? What them things are?"

"Coyotes," Don said.

"Coyotes. You got a lot of coyotes around here, so that's why you don't gotta be staying in that goddamn park." I had my recorder out, and Mae leaned in close. "Don't stay at the park because coyotes will eat your ass up!"

Don and I laughed.

"Yes, ma'am," I said.

"I just don't want to see nothing happen to you. You're a very handsome guy and you got a lot of respect about yourself and that's going to take you a long way in life. I'm telling you, baby. You're young."

A man walked past us quietly on his way to the gas station.

"Oh, you all antisocial, huh?" Mae shouted at him. "I oughta kick you in the head!" The man hadn't said hello. He backtracked, and then asked if she was working.

"Pretty as I look, do you think I'm on the damn clock?"

The man walked into the gas station, chuckling.

"So, everyone sort of knows everyone around here, huh?" I asked.

"Well, I work here so I have to learn the customers. That's what makes your paycheck. And when you don't treat your customers with the utmost respect, they don't come back. So everybody who comes in here, they know me. You see that, don't you? Because I'm very friendly. I'm nice. And I try to treat people the way I want to be treated."

Eventually, Mae decided it'd be best if I stayed with Don that night. Don smiled his acquiescence. He still had some things to do in town, he said, so I should just let myself in, shower, eat, help myself. The house was only three or four minutes down the road. Nearly an hour later, I realized he meant three or four minutes by car.

Urge-walking: when something else takes over.

There were lights ahead, red and white. A house? Slowly I got closer. Maybe it was a lawn decoration. I'd seen an interesting one earlier: a crucified skeleton dressed in camouflage holding an AK-47 in one of its bony hands. As I got closer, I saw that the red and white lights were moving up and down, slow and constant. It was a glowing Santa Claus raising a finger up to his pursed lips and then down again. "Shhh!"

Don's house was inconspicuous, easy to miss even though it was in plain sight. The windows were dark. Nobody was home. Two men stood silhouetted under a flood lamp just a stone's throw away next door. They had a dog with them. I hurried to the house, hoping they wouldn't think I was a thief.

The porch was warped and creaky. I opened the front door and walked into a small living room with clean, drying laundry draped over the couch and chairs. An artificial dwarf Christmas tree was leaning in the corner. The walls were bare. Inside the refrigerator there was a solitary head of lettuce, a gallon of milk, and a few cans of Bud Ice, not much more. Exposed wiring and plumbing snaked up the walls of the bathroom. The whole house seemed to sag. In the back room there were stacks of dirty mattresses, five or six of them. The thought crossed my mind that it was possible I'd just walked into the middle of some kind of prostitution ring, or a crack den, and that maybe I should've just camped out instead, and that maybe I still should.

I took a cold shower. I ate dinner—Uncle Ben's from the food bag. And then, with nothing else to do, I sat on the couch across from the front door and waited for Don, alone in the man's empty house. I got out my mandolin so that when he finally arrived it would seem like I was busy doing something other than just waiting for him. I also took out my knife and slipped it in my pocket. The house seemed like the kind of place where anything could happen.

My mind drifted to my father. At Christmastime before the divorce, he'd wake up early, before anyone else was up, and turn on the golden lights woven throughout the branches of the evergreen tree, and sit on the couch, just watching, thinking. What did he think in those quiet moments alone, before the rush of his life took him again when the sun rose? What was he feeling? Don's artificial dwarf Christmas tree in the corner reminded me of Dad's tiny apartment after the split, his sincere but halfhearted attempt at homemaking. It reminded me of our relationship, too, a stunted version of what could've been. He'd come to visit us right after the holidays and we'd do Christmas in his motel room. Some years we'd go to his place. Mom would drive us halfway across Pennsylvania and he'd meet us at a gas station. The handoff was the worst part. Our brokenness was on display for all to see. We never made a scene, and I doubt anyone noticed, but it still seemed like everyone was watching.

He was always excited to have us, and maybe a little nervous, too, or gun shy after getting yelled at so much. He'd be a bit jittery and short-winded on the drive back to Erie. We'd watch movies, mostly, and comedy specials. For a long time that bothered me. I didn't want to watch movies. I wanted to talk, cry, shout, do whatever we had to do to fix things and move on. We tried a few times. Once, around Christmastime at my grandparents', we took a walk at night into town and tried to work things out, really connect. Plastic, life-size nutcrackers stood in silence on the sidewalk, hungry for something they'd never taste. We weren't getting anywhere. After a mile or so we turned around.

Before I graduated from college, I finally worked up the courage to interview him for my senior essay. After my geography professor told me to turn the lens on myself, I kind of had to. We sat on a bench in the Middlebury town square, and I tried to forget I was his son. I didn't want to fight. I didn't want to grieve. I just wanted to understand.

"What does coming-of-age mean to you?" I asked him, holding a recorder like a reporter, not a son.

"I think it's learning to think for yourself, learning to voice opinions, and being willing to challenge people including those you love. It's being willing to take the heat, if there is some."

"Do you think the divorce was a coming-of-age for you?"

"There are always levels of growth. Pain is a rite of passage. Nobody likes to hear about that in the middle of it, of course, but as you work through it, what's the outcome? Perhaps more self-awareness, more compassion. It's a catalyst. So the divorce and all the circumstances around it were kind of a fiery initiation."

"An initiation into what?"

"Deeper levels of myself. I became more authentically myself. The secrecy of the affair was fundamentally inauthentic. I could have done things differently, but I didn't. I didn't have the awareness. I'm still pretty close to guilt and embarrassment, and I may always be close to that. But I'm also aware that no single event defines anybody and that we are complex processes with virtue and skill and art, and also shadow elements and limitation and need. Sometimes that can be a little vexing. So it was kind of like, 'Here I am. Everybody in the world knows about it and they can think what they think.' I learned I don't have any control over what other people think. I'd be very sad if you, for sixty years, had this bitter anger, this distance. And I can keep knocking at the door and I would always do that, but I can't change your mind."

He'd written a lot of poetry during the year of the divorce, to survive it. After our interview he sent me some. One poem stood out. It was titled "Long Distance," written to my sister and me:

A different kind of race has just begun.
And you two have sprinted far from me,
so far away, it's impossible to see my face.
I understand.
But there will be a time,
when you will see
that this is a long-distance race
with endless opportunity

for every effort,
every sign,
everything I do
to reveal
the deepest truth
that
I love you.

There was no one else in the dorm common room where I was reading, so I didn't bother trying to stop the tears that came so suddenly. He'd told me he loved me many times since the split, but as I read the poem, I realized I'd never actually believed it, and that it was largely my own refusal to believe it that was perpetuating the pain.

Don walked through the front door, snapping me out of my thoughts.

"Oh, sorry about the mess," he said. "I wasn't expecting company. This room's my dryer!" He laughed self-consciously and started folding the laundry. "I just moved in. I'm fixing the place up in exchange for rent. It ain't much, but it's home for now. You get something to eat?"

We slowly slipped into the strange moment together, but as the moment became an hour and then hours, the strangeness lifted. Don told me about the wild hogs in Georgia, how they rooted up the farmers' fields, and how the hunters went into the forests with dogs. The dogs ran the hogs down and grabbed them by the ears, and then the hunter came in with the knife and stabbed the hog in the side, the lungs.

He remembered a high school sweetheart, an epic misunderstanding, and the fortune-teller who'd said they'd end up together again one day. "By that time I might be so old I won't even be able to see what she looks like," he said.

He told me he didn't consider his day a success until he made somebody laugh, so he told the story of how he found a mannequin head on the roadside once, a blonde. His wife at the time worked nights, and he'd always have breakfast ready for her when she got back home. That morning, though, the breakfast table was empty. "Don, are you okay?" she said. She went into their bedroom and saw blonde hair spilling out across the pillow next to him. She screamed in rage and grabbed the golden locks, yanking hard on what she thought was the hair of her husband's mistress. Don and I were both laughing by the end of the story.

At one point, late, Don got up to fetch us some more Bud Ice. I was already a little buzzed, and we'd also smoked some pot out of a pipe fashioned from one of the beer cans. The toke was a gamble for me, not just because Don was a stranger, but also because I had a mixed relationship with marijuana. A brief history had shown that it sent me to one of either two places: a wonderland of giggles or a purgatory of delusional paranoia. The first time I'd tried it, in college, I ended up glued to a beanbag chair for what felt like hours, laughing hysterically. That hadn't happened in recent years. The last time I'd smoked, just the summer before, my calf had started twitching uncontrollably and I'd become convinced there was some kind of motor inside my leg, like I was an android or something. I'd just about had a panic attack. So I didn't smoke much. But Don had offered, and I wanted to be a part of his world that night, so I'd taken a hit from the Bud Ice pipe and buckled my seatbelt.

Don came back with two more beers.

"This Bud Ice is pretty good," I said when he handed me a can. "I normally go for Bud Lite if I'm drinking Budweiser."

"Yeah, they ain't bad. Better than the other kind of ice."

"You mean meth?"

"Yeah," Don said. "I don't like it. Never did. It'll have you running and running and running. Don't even think about trying to sleep, 'cause you ain't gonna sleep. I seen all kinds of shit out there you wouldn't believe. I dated a girl once who started taking oxycodone, and then she wanted to shoot it. She'd crush it up. Mix it with water. Heat it. Pour it in the needle. And then she'd stab herself. All to get high five minutes faster. If I wanted to get high five minutes faster, I'd smoke five minutes earlier, you know?"

"She all right?" I asked.

"I don't know what happened to her," Don said. "I left her. She tried to get me to buy her needles. I said, 'I'm not going to help you kill yourself. And I'm not going to stay and watch you kill yourself.' I really loved her. Well, I guess I didn't, because she didn't love herself."

"Did you ever worry about getting addicted?"

"These people who say you shoot it once and you're addicted? Bullshit. Addiction's a choice. It's you. It's what's in here." He pointed to his heart, and then he told me about a coworker who had overdosed on heroine. "These guys, they're all looking for that higher high. But it's not there. You can only get so high. I know."

I wish I'd asked him why. Why are they all looking for that higher high? Because I kind of knew what it felt like, that irrepressible urge to keep looking for something just barely out of reach, to leave everything behind each morning in search of it. A walk like this could get addicting—the highs of leaping off into unknown territory, the paradoxical power of choosing to be so vulnerable, but not so vulnerable that you had to commit to any one place or person. Maybe seekers weren't so different from junkies. If I could understand my craving, then maybe I wouldn't end up spending my entire life saying good-bye, moving on. I wouldn't have to walk across America, or prove anything, or keep quietly wondering if there was something else I should be doing, somewhere else I should explore, someone else I should be. If I could understand the slippery schemes of the unsettled mind, instead of getting swept up in them, then maybe I could just sit, and that would be enough. After all, to seek something is to assume it's not already here.

"No, this life's too short," Don was saying. "You gotta have fun. Like, look at this," and he took out his flip phone and showed me a picture of a man sleeping in a chair.

"He was on the job and I shouted, 'You're fired!'"

There was another picture of a guy sitting in a box playing Nintendo, and another of a big fish he'd caught. There was a picture of Mae, too.

After a while it was far too late to stay awake anymore. I was coming down from the weed—no psychotic breaks, thank God. Don brought in a space heater to make sure I'd stay warm on the couch through the night. The knife in my pocket felt completely unnecessary at that point, and a little shameful. I'd been paranoid even without the pot.

Don was going hunting at sunrise, so this was good-bye. I gave him one of my vogesite pebbles and thanked him for everything.

"I love rocks," he said, pulling out a few from his pocket and holding them out for me to see. They were worn smooth, and they slid easily across his calloused palm. "Yeah, I like looking at them. I just stare in and see all kinds of things."

The next morning I came across a tired gas station, and I stopped in for coffee and a Honey Bun—one of my favorite morning rituals. Before I could pay, the register broke. As the cashier struggled to fix it, more and more people kept filing inside, picking up their morning necessities and taking their places in the growing queue behind me. There was a sense of grim heaviness among many of them, dejection. Then again it was eight A.M. and none of us had had our coffee yet. But the hollowed cheeks. The missing teeth. The bodies—either gaunt or sagging in obesity. I thought of Don and his stories, and of all the suffering I wasn't seeing as I walked across America, that stayed hidden behind closed doors. We all stood together in the toxic rainbow of Pepsi and Marlboro, Budweiser and Little Debbie, and when the cashier finally fixed the register, I paid and then walked away, on to Atlanta and back into my own little world, waiting for the next person to come along and tear me out of it again, show me more of the truth about what it meant to be an American today, and what it meant to be human, just as Don had done.

MATT MATTHEWS, Presbyterian minister and author
GREER, SOUTH CAROLINA, in his kitchen, frying bacon and
scrambling eggs for breakfast
DECEMBER, a few weeks before Christmas

"*One Christmas Eve I was told by a family, 'Matt, after the service we want to see you.' And they were kind of serious. I mean, they were not kind of serious, they were very serious. And I said, 'Okay.' So we had a beautiful service, everybody's finally gone, and I went back to see this family, and I was presuming that Calvin and Dottie were going to get a divorce or something like that and they just wanted to tell me. The whole family gathered around—and I was expecting, 'So-and-so has a brain tumor,' or something—and then they presented to me an antique bedpan, as a gift, because I collect antique bedpans as a gag. That's what they wanted to see me about. That's what they were serious about. And it was just a simple moment. Twenty minutes before we were gathered around that table for communion and now we were gathered around and they were giving me a bedpan. And to me that was the crass and the holy, the profane and the sacred all stirred in together. There was not a narrator speaking Latin. There weren't smoke and mirrors. There wasn't God with a beard saying, 'Ah, bless you my child.' It was just a fun, beautiful moment of this family that would die for me, and for whom I would die.*"

Chapter Nine

"You got lots of grieving to do."

The breakfast table was even better than I'd dreamed it would be, and I was pretty good at dreaming about breakfast. Buttery grits gave rise to mountains of fried eggs. Warm homemade biscuits waited for honey from the big bear bottle, and sausage gravy smothered everything. I never got tired of breakfast on the road, but I'd never had a breakfast quite like this. The main course was deep-fried squirrel.

Bill Guy had been planning the great squirrel feast for weeks, and it was by sheer dumb luck that I wound up at his house in Shady Grove, Alabama, the night before it happened. It was January. Cold. Sunset caught me in the middle of nowhere with the mercury falling fast. Just as I was beginning to scout for camping spots, a general store appeared up ahead. I wandered in and asked if there was a place nearby where I wouldn't freeze that night—a church or a shed or something. The store owner called Bill Guy.

Bill arrived a few minutes later and immediately patted down my legs, checking for weapons. He was about eighty years old, white, and a full head shorter than I. His build was slight, almost frail, but as he appraised me outside the general store it became clear the old man was vivacious. Every one of his movements was precise and quick, the way sparrows dive and dart. He interrogated me a little more and then offered to let me spend the night in his workshop.

"It'll be warmer than the church barbecue shack," he said, but I didn't need convincing. When we arrived, the church pastor called him to make sure everything was okay. Bill explained the situation as if I weren't there.

"I had a fellow here, he's walking across the country like a dummy in this cold weather, and so I just brought him on down to my shop. He looked like a clean-cut guy, and I didn't want no bum staying here, but I believe he'll be all right.

"Huh? He's just walking across the country. He's gonna walk to New Orleans, and then he's going on to California, and he's just bumming around. Look like his pants are pretty clean. He come from Philadelphia."

The pastor asked Bill if he knew my name.

"What's your name?" Bill asked me.

"Andrew Forsthoefel," I said.

"Andrew Forsthoefel," Bill repeated dramatically. "Now ain't that a name? Yeah, you ever heard of that? Forsthoefel? Now that's a crazy name, ain't it? That's different. We ain't got nobody around here with that name have we? I frisked him down. He ain't got no gun on him, or no pistol. It's warm out here in my shop, and man he likes this. He said he might just stay here a month or two.

"Huh? I don't know why he's doing it. He's just crazy I think."

A wood-burning stove sat in the back of Bill's workshop. It was already putting out a good heat when we walked in. Two rocking chairs sat beside it, waiting. Tools hung on the walls, along with a shotgun or two. A motion-sensor Big Mouth Billy Bass fish was mounted near a refrigerator stocked with beer and moonshine.

"It's a security system for the booze," Bill said when the fish started singing Al Green. "It's for my nephews, but you can help yourself." Bill sat down in one of the rocking chairs and lit a cigarette. I joined him by the stove and listened as fragments of the old man's life filled the workshop. His words were sanded soft by an old-school country southern accent. "Children" were "chillen."

"Computers. I don't know nothing about them. My children get together and every one of them's got a laptop and a telephone. And I don't know what they're doing! Sometimes I don't like it. *Most* of the time I don't like it, because it takes up the time and they never talk to me. All that crap, you know. I said, 'Y'all shut them things off and let's talk awhile!' But computers are taking over the world. Why is that? That's the young folks for you. Like you, Matthew."

He kept calling me Matthew. It took me an hour or so to catch on that it wasn't because he was losing his mind. He was messing with me, and teasing himself, the stereotype of the forgetful senior citizen. He went on and on, and I ate it all up. It felt like I was watching a one-man show on Broadway, except the stage was a shed somewhere in the middle-of-nowhere Alabama.

"I had two open heart surgeries. The next day ain't too bad, but the second day is pretty bad. I was in the hospital on the fourth floor and I said, 'Can you get that window open over there?' They said, 'No, it won't open up.' I said, 'Well, if it did I'd want you to push me out of it.' I felt like I wanted to just die. But the third day it got to feeling better, and by the fourth day I started walking around everywhere, and I've been living ever since.

"Nothing was worse than the catheter, though. My bladder had a problem one time, and when we went to the hospital they grabbed my goober and stuck that catheter up there. But the tube was too big, and they said to get me a smaller one, and I said, 'You had a smaller one the whole time?'

"The doctors said I was going to die more than twenty years ago, but I ain't dieded yet. I don't know why I ain't dieded. I oughta been dead a long time ago, Matthew."

"What's your secret?" I asked at one point.

"Keep smoking, I guess," he said. "No, don't smoke. I shouldn't have said that."

Some of it I got on tape. Some of it I wrote down in my notes later that night. I wanted to catch everything he said because Bill had a playful irreverence I'd never seen before in an old man. It made the prospect of aging and dying a little less horrifying for me. He could talk about it, which meant we could talk about it. And I'd never really done that before, never had a frank conversation with an old person about their inevitable and imminent death.

I thought more and more about death on the road, where it felt just inches away. One little swerve from a car, that's all it would take. Feeling that fear so constantly, I began to realize I had no idea how to deal with it. When my mom had said, on the morning I left, that I was walking in an attempt to break death's hold on me, I hadn't thought much about it. It wasn't something I'd really considered before, the fact of my own death, and my fear of it. Now, I considered it almost every day. There wasn't much distraction.

The only close encounter I'd had with death was through my grandmother, my mom's mom, and it wasn't pretty. She'd had Alzheimer's disease. Her room was at the end of a long hallway at the nursing home. Whenever we went to visit, we'd have to walk down that hallway first. The doors to her neighbors' rooms were almost always open, revealing bodies sagging in their wheelchairs, or heads lolling on chests, or noses plugged up with tubes. On the rare occasions when any of these doors were closed, I assumed it meant something bad and pretended I didn't notice.

Sitting with Mimi, it always seemed she was better off than the rest, at first. It was almost as if nothing had changed. She had this prim air of propriety even as the disease was boring tunnels through her brain. She dressed elegantly and kept her hair well coiffed. She wore lipstick, if a bit lopsidedly sometimes. There was no wheelchair. There were no tubes. But after just a few minutes of conversation it would always become obvious to me that she was lost, even though she tried to hide it. I could see it in her eyes. She looked terrified, and seemed to have no idea why.

This was what I knew of death and dying. It was a terrible secret kept safely out of sight. But sitting with Bill by the fire, it felt different. He talked about aging in a way that made it bearable.

"Come on, Matthew," he said after a while, "let's go inside and meet Mother. You're probably hungry. I think we have some leftovers."

Eloise was the sweet to her husband's spice. She moved gently, a slow-motion waltz, and by the way she spoke to me I guessed she was a grandmother through and through. She loaded me up with leftovers: homegrown cabbage, black-eyed peas and bacon, pork chops, sweet potato casserole, and homemade fudge. Bill was trying to put on some weight, Eloise told me, and I should lead by example. I was happy to oblige.

After a hot shower and a tour of the walls-wide collage of family photographs, Bill and I went back to the workshop and the rocking chairs. He smoked cigarettes, I fed the stove, and the moon was high when we realized how late the night had gone. Bill said he'd be up early the next morning preparing for the great squirrel feast, and that I could come over whenever I was ready. After he left, I lay in the flickering glow of the stove, warm on a very cold night. "I don't want this night to end," I wrote in my journal.

"Matthew, would you pass the gravy?" Bill was pointing to the gravy boat. It was around eight in the morning, and the great squirrel feast was in full swing.

"His name is Andrew!" Eloise said. Before sending it down I poured some for myself, dousing everything on my plate.

"His name is Matthew, Mother," Bill said.

"It's Andrew and you know it!"

"Oh, is it?" He winked at me.

There were seven of us at the breakfast table. I was the youngest by at least four decades. Mitt Romney had been declared the winner of the Iowa caucus the night before, and that was the talk of the table. After praying over the food, one of the men read from a pamphlet on Mormonism—a good Republican Baptist trying to understand his candidate. He read for ten minutes or so while the food got cold. "There, we got all that straight?" he said at the end.

"You confused the hell out of me," said the big-bellied man to my right. His name was Jack. Bill had told me about him earlier. Jack was slipping into dementia. "I get at him and call him an asshole," Bill said, "but he don't give it back anymore, and I hate it." Sure enough, Bill had introduced Jack as "an old asshole," to no retort. The difference between the two old men was apparent by the way they filled their breakfast plates. Jack reached slowly for the biscuits and spooned his grits with tremulous hesitation, concentrating a little anxiously on everything. Bill snatched squirrel thighs with zeal, tearing into the meat as if he hadn't eaten in weeks. Jack wasn't fully gone, though. When Bill asked if he'd like some coffee, he said, "No, thanks. I'm a Mormon."

Sitting at this table, keenly aware of my youth, I found it almost impossible not to think more about death. I saw my many potential future selves in all the weathered faces surrounding me. Would I be like Bill, or maybe Jack? Would I even make it that far?

I'd asked Bill the night before how he did it. *How do you survive all the loss, all the suffering?* He'd been talking about his parents, and his brothers and sisters. All of them were dead now. He was the last one standing.

"What about your friends?" I'd asked him. "What's it like seeing, I mean, I'm imagining all my friends, and all of us growing old. What's it like seeing these friends of yours . . . you know."

"It's gone," he said. "When you get older, you forget your family. It's hard when they die, but it seems like your mind fades away from them. If I felt as bad as I did the day my mama died or my daddy died, I couldn't of lived this long."

"So there's a beauty to forgetting?" I asked.

"Oh, yeah," Bill said. "And you'll feel that way, too. When your mama and daddy die, you'll grieve. You'll grieve bad. You got any brothers?"

"A brother and a sister," I said.

"When they die, it's just about as bad. You got lots of grieving to do." He was silent for a few seconds, to let it land. When it did, I muttered, "Oh, wow," and then he leaned back and said it again, "Yeah, you got lots of grieving to do. But then time will take care of your heart."

The morning went on, and we all picked lazily at what remained of the food. I'd eaten way too much squirrel; it tasted like dark turkey meat and was actually quite good. I wasn't sure I'd be able to walk to Auburn with such a heavy gut. The sunlight in the kitchen window had lost its morning sharpness. Bill's dog, Todd, slumbered in the corner, bathed in the glow.

It was time for me to go. I wondered what these people, who had lived so long, might think of me—this young man walking from town to town, day after day, with a great load on his back. I'd never thought of walking as an act of extravagance before, almost like a superpower, but that's how it felt now, surrounded by these old people.

"Well, I think I'll take a nap," Jack said next to me. I couldn't tell if he was in a moment of lucidity or dementia. He began the arduous procedure of standing up, but Bill leapt from his chair, walked behind his friend, and then put a heavy hand on his shoulder. Jack collapsed back into his seat.

RUSSELL and JASON, best friends forever
TUSKEGEE, ALABAMA, in the parking lot of the fire station after
treating me to dinner at a nearby diner
JANUARY, three months on the road

"*Pretty much we grew up across the road from each other.*"

"*You know, BFFs, back in the day.*"

"*Right. We did everything together. We were actually blood brothers.*"

"*He convinced me he was a master of kung fu, and that I had to train every day.*"

"*I was the leader of the club, okay?*"

"*I'm gullible. I was gullible back then. You can't do it anymore, FYI. But when we were kids, he talks me into it: 'Russell, why don't you come over and play with me?' I was like, 'All right, all right. We'll come, we'll come.' We get there. He pulls out a revolver, a .22 revolver. 'All right, Russell, I found this game. I watched it on a movie, man, we gotta try: Russian roulette!' I was like, 'What is it?' He's like, 'All right, man. I'm gonna put one bullet in here, we're gonna spin it, and then we gotta put it to our heads and pull the trigger.' And he's like, 'You're gonna go first.' And I was like, 'I don't know about this.' And he's like, 'It's okay, man, I swear. It always works.' So I put it up here, and I'm like, 'You sure about this?' He's like, 'Yeah, man, just go, just go.' So I go CLICK! I was still nine, I didn't even think about it. And I go, 'All right, it's your turn.' He goes, 'No, I don't want to play this game anymore.' Takes the gun inside. I was like, 'You S.O.B.'*"

"*Sorry. I was a kid. I didn't know any better.*"

Chapter Ten

"I don't know where I'm going, but I ain't staying here."

I spent about three weeks walking through the Black Belt of Alabama, the fertile east-west cut across the belly of the state. It was a land of paradoxes. The seal of the city of Montgomery summed it up with a slogan: "Cradle of the Confederacy, Birthplace of the Civil Rights Movement."

"Rich" was a word I heard several people use to describe this place, and the soil itself epitomized this richness. The loam was so dark it gave the Black Belt its name. "You take all your footprints with you," one old woman said, because it glommed onto your soles in the springtime. Red clay infused the soil, a blood-orange tincture that mirrored the deserts out west. But whereas the deserts seemed to jeer at life, daring anything to grow, the Black Belt welcomed it with open arms: the leafy crowds of mustard greens and the waving collards of winter, the sugarcane, the cabbage heads, the okra and the butterbeans and the peas. And what lay beneath? Radish and rutabaga, turnip and onion. The soil beckoned. I wanted to go swim in the stuff, or burrow down deep to sit in silence like the Buddha-fat rutabagas.

This same dirt constituted the roadbeds in the small village of Vredenburgh. Skinny stray mutts slunk between the trailers and the rusty tin-roofed cabins, many of which were in various states of collapse. The poverty was such that I felt uncomfortable taking photographs. I feared that if anyone saw me documenting this place, they might feel ashamed of it, or of themselves. But surely I was projecting my own shame onto them. Why should they feel ashamed of themselves, of their inimitable homes and lives? If I sensed any shame walking into Vredenburgh, it was mine—of beginning to realize the depth of my previous unconsciousness to this poverty and to the struggle it implied, and to the suffering. Just a few footsteps before, I'd been blind. But to walk into this village was to catch a glimpse at the cost of my multifarious privilege, and of the great distance we all still had to travel together if we wanted to live in real peace, a peace that was inclusive and comprehensive, which had to be the only kind of real peace. It unmoored me, this glimpse, and brought me closer to a regrettably forgettable fact: that my own peace was inextricably connected to everyone else's, and that true freedom would remain illusory and incomplete until each of us was truly free.

In the shadow of this truth was my shame, itself a response to an even deeper shadow—something inside me that resented my connectedness to the whole, that wanted to just walk my own walk, live my own life, untouched by the madness of human history, excused from witnessing, experiencing, or having anything at all to do with the suffering that history was manifesting here and now. Would I choose to be so inured, if given the option? *Maybe you would*, the shame in me said. *Maybe you already have*.

There were a few street lamps, but their light was weak, and when night fell the dark was almost impenetrable. "Don't wander around in there tonight," one guy told me in the white part of town. "There are drive-bys." He was referring to the black part of town, where I was going to stay. The Sisters of St. Joseph had agreed to let me sleep in the community center—a double-wide trailer where the kids went after school to do their homework. I'd been in the trailer for an hour or two, resting, when someone knocked on the door. I assumed it was Sister Kathy Navarro, a middle-aged white woman with short, gray hair who taught karate. She almost whispered when she talked. When I opened the door, however, there was a young black man standing right in front of me. He was shirtless, muscular, and he had tattoos all over his chest. He walked right inside without an invitation—but then again it was his community center, not mine. Two of his friends followed.

"What's up, guys?" I said. I sounded a little nervous.

"So you've been walking around America?" the tattooed guy asked me, ignoring my question.

"Yeah, man. I walked here from Philadelphia. I've been walking for three months, listening to people's stories."

"You've been walking for three months?"

"Three months, man. What, you don't believe me?"

The three young men burst into laughter and started asking me questions. They'd come to meet me. Eric was the one with the tattoos, and his friends were Manny and Jay. Soon some girls joined us—Maia, Veronica, and Bea. They were all high schoolers. The trailer had been too quiet before they all showed up, and the loneliness had been murmuring; but now it was a party. The girls started up a card game, and I took out my recorder. They spoke in an accent I could hardly understand. There were no discernible breaks between words, and all the sharp edges I heard in my own voice were worn down. I started to get self-conscious about how lamely proper I sounded.

"What would you tell someone who's never been here, that would help them understand this place?" I asked the girls. They looked at me like it was the stupidest question ever asked.

"I just can't explain."

"We just party and have fun, things we shouldn't be doing. But nothing *that* serious."

"I can't tell them nothing but just walk them around."

"They have to actually come, and let us show them exactly how it is, and what it look like, even though it's a very small town. Very ghetto. It's very ghetto here."

"Black and white come through. But the whites got they own little thing. See, it was like that before my time."

"Before all our time."

"But they ain't prejudiced. Some of them aren't."

"No, no. Ain't none of them."

"I ain't never been around *all* of them, so I can't say."

"I have. Because my grandma used to go up there and clean up, and I used to go with her when I was little and help her."

"They're nice."

"They sure is."

"They got their own part. I guess that happened during slavery time, and it ain't never changed. But they ain't prejudiced. That's how I put it. They ain't prejudiced."

I thought of all the prejudice I'd witnessed on my way down to Vredenburgh. There was a white guy a few weeks earlier in Opelika who'd bought me a foot-long chili dog loaded with coleslaw. They were famous. We were having a nice conversation until he started talking about "blackfolk town." Apparently it was just a few blocks away. "I'm not racist," he said at one point, "I just don't like it when they thug out."

I'd passed old plantation estates on my way to Vredenburgh, and cotton fields. I'd passed white cemeteries and black cemeteries, black churches and white churches. All around me, the descendants of slaves and slave owners were living in neighboring communities, and sometimes side by side, forever bound together by their ancestors, many of them probably wishing they weren't. I didn't mention this to the girls as we played cards.

We all "hit the block" that night. That's what you did in Vredenburgh, they said. There wasn't much else to do. We circled the village a couple times, and then the girls took me to the mayor's trailer to say hello. Mayor Rousseau was Bea's mom.

"Forsthoefel?" she said when I introduced myself. "What's that?" I told her it was German, and then I asked her about Rousseau. Was that French or something?

"Oh, I don't know," she said. "It was the slave master's name."

I felt a confusing rush of guilt and astonishment, curiosity and shame, appreciating, for one of the first times, another regrettably forgettable fact: History is not some dead fable. It's a living reality continuing to play itself out right here and now, and I was a part of it, in everything I did or chose not to do. I didn't know what to say.

Mayor Rousseau invited us all inside and fixed me an enormous dinner plate: Boston butt, pork chops, ribs, black-eyed peas, and corn bread. She did this casually, but I didn't feel casual. I wondered, perhaps naïvely, if it crossed her mind that her ancestors had been enslaved by people who looked like me, and that the current poverty of her town was directly correlated with that history. It certainly crossed my mind. A friend in college, a woman of color, had once explained to me that white privilege was the luxury of being able to forget about your skin color, of not having to constantly check and consider your racial identity in almost every social context. She had to deal with that mental anguish and exhaustion every day, because Middlebury was mostly white, and so was Vermont. I had a freedom from that tumultuous inner dialogue; I could blend in and enjoy the privacy of my anonymity. Hitting the block in Vredenburgh, I understood my friend's words a little bit better. I'd been the only white kid in school when we lived in India, and we were one of the only white families in an apartment building in Chicago, but I'd been a child during those experiences, still in that innocence where it made no difference.

Mayor Rousseau filled my plate with seconds, and I made it a point to finish them. Soul food was sacramental in the Black Belt, a kind of communion. In this sharing, I saw how utterly dependent I was on the people around me, how I could never do this walk on my own, how none of us could.

The girls and I left Mayor Rousseau's trailer and took one more loop around the village. I knew I'd be gone the next day, so I kept peppering them with questions. What was it like to grow up in this place? What do you want to do with your lives? Who do you want to be?

"The kids are finally learning that there's nothing here to do," Veronica told me, "so they going out to get them education. Because I know most of them probably don't want to do like their parents— no job, nothing to do but sit around every day doing the same thing. I don't want to be here."

"It's a small community, right?" I asked.

"Yeah, everybody knows each other around here," Maia said. "Ain't nobody around here that you don't know, that don't know you. That's the good part about it. To me, it's nice because instead of living in a big old city where you don't know nobody, if something happens, that person see you stranded or see something wrong with you, some people be scared to stop because of all the violence going on. See here, everybody know each other. Something going on, they see you, you ain't got nothing to worry about. See that's what I like."

"So do you think you'll stay here?"

"No, I'm not gonna stay here."

"What do you want?"

"I'm gonna leave. I don't know where I'm going, but I ain't staying here."

"Why don't you want to stay?"

"Ain't nothing around here for you to accomplish. If there were like a university or something like that, I'd be happy to stay."

"If there was a mall," Bea said, "a movie theater, a Wal-Mart, a McDonald's, or something, I'd stay here."

The girls said that most kids never ended up leaving, even if they wanted to. There weren't many ways to move on.

"You're my ticket out of here, man," Eric, the guy with the tattoos, said to me that night. "I'm thinking of coming with you."

I thought of him as I left Vredenburgh the next morning, alone. It had taken me all of ten minutes to pack up and move on. For Eric, it might take years. It might take generations. In fact, it already had.

Alabama made my head swirl—the hatred, the kindness, the separation, the interdependence, the complete lack of resolution. I was walking through a land imbued with pain. Previously, the violence here had been physical. Mobs of white people had burned buses and blown up churches and lynched thousands of black people over the decades. Now, the violence was quiet, but it still felt present, a deep psychic divide. I didn't know what to do with that as I walked across Alabama. Walking and listening seemed wholly inadequate.

In Montgomery, I met Bryan Stevenson, a public-interest lawyer and the director of the Equal Justice Initiative, just a few blocks from the Alabama River. One of my mom's friends knew Mr. Stevenson, and we had been introduced over e-mail. I didn't know it at the time, but Desmond Tutu had once called Mr. Stevenson "America's young Nelson Mandela." He was an advocate for imprisoned children and inmates on death row, and he'd won widespread recognition for his work challenging the biases against people of color and the poor that riddle the American criminal justice system.

Mr. Stevenson gave me twenty minutes out of his busy day. He took me for a walk down to the riverfront and explained how he saw Alabama. His words became a compass for me as I continued across the state, a way to navigate the pain, the confusion, and the overwhelming feeling of hopelessness. We stood and watched the Alabama River flow by.

"What we don't talk about here is that this river was a very active commercial site in the early part of the nineteenth century. Slaves would be brought here into the Black Belt, which had the largest slave population in America. In the very place that we're standing, the ships would pull up to these docks and they would unload hundreds of enslaved people. The enslaved people would get off the boats and they would walk up the same path we just walked down, which would be lined with slave owners and merchants who would watch these enslaved men and women and evaluate which ones seemed strong and not strong. They would fall in behind the enslaved people and then follow them up to an auction block, which we can walk up to, and they would have a slave auction, on this street.

"Nobody wants to talk about that history. That's a very powerful history, you know what I mean? And so a part of getting people to appreciate the realities of who we are is to confront that history. People here would be angry that I was telling a visitor that this is where the slave port was and this is where the slaves came. But it's real. It's what this is about."

I told him about the prejudice and racism I'd witnessed on my way to Montgomery, and how I never knew what to say, and how I often said nothing.

"You're trying to become a witness to the reality of these communities," Mr. Stevenson said, "and that means you have to be open to hearing what people have to say. So I say receive all of that.

But I think our great challenge now is to try to address the fact that when segregation quote-unquote officially ended, we never really committed ourselves to a process of truth and reconciliation. We didn't tell the truth about what decades of segregation and apartheid did to both black and white people. We didn't tell the truth about the trauma that we created and the burdens we've inherited and the bigotry we've ingested without thinking. And that's what's manifesting itself to you as you make your tour, even in 2012. So part of our challenge is to expose that, to confront that, and to try and see if we can find a way to create some reconciliation to that history, so we can move forward."

"How do you deal with someone who doesn't want reconciliation?" I asked.

"Well, I think a part of it is they don't want truth, either. And so at first you kind of have to make truth a dominant part of the conversation. Because without the truth you begin to deny things. What's a little fascinating to me is that because we don't know how to talk about that history we just deny it. So, I think we make truth the first part of it. Then, if you can get people to at least hear the truth, even if they have a hard time accepting it, the reconciliation comes easier. You can't create reconciliation until people feel there's something broken that needs to be addressed."

I asked him about the motivation behind his work. Why do it? He grew up in the segregated South, he told me, and his great-grandparents had been enslaved in Virginia.

"I always wanted to be fully human," he said, "and I have not been able to achieve that. When you see people who are being diminished and humiliated because of their race or economic status, you either have to reconcile yourself to that reality and just accept it, or you have to challenge it, and fight it. For me, to be fully human means I have to challenge those things."

We walked back up the hill toward the center of town, treading in the ghostly footprints of those who'd come before us.

"It's eerie," I said.

"Isn't it eerie? Isn't it deep? It's a rich place full of a very rich history."

Before I left Montgomery, I decided I'd walk as far as New Orleans, where I'd stop and take stock. Maybe I'd keep walking west. Maybe I wouldn't. New Orleans wasn't quite halfway across America, but I began to see it as the halfway point of my walk. If I kept up the pace, I might even make it in time for Mardi Gras. I might never leave.

The city of Selma was about fifty miles west of Montgomery. I was heading southwest, so it wasn't on my way, but Martin Luther King Day was coming up and I decided I'd be a fool not to make a detour. Highway 80 connected the two cities, the same highway that had hosted the voting rights marches of 1965. There'd been three marches. The first, on Sunday, March 7, ended after just a mile or so at the Edmund Pettus Bridge in Selma. State troopers refused to let the marchers pass, blinding them with tear gas, electrocuting them with cattle prods, beating them with nightsticks, metal pipes, and rubber hoses wrapped in barbed wire. It was dubbed Bloody Sunday. The second march was called Turnaround Tuesday. Thousands of people marched to the bridge, prayed, and walked back. That evening, several white men attacked three white Unitarian ministers, bludgeoning one of them in the head with a club, a mortal blow. The third march was the March to Montgomery—more than fifty miles, five days, and eight thousand participants, three hundred of whom walked, led by Dr. King. I was going to walk that route in reverse and arrive in Selma just in time for MLK Day.

The city of Montgomery spilled out into the countryside for miles. I slogged through a bleak industrial wasteland of glass cutting shops and pipe threading joints, auto shops and tire repair lots. After a few hours I finally punched out into the kind country-side. It was the beginning of cotton country. The expanses bristled with stalks cut close like whiskers, stray bits of soggy cotton sagging over them. Orbs of mistletoe hung from the oak trees, and radiant green grass sprung from the red earth. The forests hung heavy with Spanish moss.

Antebellum mansions dotted the roads ahead, some still elegant, others frozen in slow-motion collapse. Their porches drowned in wisteria vine. Often, the neighbors lived in mortally afflicted mobile homes held up by cinder blocks, falling apart.

I didn't feel so alone on Highway 80 imagining the marchers here decades earlier, when things were both different and not so different from the way they are today.

About halfway to Selma, a shrine marked the spot where an activist had been shot and killed as she was ferrying people back home from the march. She was a white woman, a thirty-nine-year-old mother of five from Detroit. The memorial was on a hilltop in the middle of nowhere. IN MEMORY OF VIOLA LIUZZO, the head-stone read, WHO GAVE HER LIFE IN THE STRUGGLE FOR THE RIGHT TO VOTE. I stared in silence, haunted. It had happened here, exactly here. The scene played out in my head for the next few miles: the speeding chase, the Klansmen pulling even, the shots, the blood. I could almost see it. Something lingered here.

I walked on. At one point, bored with the silence and inspired by the ones who'd come before, I started singing "We Shall Overcome." It was full of gusto, lots of vibrato. I sounded like a seventy-five-year-old black man in a gospel choir, which I realize now might've come off as disrespectful in good company. But I wasn't in good company. I was on the side of a highway. I looked up at one point midsong and saw a herd of cows staring at me, blank-eyed. They seemed quite unmoved.

That evening around sunset, I came across a run-down gas station in the countryside. The cashier gave me permission to pitch my tent on the property. On my way out back I passed a barbershop next to the gas station. There were about a dozen guys inside, all of them black, most of them bundled up in winter jackets because it was so cold. Some were middle-aged. Some were my age, maybe younger. The bass-heavy beats of hip-hop thumped through the glass door. Suddenly, I had the same feeling I used to get cliff-jumping in college: if I didn't leap now, then I wouldn't at all, and I'd kind of hate myself for the rest of the day.

In the moments before a big jump, I've read that the human brain engages itself in a furious wrestling match. The amygdala releases cortisol, a hormone that triggers stress. However, dopamine is also released, a flow of euphoric anticipation. It's a battle between pleasure and panic, all of it jacked up on a hefty dose of adrenaline. My heart was pounding. *What am I afraid of, anyway?*

I stepped inside. Everyone looked up, and they all stopped talking. It was completely silent, except for the hip-hop. A white boy walks into a black barbershop in the middle of nowhere in Alabama. It sounds like the beginning of a joke, but it didn't feel like a joke. It felt like the room had turned into a vacuum; there was no air to breathe. *What are we about to do to one another? What can we do?* I wondered if the cosmic scales of justice would tip just a fraction of a millimeter if the men kicked me out immediately. *We don't serve whites here.* I was banking on my absurdity—the absurdity of my big, stupid grin; the absurdity of walking across America.

I explained what I was doing, and then asked if I could set up my tent outside, even though I already had permission; it was my go-to icebreaker. One of the barbers said sure, and the noise slowly started up again. No big deal. A man named Mr. Rudolph took me out back to an abandoned building where I could pitch my tent. I mentioned I was listening to peoples' stories, which was really just another way of asking if I could go back and hang out at the barbershop.

"Oh, yeah," Mr. Rudolph said, "there's lots of stories in there."

I returned, and nobody seemed too bothered by me. I took a seat next to an older man. He'd lived in the area for most of his life, he said. He remembered the March to Montgomery. "I watched them walk right by." He had a few kids. They were all living in Cleveland now. He went to visit them sometimes, and whenever he did, he loved to take his granddaughter shopping. I wrote all these details in my journal.

The floor was checkered black and white, and a haze of cigarette smoke choked out the fresh air. The music boomed and the TV blared. The local news was on, and there was a segment on Dr. King, with MLK Day coming up. I'd been thinking about him often since leaving Montgomery, trying to feel his footsteps, and now here he was, walking in old video footage on the TV.

I had a hard time understanding most of the men in the barbershop because of the noise, but also because their accent was so unfamiliar. I noticed myself saying, "What's that?" and "Sorry?" a lot, and I began to get annoyed with myself. At one point, I realized most of the guys didn't understand what I was doing. I told them that their barbershop was as far as I'd walked in three months, and that I'd started in October, right outside Philadelphia. The place erupted in laughter and shouting.

"Phila*delphia*?" one guy said, looking to his friend. "Ain't no way. Ain't no *way*. Shit, he's a walkin' motherfucker, man."

"You wanna meet someone who's walking around the world?" someone else said when a new guy came in. "He's right over there."

I smiled and waved. The guy either didn't believe me or he wasn't impressed.

I hung around for a half hour or so, mostly just listening and trying to keep up. A part of me hoped someone would point out what seemed to be the elephant in the room: that I was a white man, and that they were black men, and that we were all, at that very moment, sitting together in the legacy of slavery, which was itself the legacy of a single catastrophic idea: that all humans are not, in fact, created equal. An idea that America was built to destroy. An idea that America only reified in the way its white founders built it, and that America would continue to reify so long as its sons and daughters weren't willing to listen to one another. Who first thought this bullshit idea? Who first believed it, then acted upon it? Surely it must have arisen in some ancient place, from a primordial, lizardlike state of consciousness. It's not surprising that the idea was born, given the chaos of the caveman days. What's surprising is that it's still alive today in the twenty-first century. Evolution takes its sweet time in its work on our collective consciousness; the lasting leap from fear to love in the human mind will be its masterpiece.

I wanted to make some kind of leap with these men, but I didn't know how to do it. I wanted to have one of Bryan Stevenson's truth and reconciliation commissions, right there in that barbershop. But we didn't have that conversation. Maybe it was enough to just sit together that night. Maybe that's all we could do.

Before I could leave, a woman walked inside, and when one of the guys told her what I was doing she came over and gave me some money.

"You don't have to," I said, but she was already walking out the door, and then she said something I didn't understand. Everyone laughed. I wanted to be in on it, but I couldn't bring myself to say, "What was that?" for the ten thousandth time, so I just smiled and said thank you.

"We'll check on you later," one of the young men said as I was walking out, "to make sure you're all right."

Nobody checked on me, and I left at sunrise. Two or three hours into the morning, though, I saw one of the guys again. He was driving a steel blue Cadillac with big chrome rims. He stopped in the middle of the road. There wasn't any traffic.

"Hey, man, you walk all the way from the shop?" he said. Some of his teeth were capped in gold, and gold veins filled the spaces between them. "I took your picture. You might end up in *USA Today*."

The guy had a box of Krispy Kreme donuts. He gave me one, and then roared off down the road back toward the barbershop.

"Think about this. In 1961, I was born in Newport News, Virginia—1961. It's 2012, here in Selma, Alabama. Now when I was a young kid growing up, would I ever have dreamed of being in Selma as the police chief, having looked at the history? That would've been the farthest thing from my mind."

This was Chief William Riley. Someone in Montgomery had put us in touch, and he was housing me in an operations trailer at the police station. We were in his SUV cruiser riding through Selma. He was dressed in his navy blue uniform, bald and bespectacled, and a thin mustache lined his upper lip. He'd been the police chief of Selma for three years, one of the first African Americans to hold that position.

"What those guys and ladies that went across that bridge—that were beaten and some were killed going across that bridge for our rights—what they fought for? Yes, it is working. Because I'm here. Does more need to be done? Absolutely yes. But, we know that it is working."

I'd gotten into town an hour earlier, and Chief Riley had welcomed me with enthusiasm, and even some undeserved ceremony, considering I was just a disheveled kid on a solo walk. He'd tipped a reporter, who came to take my picture for the newspaper. Then he gave me a tour of the police station, taking me inside a jail cell where Dr. King had been incarcerated. Standing in that cell was one of the most humbling moments of my walk, getting close like that to such an important spirit. It struck me that this spirit had had a body once, just like I had a body now, hands that once touched these bars that I was touching, feet that once walked this floor. I didn't see Dr. King's ghost, but I did feel connected to him. It made me want to go out and *do* something.

The chief was eager to treat me to a rib-eye feast. Driving through town, we passed several houses in various states of dilapidation, some of them boarded up. One was sprayed with graffiti: FUCK COPS. We rolled past a housing project, where a little girl cradled her doll and teenage boys rode their bicycles. The boys reminded me of another housing project I'd passed a few hours earlier on my way into Selma. Through the chain-link fence I'd seen some teenagers riding their bikes, flashing in and out of sight behind the rows of brick houses. The houses were all dying, their windows shattered, their walls covered in vines. It looked like a ghost town, a war-torn wound in the earth, but it seemed people still lived there. I passed some of them, sitting in lawn chairs right behind the fence. One woman waved to me.

"I spent almost twenty-four years in the Newport News Police Department," Chief Riley said as he drove, "and most of my time was spent working homicides. I've seen some of the most terrible things that human beings can do to each other, you know? Now, in Selma, I don't think much is going to surprise me, what human beings do to each other. That I can tell you."

Selma was plagued by violent crime, he said, much of it coming from the housing project near the police station, a predominantly black community. But there was also another kind of viciousness in Selma. The country club, for instance. Several people told me that black people weren't allowed to play on the club's golf course. One white police officer said on tape, "The mayor has a golf tournament every year, but he has to go to Valley Grande to do it because he can't do it at the country club." The mayor was black. Someone else doubted if Tiger Woods would even be allowed to play there. It all ran quite counter to the city's slogan, "Historic Places, Social Graces." Social disgraces, maybe.

"But, the good outweighed the bad, in my lifetime," the chief continued. "The good totally outweighed the bad. I've been approached by people who said, 'You know, young man, it looks like you've got something on your mind. Everything will be all right.' Somebody who doesn't even know you! We got to where we are today because someone helped us. We are our brother's keeper. Some people don't agree with that, but we are, because everything we do will have a ripple effect. I don't care where we are. It's going to have a ripple effect. One act of kindness may conquer an army one day. We don't know."

Listening to the tape of this conversation years later, I'm still surprised at how hopeful the chief was, given everything he'd seen in his lifetime. Later at the dinner table, I asked him what he meant by "the most terrible things that human beings can do to each other," and he said he'd seen people "beat up, cut up, shot up, drained up, drowned up, hung up, burnt up." I lost some of my appetite after he told me a story about an old man who'd been doused in paint thinner and then lit on fire. They had to cut him so he wouldn't burst from the bloating. There were lots of stories like this, involving crack cocaine, trains, knives, cliffs, and a Freddy Krueger comparison. *One act of kindness may conquer an army one day.* Those were not the words of a naïve man.

"It's amazing how life changes," he said. "That's just part of living. I try to impress that upon my kids. Live! Really, just live! I want you to go to college, but I also want you to *live.* I've always told my son and my daughter, Malcolm and Amani, that the world is huge. We're just a small speck on this earth and you have to go and see it. We've always encouraged them to see the world. We all have a history and a story to tell. My son is at Faith Baptist down in Florida. On his basketball team he's got guys from South America, Europe, and whatnot. He's hanging out with a guy from Ukraine. And I just thought that was the neatest thing. You know? It's like, 'Yes!' Because I'm like, 'Yes!' Okay? That's what I want. The world. My daughter, she's eleven. I always ask her what she wants to do, and she always says, 'Daddy, I want to be a chef and I want to cook in Paris.' And I'm like, 'Okay!'

"I look at you. You're a young man out here, you're walking across America, and you're going to have experiences that I will never have. Okay? And, of course, you'll be richer for them. I definitely wish you well. And keep going."

Before we got to the restaurant, we stopped to visit the town's World War II memorial. The names of the fallen were carved into the stone, separated into "Whites" and "Colored." Next to this, the inscription seemed painfully ironic:

TO THEIR MEMORY THIS MONUMENT IS HUMBLY
DEDICATED,
WITH THE DETERMINED PLEDGE OF THEIR COMRADES IN
ARMS TO PERPETUATE AND PROTECT THE AMERICAN WAY OF
LIFE FOR WHICH THEY SO VALIANTLY DIED.

"It's like a slap to the face," the chief said. "These people gave their lives, and even in death they're not equal. So long as that's in public it's a statement about what we believe, what we think is okay. It's shameful. This thing should be in a museum."

The chief told me about a ritual at the high school where the senior boys rode around in their pickup trucks flying Confederate flags. Some kind of pep rally.

"The Confederate flag isn't a 'Southern pride' thing," he said. "It's a 'We-used-to-own-your-asses-and-we-will-again-if-we-get-the-opportunity' thing."

I recorded more interviews in Selma than anywhere else in the country. I stayed for three days and bounced around between Church's Chicken and a few actual churches, the police station, a museum, the welcome center. I listened to anyone who wanted to talk.

I met Quentin Lane at a coffee shop downtown. He was an organist across the street at the Presbyterian church, and he offered to give me a tutorial in the "king of the instruments," as he called it. The church was empty, and the silence was all-swallowing until the organ grumbled awake at his touch. He didn't have his organ shoes, so he played without them. A cascade of invisible notes washed over us. He explained how it worked: there were buttons and levers that you could push and pull, and the different combinations transformed the sound—mellifluous and shy, warring and triumphant, sweet, blatting, squeaky, and when all the buttons and levers were pressed and pulled, utterly magnificent. "It's whatever you make it," Quentin said.

I met Dr. Frederick Douglas Reese, a reverend who had helped organize the march to Montgomery in 1965. He was leading a Bible study in the basement of his church, and he took a break to tell me the story of Bloody Sunday. I didn't have my recorder. Later that night I wrote his memories down in my journal, frantically, before they slipped away.

"Apex of the bridge a sea of blue, the troopers and their cars lining the highway, beat us all the way back to Brown Chapel' got hit in the head and the shoulder, holding the billy club at both ends and plowing them over one by one down the line."

I felt a bit like Forrest Gump around Dr. Reese, finding myself in the presence of a man who'd directly influenced the course of American history. The strange thing about Selma was that lots of people had. So many of the protesters were still alive. Plenty of the counter-protesters were, too. They all had their stories. Dr. Reese gave me a black-and-white photograph. In it, he's walking at the front of a large crowd of people, his right arm linked with Coretta Scott King, her right arm linked with her husband.

On MLK Day, a crowd of a hundred people or so walked to the Edmund Pettus Bridge, an antiviolence march. The only white people I saw were police officers, a reporter, and a judge who was there to give a speech. Little children were holding posters printed with the portraits of young men and women, along with their names, birth dates, and death dates. More of these portraits were taped to a wooden coffin that lay in the center of the crowd. Women—mothers and aunts and sisters—were wearing T-shirts printed with the faces of the slain. I asked one woman about the young man that her shirt memorialized. He was her nephew, she said. "They shot him in the back of the head. His mother's right over there." She shouted out to his mother, who smiled and waved at us.

A large bald man stepped up to the podium to speak. He was introduced as Silky Slim, and his name was Arthur Reed. He began quietly, but after the first few sentences he spun into an extemporaneous fervor, in the tradition of the Southern preacher.

"One of the things that I do is I go around and I talk to individuals about violence. I was a twenty-two-year gang leader. And we, as black folks, of course we want to get away from everything that has happened to us. But we gotta know that whether the bite comes with a growl or a smile, the bite is still the same when we look at what's going on in America today. See, I, for one, know that the criminal justice system is exactly that. It's a justice system that's being ran by a bunch of damn criminals, and until we get up, stand up, and make ourselves the strong people that we are, we will never ever see change. People want to get mad when you speak the truth, but the truth has to be told! I have to tell you that they got too many pimps in the pulpit! Everybody's talking Jesus, ain't too many walking Jesus! It's easy to say you're a Christian, but if your heart is not what a Christian heart is, then you find yourself among wolves in sheep's clothing! No, I'm not a racist, I'm a realist, and I always have to speak real! If you stop talking Jesus, you start walking Jesus, you will see a change in your hood! It's not the police's responsibility! It's not the judge's responsibility! It's your responsibility to take control of your kids! Raise your kids! You can raise a beer bottle up but you can't raise your kids! You walking around, your pants sagging in 2012, looking like a slave! It's time for us to raise up our knowledge! Pull our pants up! It's time for you to put down Lil Wayne! Pick up Jesus's cross! Follow him! The biggest problem of the world today: Jesus got too many worshippers and not enough damn workers! Let's get to work!"

He stopped abruptly and walked off the stage. The emcee took the mic and said, "My Lord!" which was exactly how I felt.

The day before I left Selma, James Perkins invited me out for dinner at a Chinese restaurant. He was the former mayor of the city and the first African American to hold that office. We were in the parking lot of the restaurant when his cell phone rang. "Sorry, I have to get this," he said. It was the daughter of Viola Liuzzo, the civil rights activist who'd been assassinated and then memorialized on Highway 80.

Mayor Perkins introduced me to Mary Liuzzo Lilleboe, putting her on speakerphone so I could hear, and then they continued as if I weren't there. Recently, Mary had lost her temper at a city councilman because she was convinced he had known of the KKK's plot to murder her mother. She regretted her outburst, and wanted to recant some of her anger. I was stunned as Mayor Perkins and Mary went back and forth. It seemed like Viola Liuzzo was right there, and that a strange communion was taking place between all of us, the living and the dead, the past and the present.

"It's okay to hurt," Mayor Perkins said to me afterward. We were still sitting in the car, and I'd asked him about the conversation with Mary. It was my last interview in Selma. "That hurt does not constitute hate. It's okay to hurt and it's okay to express that hurt, because the expression of it is a part of the healing. The pain that we experience, physical and emotional pain, is real. And part of the healing process is acknowledging that it's there, and being able to speak to it, about it, so that you can better understand what's going on inside of you.

"One of the challenges in Selma is when you go around and talk to people, it's common to be speaking to someone who was here in 1965, who was a part of the movement, on both sides. And the consequence of that is there's still this healing process. And we're going to have to talk about it. Talk about the pain that it caused, talk about how it makes me feel. It's one thing to know my history. It's another thing to feel what I feel about my history."

I mentioned my anxiety about speaking up, as I had with Bryan Stevenson in Montgomery.

"One has to really look inward to make those decisions," Mayor Perkins said. "When's the best time to speak? What's the best way to express how I feel? There is a tremendous amount of focus on knowledge, but I go back to the fact that human beings are also equipped with feelings. That's why words mean something to us, because they make us feel a certain way. And until we're willing to sit down and really address how these things make us feel, then we're going to come up short on the healing process."

His words hung in silence. I'd never thought of healing as simply the willingness to fully express pain, and the ability to allow someone else the opportunity to do the same. It sounded so easy, but of course it wasn't, which was exactly why the healing still hadn't happened. It made me think of my own pain, and my dad's, and I realized that the physical pain I was experiencing on this walk every day was an oblique way of processing the pain I'd neglected to feel or express, a sideways entering of the old wound. And I realized I'd never allowed my dad his own pain. I didn't want to see it, refused to see it, and surely that contributed to its power. Looking at it like this, it all felt like an impossible knot. And the South, too, and all of America. The collective pain was as tangled and interconnected as the U.S. highway system, but it was invisible, and few seemed to have any idea how to navigate it.

"Come on," Mayor Perkins said. "Let's go eat."

The next morning, I decided to get breakfast at one of the diners before leaving Selma. I sat down in a booth by myself. Across the room there was a big table full of older men, all white. I recognized one of them. We'd met at the coffee shop a few days before. I really liked him.

"Selma is a great town," he'd said over coffee into my recorder. "Everything is fine here." He saw me sitting alone in the diner and waved me over, and then introduced me to the table. Everyone greeted me warmly. They were as friendly a group of regulars as I'd ever met, and I was glad for the company. At one point, the old man leaned in and whispered to me, "They're a bunch of good old boys, didn't I tell you? But some of them are still living in the past, if you know what I mean. So don't bring up integration. Just play it cool."

I didn't ask any questions. I stayed quiet. *What a way to leave Selma*, I thought. I spent most of that morning disgusted at my silence, stunned by the power of my fear, wondering how this walk would've been different if I were black.

I wondered about my own freedom. Could I really say that I was free if I always played it cool when I was told to, if I couldn't bring myself to ask certain questions? *"Are you* sure *everything is fine here?"* The appalling silence was a prison, a prison that I reinforced each time I didn't speak up. It hurt, to lock myself up like that, to go mute, and the consequences of my chosen confinement hurt others, too. It wasn't just my own freedom that was at stake in these little pivotal moments, but America's also. American freedom was a collective dream that would remain a dream until all the silent dreamers did the work of waking up from their respective prisons, the work of seeing and grieving the truth of how things actually were, which was, perhaps, the work of freedom. But it was hard to wake up and work if you didn't have to, dreaming such sweet dreams like the one with the good old boys at the diner, a dream that said everything was fine here. We all remained prisoners that day, of ignorance and denial, of silence, and the dream of freedom in America stayed exactly that in our little corner of the nation, a dream. Or maybe it was a nightmare.

JESSE MOTON, small-time cattle farmer, raccoon hunter
CAMDEN, ALABAMA, in the country outside town in a field among
his cows
JANUARY, far enough south to be safe from the cold

"*They got this thing they call a 'coon hunting club, and it be a bunch of fellas get together, you know, I may have my dog, you got your dog, she might have her dog, and all of us turn loose the same time and see whose dog can tree the 'coon the first. It's just a lot of fun. We listen. Some people will hoot, but I don't hoot to my dog. They'll hoot to them and let them know they're still in the woods, but I don't never say nothing, till my dog trees him, and when he trees, then I go to him. It's a lot of fun. At night. Sometimes a lot of people will go, and they like it. You know, after you come back, you may have a little party or something like that, a little get together, eat and drink and tell stories about your dog. It's a lot of enjoyment.*"

"*So normally when you tree a raccoon finally, you take it down?*"

"*We usually shoot them down, yeah. I like to eat them.*"

"*What do they taste like?*"

"*I don't know. It's good meat to me. It's hard for me to tell you what it tastes like, but it's real good if you cook it right. I love it. I eat me about two or three a year. I got my traps set now, try to catch me one. I ain't got no dogs no more.*"

"*Oh, you're not running any dogs right now? Do you miss it?*"

"Do *I miss it! I go now with my nephew, but I can't do all that walking like I used to. I just sit in the truck and listen at the dogs. I wish my health was able to let me do like I used to, but it don't, so you got to live with whatever's wrong. I can do everything except walking. That walking gets on me.*"

Chapter Eleven

"And it's real."

South of Selma, pine plantations thickened the hills, tunneled through by quiet country byways. Logging trucks thundered down the roads, their steel-armed trailer beds stacked high with tree trunks stripped naked. Some veered into the far lane away from me as they passed. Most didn't.

"Be careful not to get hit out there," one old man told me in Selma, referring to the trucks. "We won't find you till next deer season."

As the day fell, turkey vultures flew halos over the heavy oaks, and little Baptist chapels hid among the trees, patiently waiting for Sunday. To the west, the Alabama River churned. To the south, the Gulf of Mexico. In the dusk, I dream-walked, letting loose my imagination: my pack was a living creature, its tentacle straps suctioned tightly to my back, quietly riding along. I saw a stubbly cotton field as the close-shaved cheek of a giant, the rolling road his lolling tongue pebbled with taste buds. I thought of the shack I'd been to earlier for lunch, and the woman behind the buffet serving the soul food, her black hair in a black net, a red apron wrapping her motherly girth. She'd asked me, "Whatchyou want, baby?" and in the dream-walking I imagined this blown through the dead rattling leaves, something calling me baby and child, something calling me home.

But it didn't seem I was getting any closer. What was home, anyway? What did it really mean to belong? The constant movement of this walk, each day's good-bye, the untethering and uprooting of every footstep—I was a stranger wherever I went, unmoored, ever-leaving, and I began to wonder if that's how it had always been, but I'd just never seen it before, my own true strangeness here. I was passing through, passing on, passing away, and that state of flux would remain, even when I stopped walking. How could you belong if you were destined to leave, or leaving already, so slowly you couldn't even see it? This was a world of wayfaring walkers and each home was nothing more than a way station, a place to rest for a while before moving on again. Even if I did find home somewhere, it wouldn't last; but still, I sought it with a hope that almost hurt sometimes.

"Will you seek afar off?" Whitman wrote.

You surely come back at last,
In things best known to you finding the best or as good as
the best,
In folks nearest to you finding also the sweetest and stron-
gest and lovingest,
Happiness not in another place, but this place ... not for
another hour, but this hour.

Home was here. Home was this. Home was now. There could be no other answer, but something about that felt disappointing. Home was supposed to be solid and unchanging, not the unpredictable fluidity of the present. It was supposed to be a place, not a state of mind. It certainly wasn't supposed to be a mix of Dad's apartments and Mom's rental houses, all tied together by the bitterness and grief. Home probably had something to do with forgiveness, moving on from the resentment that made me want to keep seeking until I became someone else altogether, with a different story and a better home that was always just a little further off.

There was a certain futility to seeking, without that forgiveness. How could I find my own home and be at peace in it with such unfinished work behind me? That work involved accepting my dad just as he was, which included the divorce, and everything that led to it, and everything that came after. That split had created me, after all; in hating it, I was only hating myself. But forgiveness felt more daunting than walking across America. You can't pretend to walk across a continent. It's simple: either you do it or you don't. But you can pretend to forgive, or convince yourself you have when in fact you haven't. How do you do it? How do you know if it's the real thing? It was the same with falling in love, it seemed to me, and the same with finding home.

In the countryside south of Selma, I was taken in by a pair of grandparents who lived in an old farmhouse they called the Homeplace. They were known for putting up travelers. The house had developed its own gravitational pull over the decades. Peter Jenkins, a famous transcontinental walker of the 1970s, had found his way to the Furmans, too.

Sister Kathy in Vredenburgh had put us in touch, and I got to their back porch at sunset. The place was decorated with retired artifacts from a different age. There was a pecan cracker next to a homemade basket of oak strips, a stirrup, a scythe, an ox-training bow, the arm of an old Victrola record player, a coffee percolator, a sheep's bell, a giant cast-iron skillet scabbed with annealed grease. Each carried its own history silently.

Marian met me at the back door and welcomed me into the kitchen, where I shook Herb's hand for the first time. I liked the

Homeplace so much that I went back there for a few months when I was done walking. Herb, I've learned, is a slow talker, a gentle man. He sits in his chair by the fire, reading the paper or watching Fox News, fading in and out of sleep. His eyes are squinty after a lifetime of sun exposure. He was a pilot, and a land surveyor. He'd only just retired when I first met him, and he was spending his time splitting wood, monitoring the weather, and leading the blessing over every meal. "Bless us, oh Lord, and these thy gifts . . ." He takes his time with it.

Marian is tall and wears her long, gray-brown hair in a bun, always covering her ears. She's beautiful, but she either doesn't know it or won't admit it. "I'm gangly," she's told me. "The kids all called me Ichabod Crane when I was coming up." She's a mother of ten and a grandmother of twenty-seven. When her own mother died, she went to her priest and told him she felt like an orphan. "You're not an orphan," she tells me he said, "you're a matriarch!" She says this with a laugh, but that's exactly what she is: a matriarch. She's also a world traveler—Mongolia, Iran, Antarctica. Her collection of *National Geographic* magazines is approaching one thousand issues. She bakes a mean batch of biscuits and offers them up right out of the oven. I'd slather them with butter and molasses, or her homemade whole fig preserves. "Praise the Lord," I heard lots of people say in Alabama, and that's what I had to say about those biscuits. *Praise the Lord.*

When I returned to the Homeplace, it was ostensibly to work on this book, but it was also because I wanted to feel it again, that suggestion of home. I'd never felt anything quite like it in any of my family's apartments or rental houses growing up, not even in the house Mom and Dad bought a few years before the divorce. We never lived in any of those places long enough to create what the Furmans have created in the Homeplace. There's something written in the peeling walls of the old farmhouse, a sense of belonging. Each object belongs, sometimes far beyond the realm of the superficial. The beds aren't just beds; they're the bookends of life and death itself—Marian's mother was born in this one, Herb's grandmother died in that one.

The patina on the smooth pine floors has been worn by a hundred years' worth of family footsteps. The draft that chills the front living room is the same draft that has chilled so many others before me. In the den, a wood-burning stove puts out a strong heat, and in that heat, too, is home—so many hands have kept that fire. Most often it's Herb now, prodding the pecan logs he's spent hours tenderly splitting.

One night I was sitting with Marian on the couch and I asked her about her own travels. She spoke in spontaneous poetry.

"The world is so big and so wide and beautiful and exciting. There's so much out there that you want to see and do and experience. I even skydived. I did. It was fantastic. I did it twice, and the second time I knew, not that I'd ever been afraid of dying, I just never have, I hadn't thought a whole lot about it . . . but there was something about voluntarily stepping out of that airplane and falling through the sky. It was like another dimension. You have stepped through into another way of existing, just temporarily, for those minutes of free fall. And it's a total and absolute trust. And I think that kind of goes in with the travel. The unknown. The maybe-a-little-bit risky. But it's the unknown, the uncharted, the unadvertised. And it's real. In the Gobi Desert, these are real people living real lives. And the icebergs and the penguins and the sea, and how clear and beautiful it is. Did you know that ice sings? Ice sings. It has a song and a voice. And it has different colors. I never knew ice had different colors, and you don't know that or appreciate it until you're there, seeing it and hearing it. And there's just so many wonderful places in the world, and I love going there. It's kind of like, well, if you get swept away in a river and you got to cross in four-wheel drive, oh well! You know? At least you didn't trip and fall over your vacuum cleaner! I have this thing, this angst about vacuum cleaners. Anyway, that's a whole 'nother story. But I think when I leave this world it will not be tripping over a vacuum cleaner, if you got that. It may be falling out of a plane over the Serengeti into the Great Migration. And you know, at seventy-six, what have you got to lose, really? I guess I felt that way at fifty, also."

While Herb tended the stove, I asked Marian more questions, and she told me family stories. Their daughter Anne Marie loved animals as a child. She had a ferret named Ringo who slept in a pie pan under the stove, a descented skunk, a parrot named Joe who ate the wallpaper near the ceiling, and Hope, the doe who ran with the dogs and slept in the house by the fire. Hope was struck by a car when she was with fawn for the first time. Herb was the one who had to bury her in the dry August ground. It was one of the only times Marian ever saw him cry. "He just never cries, ever," she said.

One year, their son Stephen lost a fingertip in a slammed car door and kept it in his shirt pocket to show his friends at school. Marian found it days later in the laundry and didn't know whether she should bury it or compost it or throw it in the trash. "What do you do with the tip of your son's finger, anyway?"

There were countless more stories: the children rushing into their bed at night during thunderstorms, dancing the jitterbug on the back porch as teenagers, the family garden and its bumper crop of snap beans in 1970 when they pressure-canned 384 quarts after picking, washing, and snapping every single solitary bean. It was an all-time high.

With each story, their lives expanded before me, and I realized I would never know Herb or Marian in their entirety. My image of them, even after all the listening, was composed of just a few specificities fattened up with so many approximations that filled the gaps. I could never hear all their stories, so how could I ever really understand them? How could I understand anyone for that matter, and be understood? For me, this was important to the question of home, because what's home if not the place where you're truly understood? There would always be a space within each of them that I could never enter, no matter how long I listened. And I had that same solitary space inside me. Even if I tried to show it to them, they wouldn't see it. How could they? No words could ever fully describe it. It was just mine, impossible to be shared, and perhaps not meant to be. This space was where I lived on the road. It was my only constant, besides the walking itself. I was getting a little more comfortable there, and it made me wonder if perhaps there wasn't any other home than the one I might find inside myself. Hadn't it always been that way? Would it ever not be? The cliché goes, "Home is where the heart is," and the heart is inside, not out.

But the Homeplace felt like a heart outside of myself, and its chambers were the kitchen and the den and the bedrooms. I felt hopeful inside it, because I wanted to believe that home wasn't just something floating around inside my head, pumping through my own hidden heart. The Furmans made me think that I might actually be able to make a home someday with someone else, a family. At the same time, I saw that I couldn't do that until I found it in myself. It'd be like offering to put up a traveler for the night when I didn't have a house of my own. I had to build that house first, and no one else could do it for me.

"Your solitude will be a support and a home for you," Rilke wrote to the young poet, "even in the midst of very unfamiliar circumstances, and from it you will find all your paths."

"But what if it's lonely in there?" I wanted to ask him. "What if it feels broken and afraid? What if there's nothing but doubt in my solitude?"

Rilke had an answer for that, too, as he did for most of my questions: "Be attentive to what is arising within you, and place that above everything you perceive around you. What is happening in your innermost self is worthy of your entire love; somehow you must find a way to work at it."

KARIE FUGETT, *writer, college student, widow*
FOLEY, ALABAMA, at an RV park near the Gulf of Mexico, sitting at a picnic table after a dinner of fried crawfish with her friend Melissa File
FEBRUARY, four months on the road

"He was driving the Humvee and there was a roadside bomb. He got the worst of it. He was kind of like a cool dude so he would drive with his leg propped up on the steering wheel, just cruising. And I guess when it blew up, his leg had gotten tangled, and in his words, it was like a noodle. Eventually, a year and a half later, infection set in and we ended up having to amputate.

"He was the life of the party. He was funny. He was outgoing. He was lively, optimistic. I mean, he just lit up the room. Even when I was thirteen that was what attracted me to him. When he came back, it was like slowly but surely you could just see his soul being sucked out of him, if it hadn't been already. He started out fairly optimistic about his injuries, but eventually we'd been in and out of hospitals for years and he started to get mean. He didn't care about much anymore. He wouldn't bathe for weeks. He started getting addicted to his pain medications. He just, I don't know, it was like he got lost somewhere in Iraq and never came back.

"And then I find out he died. Didn't really believe it. Once I did, the next day I was at my friend's condo and I just sat out in the sun, no sunscreen or anything. I just laid there, hoping that the wind was him or the bird flying by was him, and I was trying to, you know,

hopefully he would hear me because I just felt like I had to say I'm sorry.

"There's a part of me that's like, 'Why did we have to suffer for so long and why did we have to treat each other the way that we did? Why couldn't it have just ended in Iraq and he would've been a hero and we wouldn't have all these struggles that didn't have to be there?' I just didn't understand. So, yeah, I had a lot of guilt. But I've come to terms with it, for the most part. I just feel like there's only so much you can do, and someone dying doesn't change that. It doesn't make them perfect.

"After everything, there's a part of me that's kind of shut off a little bit because there's a tiny fear, like the more people I get close to, if they were to die I would just hurt all over again. I know that's so morbid, but on a day-to-day basis I just try to appreciate things and I try to just, you know, if I want to meet someone on the side of the road I'm just going to do it. And, if you care about someone, tell them. Don't leave anything behind that you wouldn't want someone to see if you were to die. There are so many little lessons, but I don't know. I don't know what the big life lesson is."

Chapter Twelve

"I'm looking for a great day."

The top-heavy tulips in the flower section of the Piggly Wiggly glowed fierily in their pot, red and orange. They were perfect. Better than the bouquets, at least, because the tulips in the pot were still living out their lives. It seemed a hopeful offering for a woman so close to death—just a few months, it turned out. I bought the tulips and left for the Monroe County Hospital.

I'd visited Emma Lou Dailey the morning before in Monroeville with Jeff Robison, a Baptist pastor in the nearby village of Beatrice. Pastor Jeff had taken me in with his family when I passed through town, and over dinner he'd told me about Emma Lou, "the most interesting person in Monroe County." She was ninety-one years old, he said. She'd been a sharecropper, a nanny of many children, and the caregiver for her great-grandfather, a first-generation enslaved man.

Her hospital room was like most hospital rooms—sterile white, nauseating smells masked by bleach. She was alone when we arrived, sinking into the hollow of her bed. Her face was lost in its own wrinkles, and her hair was gray, tucked into a black hairnet. She had scaly, papery skin, and she looked so frail, so featherlight it seemed she might just float away at the end of a breath. It was only a foot infection that had landed her in the hospital, but there'd been a string of scares before, and at her age she had to be careful.

Emma Lou labored herself to the end of the bed where she sat as we talked, her legs dangling above the floor, her back bent forward like a C. Pastor Jeff and I sat in chairs beside her.

"You been walking since October?" she said. "Oh, God. Oh, God. God be with you and bless you and keep you. Oh, God. You got nerve." Her voice was thin and it wavered. She said, "Oh, God" all the time, as if it were the refrain of a sad song.

Sitting next to her, I held my recorder with a mix of reverence and trepidation. I felt the former as soon as I walked into the room and saw her lying withered on the bed, a kind of hyper-attentive presence demanded by the close proximity of death. I wanted her to feel recognized and celebrated and understood. But how to do this respectfully? How to empathize, and at the same time honor the fact that her past was ultimately inscrutable to me, coming as I did from such a radically different background? This was the latter, the trepidation. I didn't know if I'd be able to do it right.

"I was telling him how when we first moved here you wouldn't even come into my house," Pastor Jeff said. Pastor Jeff was white.

"Well, you know, I wasn't allowed to in days back," Emma Lou said. "We would go in the back porch. Oh, but they kept begging me to come in. And I thought, 'Oh, God, what would happen if some of these others catch me in there? They're likely to skin me.' And I said, 'Y'all just go ahead.' I tried to figure about all kinds of lies to tell them. I might start coughing. I might start doing this and doing that. I'm scared, looking out the corner of my eye. Because there's some of that still makes me feel that way, like if some of them caught me in there what would they do to me?"

"So, what was it like in the old days?" I kept the question open-ended. We'd just met, and I didn't assume she wanted to discuss past traumas with a stranger. But she answered quite specifically.

"Oh, God, honey. I never will forget. We was picking butter beans in the garden for a white man and the wife told us to go bring in some water. And we got the buckets out the kitchen and went sailing down the hall to the well. Got the buckets full and when we got back to the steps he said, 'Don't y'all niggers come back up them steps. Go on around the house with that water to the kitchen.' We said, 'Yes sir.'"

I couldn't stop thinking about how Emma Lou was looking at me with the same eyes that had looked at her great-grandfather. Pastor Jeff had told me that he'd been taken from Africa and enslaved as a boy. It seemed like an impossible connection to the very distant past.

"Did you ever know him?" I asked her, just to confirm.

"Oh, yes, sir," she said. She kept calling me "sir." I didn't want her to call me that, but I also didn't want to ask her not to, so I started calling her "ma'am" as much as I could. "I used to wait on him when I was, I reckon I was about thirteen or fourteen. He had a thing on his shoulder. Back then they used to call it a carbuncle. It was a big knot. I would have to go and dress his shoulder every evening and kind of bathe him up and put his clothes on and get him ready to go to bed. He used to tell us how he cried when they rode him from his African home to our world. Said a white man had control over him and would tell him, 'You better stop that crying. If you keep that up we're going to throw you off in that water.' And he said he would get scared and hush."

"What was his name?"

"Jeff. They all called him Jeffrey. Jeffrey Montgomery."

Maybe he was sold at the slave auction in Montgomery where I'd walked with Bryan Stevenson. There was an inconspicuous sign near the center of Montgomery where the market used to be:

SLAVES OF ALL AGES WERE AUCTIONED, ALONG WITH
LAND AND LIVESTOCK, STANDING IN LINE TO BE
INSPECTED. PUBLIC POSTERS ADVERTISED SALES AND
INCLUDED GENDER, APPROXIMATE AGE, FIRST NAME
(SLAVES DID NOT HAVE LAST NAMES) . . .

"He was the first in your family taken from Africa?" I asked.

"Yes, sir."

I still wonder about that. In 1808, a federal law was passed prohibiting the trafficking of newly enslaved people into the United States. If what Emma Lou said was true—that her great-grandfather had been taken from Africa—then perhaps Jeffrey Montgomery had been smuggled into the country.

There was a knock on the door.

"Come in!" Emma Lou said.

A nurse peeked her head inside. "You have a visitor?" she said. "I was just going to take your blood pressure." The nurse walked over and began strapping the cuff around Emma Lou's arm. "You getting interviewed, Miss Lou? You famous?"

"She's famous indeed," I said, jumping in, even though she wasn't. It sounded like she hardly had anyone there for her at all. She'd never had children of her own; her husband, Moses, had died years earlier; and when she was released from the hospital—or if— she would return to the isolation of her empty house, bound to the den because it was the only heated room and it was January. *You famous?* I thought she deserved fame more than most, because of her age and experience and resilience, but there weren't any crowds outside cheering into her window, no lines of people waiting to hear what she had to say.

The hospital buzzed and beeped around us.

"I'll come back in a few minutes with your pills," the nurse said, finishing up the blood pressure reading. Emma Lou nodded.

"Andrew's going to walk right through Uriah," Pastor Jeff said, "right past those cotton fields up on the south hill where you used to work."

Emma Lou told me how the landowner would pick up the sharecroppers and take them to work. "We'd all get piled up back down in that truck, and he kept cotton in there so it would be kind of comfortable for us. We had it kind of made when we would go out to his field, because Miss Ira would have us the best old food. I don't think there's no woman in the world who could cook better than her mother and her sisters. Oh, them womens could do it. I can see me right now with a huge sweet potato, getting the hull off it, and just smiling. 'I'm going to eat all this by myself. If I was at home I'd just get a piece of it, but I'm here where it's plenty and I'm going to get the whole sweet potato and eat it all by myself. And drink me a big glass of milk. And have me a big slice of butter between my corn bread. And my good butter beans and okra.' Oh, that's glorious and heavenly."

There was another knock on the door: the nurse with a little cup of pills and an old banana to help with swallowing. Emma Lou struggled down the pills. I watched, struck by the gratitude with which she'd spoken about the food from her past. The beauty of that was self-evident, but it seemed damning, too, of the world she'd lived in, a world in which getting a whole sweet potato to herself was an event of significant consequence. But maybe I misinterpreted that. In a college class on Buddhism I'd learned that one of the Buddha's first teachings was about a tangerine. Eating it with awareness, he said, could reveal the wonders of the universe and the interconnectedness of all things: the tree that bore the fruit, the soil that grew the tree, the water that fed the soil, and so on forever, all of it culminating in that little wedge of tangerine. That sweet potato. *Oh, that's glorious and heavenly.*

It was nearly noon, and I hadn't yet made the walk to Monroeville. Pastor Jeff had driven us to the hospital from his home in Beatrice, and the plan was to shuttle me back so I could return to town on foot. But I didn't want to leave. Emma Lou was talking about her firsts: first radio, first car ride, first phone call. And then there was her first trip to a movie theater, with Pastor Jeff and his family.

"Oh, that was a sad time and a joyful time, and I cried all the way through the program."

"Why did you cry?"

"Because I was so . . ." she trailed off. "They said, 'You oughtn't be crying. Why are you crying?' I said I wasn't sad I was there, I was glad. But all these years I lived in this world and that was my first time going in a theater. And I was in my eighties when I got to do that. Well, you know I was happy to be there and just enjoying it so, but then I would think about what a tough time we've been having all these years. There's been movie theaters and nobody thought enough of you to tell you."

"And she was mad when we made her ride up front in our van," Pastor Jeff said.

"That's right. It ain't been too many years ago when I started working for the garden club up there in Beatrice. One of the women, she said, 'Get in the back!' I said, 'Yes, ma'am, I am.' So I opened the back and got in, because I know that was my place. If I got in at all, it was going to be in the back. And now here these people come. I said, 'Y'all know I can't be sitting up here with the preacher, and his wife sitting behind me. Y'all know I can't do that.' Oh, God. I couldn't get them to see my point, no way I did. They just wasn't scared.

"I never did no harm to nobody. Nobody. And I've always took a lot of wrong for right. Always was scared for peoples to dislike me.

It's dangerous to go to bed when you got enemies. Somebody could come while you sleep and set you afire. And I didn't want nobody to have that kind of feeling toward me. I wanted them to love me."

"What do you think about those people who were so mean and hateful?" I asked. "What do you feel about them?"

"I feel like this: They ain't looking for a great day. I'm looking for a great day, when I see my Jesus face to face. Our parents taught us to not do evil for evil. Said they hate y'all, y'all love them. And I thought, how could I love somebody tell me, 'Little nigger don't you come back up them steps, go around the house.' Now how could I love somebody, Lord? And he said, 'That's the rule. That's the golden rule. Love thy neighbor as thyself.' And I got to do what he say. I got to love them."

Before I left with Pastor Jeff, I asked Emma Lou if she would sing one of her favorite hymns, "Amazing Grace." She was hesitant. "Oh, God. I don't know how it'll come out," she said, but she agreed after I promised to accompany her. She began quietly at first, a sweet and sorrowful trickle of water. I broke my promise. I didn't sing.

"You didn't join me," she said after the first verse, and so I joined her, and her song grew stronger, quite noticeably, swelling into bellyful vibratos and dancing out triplet riffs on the pickups. It dipped low and soared high without a crack, free and easy. And she didn't stop. Verse after verse, she kept singing. I didn't know the words, so I stumbled along on harmonized hums trying to keep up with the rolling flow, the amazing grace, so many years and so many miles and all of them pouring into the hollow hospital room, sung out into my ears and eyes and skin. As we neared the final verse, she pulled back and slowed down and came in for a landing: "Have mercy, Lord, have mercy, Lord, have mercy, Lord, on me."

* * *

The walk from Beatrice back to Monroeville was a nightmare. I took an abandoned railroad line instead of the highway. Half a mile in, the tracks were choked with barbed vines. I did battle with the thorny hydra, oblivious to the deer hunters, indifferent to the rattlesnakes, cursing and bellowing because you can do that in the backwoods where no one can hear you. This was fury-walking. War-walking. Scream-walking. Maybe I was venting, too. The listening that morning had been so heartbreaking.

I stayed in Monroeville the next day instead of walking on. I had some free time, so I bought the tulips and went to visit Emma Lou again, to say good-bye. It was late afternoon, overcast. Emma Lou's room was dark. She looked worse: unable to sit up, heavy eyelids, a tight winter hat hugging her head. I put the tulips on her bedside table. They'd closed up from the cold outside.

"I thought I would never see you again," she said, "and I thought, 'He was such a beautiful, handsome face,' and I wanted to remember that in my mind, and sure enough you come bursting in today."

Her head was cold, she said, and her hat kept falling off, and she couldn't sleep for the chill. Her stomach was unsettled, too. The hospital wouldn't give her the corn bread and buttermilk she wanted, and they were out of ginger ale.

"The Lord will take care of me," she said. "He always does."

BONG GEUN SONG, *a South Korean cyclist on a bike trip around the world*
PASCAGOULA, MISSISSIPPI, *on the side of Highway 90, a few miles from town, sitting on the grassy shoulder by the swamp*
FEBRUARY, *Mardi Gras just around the corner*

"I'm on the way to the Miami. It's about eight hundred miles left. I have to be there until twenty-second of this month because I already booked a ticket. Usually I cycle just sixty miles or seventy miles a day, but yesterday I miled one hundred. So probably I have to keep cycling to be there."

"What is it about this type of experience that you love?"

"I will have to say, before this traveling I was just half blind. I didn't know the world at all. I knowed only the Korean. Now I think I know a bit about how to make a better life. I learned, from this trip."

"What's the secret? What'd you learn? Because I'm trying to learn all this, too."

"Okay. I'll have to say love. I think I learned the love from the people. That's what I was looking for, for this trip. I think I found it. So it's time to go back to Korea. Yesterday, I cycled, and I have just one more page of map, about ten days, just left one hundred dollars, and just left one thousand kilometers. I almost dropped my tears."

Chapter Thirteen

"Sleep tight."

"All forces have been steadily employed to complete and delight me, / Now I stand on this spot with my soul."

I'd never seen that line in *Leaves of Grass* before, but I caught it when I was camping out behind a fire station one night not far from the Gulf of Mexico. That "spot" seemed to be following me wherever I walked. Everything I encountered on the road was employed in the process of my completion, that's how I was coming to understand it. There was nothing that didn't serve me in some way. I was learning from all of it, even the shitty stuff. The pain in my feet taught me about what it meant to inhabit a human body. The act of saying good-bye was a master class in the transitory nature of everything surrounding me, and my sadness during these departures revealed the intensity of my longing for something that would last (and suggested I had work to do when it came to accepting the fact that nothing would). Even the fear played a role in my completion, although that didn't diminish its power. But still, there was a kind of delight in knowing that each moment was a loaded one, a classroom in which I could learn from these teachers and perhaps even outgrow some of them, like the fear.

I hadn't been attacked yet, or robbed, but that could change. Something really bad still might happen. Most people kept telling me it would.

Not far from the Gulf, walking into the little town of Stapleton, Alabama, after the night behind that fire station, I came across a young guy who looked quite capable of killing me with his bare hands. He was stout, leaning up against a fence sipping a bottle of Budweiser. A tattoo of the Chinese character for "respect" was inked under his jaw, and a camouflage New Orleans Saints cap was cocked low over his eyes. His head was shaved bald except for an orange-dyed ponytail. He was watching the cars go by, and he looked rooted, as if he'd been there for a very long time. I decided to approach him instead of hurrying past, to challenge the seemingly uncontrollable assumptions that my mind was spewing out like toxic waste. The Whitman line I'd read the night before at the fire station was running in the back of my head as I got closer.

"They got any food up there at the gas station?" I asked the guy. "Po'boys or something?"

He took out an earbud. I could hear a metallic blasting.

"Huh?"

"They sell food up at the gas station?"

It didn't seem like English was the guy's first language. On top of that, he was extremely drunk. He spoke in a slurred fog, asking me what I was doing. When I told him, he took out his other earbud.

"You been walking since Pennsylvania?"

"Believe it or not."

"You carry that big motherfucker the whole way?" He nodded at my backpack.

"Yeah, man. And I was just looking for some dinner. Figured the gas station might have food."

"Fuck the gas station, man." The guy swatted at the air, almost throwing himself off balance. "Gas station don't got shit. I got some food, man. Good food. I'm a cook. A chef. Come on, man. Come inside."

It was happening again.

"You're a crazy motherfucker, man," the guy said over his shoulder as he staggered toward the house.

His name was Phil, he told me. His house was empty. It felt unlived-in, like a motel room or a house for sale, but he'd been living there for several months. He'd moved from Hawaii, and before that from Micronesia—a sixteen-year-old immigrant. Several years had passed since he'd left home, and he was now working as a cook at a nearby Japanese hibachi restaurant.

The refrigerator was barren: a Tupperware container full of fried rice, some hot dogs. There was plenty of Budweiser, though, and a gang of liquor bottles. Phil microwaved a plate of rice for me, tossed in a few hot dogs for good measure, and then handed me a beer. It was almost everything he had. We clinked our bottles and sat down at the kitchen table.

I asked him if he ever missed home.

"Fuck yeah, man. It's home," he said. "My island is Pohnpei. It's paradise, I guarantee you. You gonna know, man, when you search it on the Internet. You gonna know about us." He loyally beat his chest with a fist. Later, I looked it up and Wikipedia had a line that stuck out: "The islanders of Pohnpei have a reputation as being the most welcoming of outsiders."

Phil talked about how he wanted to go back and marry a Micronesian girl and open up a store. He didn't want to be a cook, but it was good money for now, and his schedule was such that he could drink after work and sleep in late the next day, and he liked that. But Pohnpei. It tugged at him.

"You'll go someday, man. You'll see. But it's violent, though." He held up his arm, revealing a massive scar from wrist to elbow. A blocked throat slash, he said. Apparently there were endemic family feuds on the island. He explained it to me:

"If you come and kill one of my family, what am I gonna do?"

"Come kill one of mine?"

"That's right, man. But, actually that's not good. You kill someone, man? That's bad, man. You gotta respect people."

I agreed.

"But someone don't respect me? I don't even talk. I go up and knock 'em out in the face, man. You don't respect me? You gonna get . . ." and he trailed off here, as if he'd lost his train of thought.

"Fucked up?"

"Yeah, man. You gonna get fucked up." He took a swig from his bottle, slipping deeper into the haze. I ate my fried rice and hot dogs.

Phil kept his earbuds in as we talked, the continuous noise a tinny ringing in the background that robbed our lulls of silence. Adding to the din was a flat-screen TV in the living room, flashing a reality show about prisoners in their first week of incarceration. It played on repeat throughout the night, the volume turned up. I had no idea how Phil could hear anything I said.

After dinner, Phil showed off his hibachi moves using two wooden salt and pepper shakers—no knives, thank God. They twirled in his hands, spinning and flipping and clattering to the floor.

"Shit, man. I'm too fucked up."

He tossed the shakers aside and took out some betel nut, limestone paste, and a sliced palm leaf, fixing himself a quid to show me how they did it in Pohnpei. I almost wanted to try it, but when Phil said I wouldn't like it, I took his word for it.

At one point during the night I took out my map and spread it against the refrigerator, tracing the route I'd walked from Georgia: entering at West Point and Opelika, heading through Tuskegee and into Montgomery, past Selma, past Monroeville, and then through the backwoods to Stapleton and right up to Phil's house. He placed a hand over his heart.

"You give me a good feeling, man. I worry about you. I'm gonna miss you when you leave. If you were my brother, I wouldn't let you do it. There's too many crazy people out there. You're so young, man. You're so young. If it was me, I couldn't do it. I'd be out there and I'd wanna stop. I'd be crying, man. I'd be crying."

"No, you could do it. You are doing it, man!" I tried to explain that his path was far more epic than my own: crossing an ocean, learning a language, supporting his family overseas and doing it all alone. And he was younger than I was. But he shook his head.

"No, man. I couldn't do it. Not me."

That killed me, the blindness to his own magnificence, to the radical courage he was embodying in that very moment, taking in a complete stranger off the road. The extraordinary kindness.

He said I could crash on the couch for the night and shower if I wanted. I took him up on both offers. When I came back out into the living room after a blissful shower, I noticed that a blanket had been laid on the couch for me.

"All right, man," Phil said, "you want to watch a movie, you watch a movie. You want to sleep, you sleep. Whatever you need, take it." He gave me six dollars and a pair of Hawaiian-flowered swimming trunks.

"Don't worry about me, man," Phil said when I told him good night and to take care. "I'm a survivor. You're the one who's gotta be careful. When you're out there fuckin' walking and shit, don't trust nobody." He raised his hand. I connected with the high five, and he brought me in close, wrapping his arm around my shoulder.

On the couch, I sunk into sleep, drifting back every so often to see Phil swigging his beer, or sleeping in the kitchen chair, or walking into the bathroom to retch. Sometime around three o'clock I dazed into semiconsciousness and he was covering me with the blanket. It had fallen off.

"Sleep tight, motherfucker," I heard him say.

VINCENT and FRANCES BOSARGE, old lovebirds
CODEN, ALABAMA, in the swamps of the Gulf Coast, on the couch
next to Frances, Vincent sitting on the floor leaning against her legs,
her hand on his shoulder
FEBRUARY, and actually quite warm

"Well, one good thing: you make a lot of good memories."

"Oh yeah, that's true."

"I know we've got memories, so many we've just forgot some of them once in a while."

"You don't forget nothing."

"The things we've done around the home here, and stuff like that. Just all good memories, like us going out in the woods just hunting old bottles. Just things like that. Just good, time-killing fun."

"Was there ever a moment where you two felt overwhelmed? Like, you didn't know how you were going to do it?"

"Oh, yeah. That was a lot. That doesn't stop. We're back at that point again right now. It's funny, isn't it? I told him the other day, I says, 'You know, I feel like I'm still just a little kid and we just got married.' Because life doesn't change that much. It does. But it doesn't. Not really. It's all according to how you look at it, I guess, and we look at it like: We just like each other. We like being around each other, and that does make a difference. He's awful good. He still does the same as he did when we was young. He's always there. And he likes being there, and that makes me like being here. It makes a difference. You do have to put up with a lot, but it's worth it. Isn't it?"

"*Yeah.*"

"*Every bit of it. Look how far it gets you. Before you know it it's done turned around and you're there. And it does, it seems like yesterday. It really does. Look forward to it. You'll see. You'll see. You will see. Because you're interested now. You got a lot you're going to see. You got a long way to go and a lot to do. I can see that in you already.*"

Chapter Fourteen

"There's no room for being scared."

"Why don't you just drive?"

That was one of the first things some people asked me when I told them what I was doing. The answer was simple: Sure, driving would get me there faster, but it would cut me off from everything in between the beginning and the end. And where was "there," anyway?

Something human is sacrificed traveling at high speeds, I came to believe, because humans are actually quite slow. When we walk, we are brought back to ourselves again, immersing our awareness in the body and all its sensitivities, creating space for the mind to breathe and explore and play. There's so much to feel, and there's nothing to distract you from feeling it. Walk long enough and this immensity of feeling begins to blur the boundaries between you and everything else. One elderly man called it "the white time." His name was Jerry Priddy. He walked two miles every morning, hadn't missed a single day since 1995. That was like walking across America four times.

"You amble along," he said, "and it's like being whited out in a snowstorm. You can't see anything and you're not aware of anything, and it's going on around you. It don't amount to a whole lot, but the sum total is it's a beautiful experience when you get through. It clears your head. You're there."

There was no such thing as boredom in the white time because everything was always in flux. The white time demanded my engagement. I couldn't just sit in it, as I would in a car, because I was my own vehicle. I was married to the movement. I *was* the movement. Each and every stride was an active stitch binding me to the land and to everyone I met. In this way, the road wasn't a contradiction, like it would've been at car-speed. When you drive, the car isolates and insulates you from everyone and everything you pass; it's a severing from the surrounding world. When you walk, however, the road takes you from the beginning to the end not by severance but by connection—connection to the people you meet, to the land you touch, to the sun and the wind and the rain.

Despite the growing magic of it, the walking was, at the very same time, still utterly miserable at the end of most days. I'd been walking all through the winter by now, and it hadn't gotten any easier. By dusk, I was always ragged and raw. The blisters kept coming, and I hadn't gotten used to the ass chafing yet. I gave up hope that I ever would. The worst, however, was the Deep Itch. I won't elaborate, but a piece of advice if you're heading out for a long hike: bring baby wipes.

There was, in fact, something worse than the Deep Itch: mosquitos. It was February now, warm enough for them. They could fly faster than I could walk, which was unfortunate because I was about to walk through the swamps of Mississippi and Louisiana.

I'd heard horror stories about the breeds on the Gulf Coast. "They're bigger than VW bugs." "They drink DEET like blood." "They'll carry you away." They only caught me twice. The second time, I was in southern Louisiana setting up camp in a field shielded from the highway by a grassy berm. When the steady pestering became a full-fledged attack, I took refuge in my tent. I lay naked on my back, watching the mosquitos slowly flood the space between the mesh ceiling and the rainfly outside. There were hundreds.

They floated so delicately, silent little sprites poking at the mesh skin, hopeful for a drink. I watched them for nearly an hour, the ballet of bloodsuckers.

But the first time the mosquitos swarmed me, almost in Mississippi, I was on the road, exposed. I put on my rain jacket. It didn't do much. Now they all just went for my face. I started swatting at the air and slapping my face, bellowing. This was craze-walking, a manic, delusional unraveling. If I found myself babbling in an argument with the headwinds, begging aloud to the rain for mercy, or nursing personal grudges against each and every mosquito, I was craze-walking.

The mosquitos abruptly disappeared at around five P.M. I peeked out from my rain jacket. An egret was standing in the marsh, its ivory white shocking against the tall brown grass, and two blue herons burst out of the forest. Pelicans cruised above, joined for an improbable moment by a bald eagle. I started shouting, "Yes!" over and over again. Perhaps a side-effect of the craze-walking.

This was the real-life swamp, the bayou. The mosquitos were benign compared to the bigger beasts lurking deeper inside. There was legitimate cause for concern with the alligators. Wild boars ran free, and bobcats, too, and packs of stray dogs. Somewhere in the murky waters swam saw-toothed monstrosities called alligator garfish. There was even rumor of a panther, I would soon be told. And everything was soggy, which meant there were precious few camping spots. Not that it mattered. I wasn't going to sleep on the ground in that hungry place. The tree canopy seemed much safer. Then again, there was the panther.

When I first crossed into Mississippi, I was spared a night in the swamp by a benevolent alligator rancher named Allen and his girlfriend, Addie. Allen ended up letting me stay in the guest room of his apartment above the ranch's showroom. He had a few alligators in captivity, including a thirteen-footer called Big Bull, but those weren't the ones to worry about. There were others outside the fences. Hurricane Katrina had flooded Allen's compound when it blew through, raising the swamp right over the pens. When the waters subsided, the alligators were gone, all 150 of them. Allen had recaptured forty in the seven years since the hurricane. The math didn't favor camping.

The ranch was right on the edge of the swamp next to Highway 90 outside Pascagoula. Out back, a small fleet of airboats propelled by gigantic fans bobbed by a dock, and a swath of mucky marshland was fenced off for the alligators. Shining a flashlight that night from Allen's porch, I could see their eyes gleaming.

The TV played in the living room, a show about passion killings. It was part of a series called *Deadly Women Tuesday Marathon*. Sitting between Allen and Addie, watching the grisly reenactments, I wanted to crack a joke—"I promise I'm not taking notes"—but I thought better of it. We were all sleeping under the same roof that night, and I didn't want to put anyone on edge.

"Allen watches this to make sure none of the women he's fooling with are on there," Addie said. She had a riotous laugh. She called me "kiddo" and "dear," and earlier, before Allen invited me inside, she had come out to my tent and brought me a plate loaded with lasagna. And then another one. After the second plate, I started calling her my Mississippi mother. She said that if her son were walking across America she'd inch along behind him in her car the whole way, shouting advice and honking at strangers. "You stay away from that boy!" "Drink some water, honey!" Addie reminded me of my aunt Ginger back home. She'd said she was going to follow me in her minivan. My aunt Janet had promised to join her.

"Your poor mother," Addie had said when I first met her. "I don't know how she's doing this." That was probably the most commonly asked question of all: "How is your mother doing this?" We talked often, and I asked her once myself. *How are you doing it?*

"If I don't let you die," she said, "if I don't embrace that the end of your life could be at twenty-three, then it'll be a lot harder. I'll freak out. So I have to completely let go and say yes to anything. I have to say the same yes you have to say, in a different way. I just have to work very hard to stay still. There are times where inside I'm like, 'No! No! No!' and I have to lock her up in the bathroom, that animal mother.

"So at night I assess: 'What's the fear? What's hard about this?' I'm worried about you being outdoors. It's so anti-intuitive for me, because you were in my womb. You need to be sheltered somewhere, but you're on a road without a shoulder with freaking eighteen-wheelers. That's the hardest. 'How will it be if he dies, or if he gets seriously, seriously injured?' And I say, 'It will not be good, *and* he can't not do this.' Because I know that if you don't do this thing, it won't be good for you. So it's really about letting you not come back. It doesn't fit with the animal mother in me, but my yes is becoming stronger than my fear. It's a process. Every day is, 'He could die today.' I feel very alive. Awake. I literally feel like I'm in two places at once—where I am and where you are. I think that's just love."

The night before I left home, we had a bonfire out in the backyard. It was at the fire that I first felt, somewhere beyond my intellect, that I might actually die on this walk, and that this might be one of the last times I ever saw my mom. We prayed. I wasn't entirely sure to whom or to what, but that didn't matter to me. All the discussions I'd had in high school and college about the existence of God seemed so trivial now, even moot. I wasn't interested in proving or disproving anything. I only wanted to start this walk on the right foot, and that meant acknowledging my own tininess, honoring the fact that I couldn't do what I was about to attempt to do alone. At the end of our homegrown backyard ceremony, my mom washed my feet with warm water, a Catholic ritual that seemed relevant now given all the walking my feet had in front of them. That was when Mom first let me die.

I found many mothers on the road, and Addie was one of my favorites. She kept making me laugh. On the TV, a woman was braining her sleeping lover with a cricket bat.

"God, this is insane," I said, looking away.

"Well, I lost my sanity a long time ago," Addie said. "But don't worry, I found it again. I keep it in a little bottle at the bottom of my drawer, so it's not lost anymore. I just don't have it on me. I'll get it out when I'm ready. Until then," and here she leaned forward to look at Allen, "watch out, baby."

We both laughed. Allen shook his head and grunted.

"Oh, he's an old crank," Addie said. "But I'm an old bitch, so we get along."

Allen wore cowboy boots and a big belt buckle. He was from southern Louisiana, the first Cajun I'd met, born and bred on the bayou. He'd suffered a couple of alligator bites in his lifetime. The worst one was from a seven-footer. It almost took his hand off.

"It wasn't no big deal," Allen said. "He didn't do it on purpose."

"You ever wrestle any?" I asked.

"No, not really. Just when we had to go out catching them after Katrina. You gotta jump on they backs and hold them down. I don't do tricks anymore, like them guys like they do? Put them heads in they mouth and all like that? That's people that ain't got no brains. That's crazy."

"What do you do if you get caught by one?" I asked. "A big one, like that guy you have out there?"

"Gator like Big Bull grab you? They ain't nothing you can do."

Allen told me a few more swamp stories into the recorder. The conversation drifted into nostalgia—how things used to be, how today's just not the same—and then, rather abruptly, we were talking about the apocalypse.

A Great Tribulation was on its way, Allen said. An Armageddon. A God War. I would know it when it came. It wouldn't be tornadoes or earthquakes or another Katrina. It would be like nothing anyone had ever seen before, something unbelievable, like fire raining down from the sky.

"Says in the Bible, 'One will be taken along and one will be left behind.' So if you're left behind that means you're probably going to be destroyed. Bible says that God separates people, just like a shepherd. Separates the sheep from the goats. Says the sheep know his voice. The goats? Well, they're gonna blow off into everlasting destruction. The sheep go off into everlasting life. God already knows who the sheep are."

Allen spoke quite matter-of-factly about the end of the world, but perhaps that was to be expected from someone who'd nearly lost a hand to an alligator and didn't think it was a big deal.

"No one can know for sure," he said, "but I think it's coming soon."

I could see how the promise of an apocalypse was comforting as Allen described it to me. It explained the baffling complexity of the world. When Armageddon arrived at last, everyone would know the truth of this mystifying human experience. It would be absolute—there'd be winners and there'd be losers, the ones who just never got it. Sheep were sheep. Goats were goats. That was that. I almost wanted to believe it myself.

I didn't know what to say as he expounded. Mostly I kept quiet, wondering if he thought I was a goat. To me, he was neither goat nor sheep. He was Allen. I was Andrew. We were each our own kind of animal, a tiny, unique branch in the dendritic evolution of humanity. Walking the country was like an exercise in taxonomy, cataloguing the varieties of the human species. I'd already encountered so many, and would meet many more as I continued: hitchhikers and hobos, waitresses and their regulars, road-trippers, ranchers, and roughnecks, raccoon hunters, deer slayers, hog stalkers, mothers of five and seven and ten, firefighters, police officers, professors and pot growers, laughing cowboys and solemn mechanics, the hippy-dippy ice sculptor, the drunken hibachi chef, the farmers of cotton and corn and goats, fledgling sweethearts and ancient lovebirds, an old-time bounty hunter, a small-time shrimper, a homemade-ice-cream maker and a biscuit baker and a master of crawfish étouffée, a Hopi glassblower, a Navajo medicine man, a Cajun mystic, an ex-con, an ex-president, preachers of fire and brimstone, football heroes fallen from glory, mariachi DJs, a deluded messiah, cosmetologists and embalmers of the dead, wannabe crop-dusters, would-be walkers, the lost, the found, the saved, the damned, and an old man on the highway called Nowhere.

And then there was Addie, my Mississippi mother, and Allen, the doomsday alligator rancher. Of course, all these people were far more than the titles I've just given them, but that's taxonomy, finding some kind of order in the chaos and classifying it. Why bother, in this case? Because then an amalgam of indistinguishable faces splinters off into hundreds of millions of fragments—individual human beings. The closer you look, the more varieties you find, and any goat-and-sheep dichotomy starts to look completely absurd. Americans become Mississippians, who become alligator ranchers, who become Allen, who likes hunting in the swamp on his airboat at dusk and watching the *Deadly Women Tuesday Marathon*; who believes in goats and sheep, and probably thinks you're a goat; and who feeds you a huge breakfast in the morning anyway.

Reaching the Gulf Coast was bizarre, like crossing into a new state. *Did I really just walk to the Gulf of Mexico?* A bit to the north I'd begun to see seafood joints and Cajun markets and billboards for beaches. It seemed impossible. My footsteps were actually covering ground, one by one making finite that which had once seemed so infinite.

On Highway 90 I passed through Pascagoula and Biloxi. The signature of Hurricane Katrina was still written everywhere, almost seven years later. Twisted trees kowtowed at absurd angles. Buildings were flayed down to their structural skeletons, or being built anew. In the bayou country just north of New Orleans, fishing boats lay beached on the marshy banks, rotting.

Pearlington, Mississippi, had seen the worst of it. The quaint little bayou hamlet had become a war zone. Those who'd stayed for the hurricane had stared straight into her furious eye. I'd arrived in the town at sunset and, as always, I needed a place to camp out. A bar was on my left, a church on my right. I went left.

The bar was called Turtle Landing. I took a seat next to a tan, rough-faced man with an aquiline nose whose cigarettes smoldered in the dark. His name was Randy Turpin. His partner, Susie Sharp, looked strong and sturdy, and smiled a lot. She wore glinty glasses. They'd both just come back from the Mardis Gras parade in Bay St. Louis, the same one I'd walked past that morning. When I admitted I'd never really taken part in a Mardi Gras parade, Susie festooned me with a bunch of beads and a crown of purple panties, thrown from the floats. Everyone at the bar seemed to be wearing some mark of Louisiana loyalty—Saints sweatshirts, LSU hats—and although no one else was wearing panties like a swim cap, I thought I fit in better with them on.

After a few beers, Randy and Susie offered to put me up at their place for the night. At their kitchen table, they told me their Katrina stories. Everybody in town had one.

"You ever have one of those dreams where you're falling and wondering whether you're going to hit the ground or not, and you just won't wake up?" This was Randy. "We never had a chance to figure out whether we were going to hit the ground or not. You just can't wake yourself up from that nightmare until it quits. I've had over six years to think about it now, and that's as close as I can put it. That falling dream. You know you're falling, and you know you're dreaming, but you won't wake yourself up. And then the pressure changed, and it was like you were taking off vertical in a jet and your ears just go POOF!"

He spoke with little emotion, his voice sandpaper rough. He was the kind of guy I'd want to be around if I ever found myself trapped in a Category Five hurricane, the kind of guy who takes an ax into the fray, which was exactly what he did. I wouldn't have thought to do that, but it made sense: if the water rose too high, you'd have to get to the roof somehow.

"And then everything got calm," Randy said. "Dead calm. They tell you about the eye of the storm? That's what we was in. Pretty blue sky above you. Someone said, 'It's over!' and I said, 'No, we got the other side of this sombitch to go through. Something bad fixin' to happen.' About ten minutes later, something bad happened. That's when we seen the water. It just rose up so quick. You either moved right then or you drowned. You were past the point of being scared. There's no room for being scared."

"Everything that was down went up, and everything that was up came down," Susie said, showing me pictures of the aftermath. It didn't seem possible that water and wind could be responsible for such devastation. It looked more like the work of mercenary giants, legions of them. The bartender at Turtle Landing had told me that the whole bayou had emptied itself out onto Pearlington, the water climbing as high as twenty-eight feet. Houses floated off their foundations, crashing into telephone poles like possessed pinballs. Trees snapped. Refrigerators shot through the roofs of flooded homes, propelled by their own airtight buoyancy. After it was over, sludge coated the town. Dogs lay dead. Fires burned.

"It looked like a nuclear bomb went off," Randy said. "But we know how to survive in the woods and on the water. Hunting, fishing, trapping. Nobody went hungry. There's no 'me' in this town. It's 'us.' Because it's us against the elements down here. It ain't us against the government. It ain't us against the blacks. It ain't us against the whites. It's us against what we got to deal with out there." He pointed in the direction of the swamp. "Yeah, we just know how to get along. You do what you do with what you got. You have food to spare? You spare it. That's just the way it goes."

"Everybody knows everybody," Susie added. "And if you don't know somebody, somebody you know knows them."

"So somebody like me sticks out?" I said.

"No, you don't stick out," Susie said. "You're just . . . noticed."

"We trust in people," Randy said. "It costs us a lot sometimes, and sometimes it don't cost us nothing but a handshake. It might be our curiosity. It might be just the way we are."

On the approach to New Orleans the next day, Highway 90 cut through the bayou, brown and bare with winter. Bridges hopscotched the checkerboard wetland. Not many cars seemed to know about 90. It felt like a secret, and I wished it would go on forever.

Across one of the final bridges before New Orleans, another bar was nestled among a colony of stilt-legged fishing shacks: Crazy Al's.

Inside, a long-haired man named Rapp gave me a bowl of chili and a piece of advice: "Don't walk through New Orleans East. They're all niggers, rapists, and crackheads. They'll take everything you have." I'd been hearing the warnings for weeks. At Turtle Landing just the night before, another guy had told me that if I walked into New Orleans East it'd be like a rookie walking into prison.

At first I thought the warnings were just unfounded and disgusting manifestations of racism, but so many different people had spoken up. Plus, I'd begun to develop a real fear of dying, which had taken root somewhere around the time I ate squirrel with Bill. *You got lots of grieving to do.* It was new for me, to go through my day afraid I was going to die. Sometimes I was really in its grip, other times I had more distance from it and could see it as fear rather than as reality. But the thing about a so-called irrational fear of death is this: we are all, in fact, going to die, and lots of us die early, from accidents or illness. So there's always the bit of you that thinks, I could actually die at any moment, so why would I walk around thinking about anything else? In any case, I began to worry about the next leg of my walk, rationally or not I didn't know. I reviewed the plan over and over in my head: I'd find a safe place to camp that night on the outskirts of town, and then I'd wake up before dawn and reach the French Quarter by noon, where a friend had an apartment nearby. The morning would be safe. All the dangerous people would be asleep. I explained my logic to Rapp over chili at Crazy Al's.

"Crackheads don't sleep," he said.

Across the final bridge before New Orleans, the bayou faded into suburbia. There was a fire station a mile or two ahead, I'd heard at Crazy Al's. It was almost dark.

"Hey!"

Someone was shouting at me from across the road. I gave a sidelong glance. It was a white guy standing on his front porch, staring at me. His wild blond hair was receding and electrified, a combination that lent him an air of madness. He'd sounded more accusatory than inviting, so I pretended not to hear.

"Hey you! Walker!"

There wasn't anyone else walking on Highway 90, and after the second shout, ignoring the guy felt riskier than acknowledging him. I waved and crossed the road. His house was on a small hill, so he spoke down to me from his porch, asking what I was doing.

"You're from Pennsylvania, huh?" he said, after I explained. "So you're a fucking Yankee. Who the fuck invited you down here? Take a look at where you're standing." He pointed to the grassy median between the road and his yard. "That's the neutral zone. You cross that and you're in my territory."

This was the kind of thing everyone had been warning me about. Time to go. "All right, man, I'm not trying to cause trouble," I said, turning to walk away.

"Hey, wait," the guy barked before I could get far. "You, uh, you like beer?"

"Um, yeah."

"You want one?"

I said sure, before I could think too much about it. I heard Randy from the night before: *We trust in people. Cost us a lot sometimes, and sometimes it don't cost us nothing but a handshake.*

"Am I allowed to cross the neutral zone?" I asked.

"I never said you couldn't. As soon as you do, though, that's my taxed land. Don't forget that."

I walked up to his porch. He told me to leave my backpack outside—"Don't want you pulling a gun on me"—and then he asked to see my ID. I gave him my driver's license, as if he had some sort of authority. He looked at it for a long time, squinting his eyes and wrinkling his brow, twisting the card suspiciously.

"You know, I used to work at a liquor store, and this looks like a fake," he said.

I reached for the license, but the guy pulled it away, and we locked eyes for a second.

"Come on, man," I said. "It's not a fake. Are you serious?"

He narrowed his eyes at me, gave the license one more glare, and then handed it back. We walked into his house.

Stray papers littered the front living room. Cat toys lay scattered across the floor of the hallway that led into the kitchen. He had a small backyard where a pool glowed neon blue. It was a small ranch-style home that wouldn't have been out of place in most suburban developments. The guy got two bottles of dark beer from the refrigerator, lit a cigarette, and joined me at the kitchen table.

"You'll like this beer," he said. "Trust me. It's my favorite."

He was a computer programmer, but he used to teach skiing in Alaska. He should have stuck with the skiing, he said. He'd fought in Korea before that. Now, he lived alone. At the table, the tension dissipated a bit, probably because we were inside his home. He was exposed now, too, as I had been out on the road. The vulnerability was shared.

The beer was perfect—a cold, crisp wash, and the faintest floating buzz. A blue-eyed, buxom blonde smiled at me from the label, holding several steins overflowing with foam. I told the guy what Rapp had said earlier at Crazy Al's, and that I was worried about walking through New Orleans East the next day. He chuckled.

"I'd do it, but that's coming from me, and you gotta take that with a grain of salt. A whole bag full. When I was in the army in Korea, I'd make them drive me way out there and just drop me off.

And then I'd walk back. 'Fuck with me, I dare you,' that kind of thing. And New Orleans East is just as bad as that. Worse. Yeah, you better get a ride. Those people down there'll shoot you for the shirt off your back."

"That's what everyone keeps saying," I said.

"Fuck it, man. Do it. Maybe you're crazy enough. Do it right now. Do it tonight. I like to go where people tell me not to."

The beer slowly sank in our bottles. We'd been sitting together at the table for ten minutes or so when the guy abruptly went silent and narrowed his eyes again. They darted back and forth as if watching ghosts running amok in his kitchen.

"Where's my cat?" he said. "He's hiding. He must not like you."

I finished my beer. I'd come this far without getting stabbed, and I wanted to get out while I was ahead. It was twilight and the fire station was still about a mile away. I began looking for an opening in the conversation to initiate a graceful departure. It couldn't be too abrupt or the guy might get agitated. He was telling a story about one of his death-wish walks, this one in Texas, and I was about to interrupt when he mentioned, as if it were a footnote, that he'd lost a child.

"I was hoping somebody would jump me that day because I wanted to kick somebody's ass. I was pissed off because I had to bury my son. Three niggers jumped me so I did. They all ran away. One ran away with a knife up his ass."

I saw him differently, for a moment. He was a mourning father who lived alone with a cat instead of a son. It did absolutely nothing to justify his paranoia and violence and racism, but it cast a little light on the pain that was its source. For just a moment, he'd opened the barricaded trapdoor to his hidden, private hurt, let me gaze down for a second in wonder at how terribly deep it went.

And then he slammed it shut again. To think that everyone I'd met on the road, and everyone I hadn't, everyone who had ever existed and would ever exist, to think that we all carried this pain in some way, the pain of being human, which perhaps is the pain of loving. What a double bind, being human: the more you love, the more you hurt. I thought of all the people who'd told me stories of heartbreak, and how connected I felt to those people as they opened up. There is some emotional alchemy that occurs even just listening to heartbreak, let alone living it. Because it's when your heart gets broken that you know, without the slightest shade of a doubt, that you have one. It feels good to know you have a heart, even if that heart hurts like hell. That's the emotional alchemy. It's far better than the hell of not feeling anything at all, or the purgatory of denying the hurt, which is the denial of your very own heart and its astonishing capacity to care.

I looked at the guy across the table. He was looking away. Maybe it wasn't me he saw walking out on the road. Maybe he saw his son.

It reminded me of an old man I'd met at a diner in South Carolina, months earlier. He asked if he could join me at my table. His name was Paul. Paul had been a widower for sixteen years. "It gets lonesome being up at the house all alone," he said. "You can always talk to God, but it's not the same as talking to someone else, like you." Paul carefully selected a potato chip and lifted it to his mouth. I realized he probably hadn't come to the diner for a hot dog. He'd come just to be with someone. I wasn't so different, really. Outside New Orleans, maybe it was the same with this guy.

"It's a good thing they fed you at Crazy Al's, or else I would've had to," he said. He'd finished his beer. "If the fire station down the road doesn't let you camp out, you can pitch your tent in my backyard. There's a fence so you'll be safe."

I took that as my opening, and said I'd better hit the road. Before I left, I realized I still hadn't gotten his name, so I asked him for it. He looked at me, suspicious again.

"My name's Bond," he said and paused, "James Bond."

Half a mile down the road, James Bond pulled up in his pickup truck, slowing down in the opposite lane and crawling along at my walking pace. I was not thrilled to see him.

"Hi, Mr. Bond," I said.

"You walk slow, man. What'd you do, take a ten-minute shit or something? I'm gonna ride ahead and check in with the fire station for you, see if you can camp there."

I assured James Bond he didn't have to do this—suggested, in fact, it'd be best if he didn't—but another car pulled up behind him and he drove off.

The fire station was set up in a makeshift warehouse built in the aftermath of Katrina. A high chain-link fence topped by a writhing snake of barbed wire protected the compound. The gate was open. James Bond's truck was parked by the fire engine. I saw him standing in the doorway of the mobile home headquarters, his electrified blond hair unmistakable. Inside, two firefighters sat on a couch. They were looking up at him like they'd just seen something highly inappropriate, maybe even horrifying.

"Speak of the devil," Mr. Bond said, gesturing at me as if to say "Ta-da!" I made my own case to the firefighters, and they said I could stay.

"Looks like that guy played with too many detonators that went boom," the fire chief said after James Bond finally left. He asked me if I knew him, and I said no, which felt a little bit like a betrayal.

I sat with the firefighters in the lounge. They were watching a reality show that involved jousting. I hoped in silence that someone would turn it off, so we could all enjoy our own reality in peace. Someone had donated a king cake to the fire station, frosted gold and green and purple—a Mardi Gras tradition. The fire chief said I could have some.

"You can go serve yourself, though. Who do you think I am, your fuckin' mother?"

I was eating my king cake when the siren sounded—an emergency call. The firefighters started rushing to the truck. On his way out, the fire chief told me they'd be back soon. "You unlucky son of a bitch," he said, shaking his head. "It must be you. We never get calls out here."

When they were all gone, I turned off the TV and an uncanny silence filled the lounge. It crossed my mind that perhaps James Bond had faked an emergency call, and that he was now coming to kill me. I got up from the couch and locked the door.

"Just an old lady," the fire chief said when they all returned a half hour later. "Heart attack scare. No problem."

I didn't sleep well that night, worried about the next day's walk through New Orleans, but it turned out to be completely uneventful. Just another fifteen miles. Maybe there was never a need to be afraid, or maybe I got lucky. I expected to see James Bond roll up beside me in his pickup truck all day, but he never did come.

WENDELL LEE, retired bounty hunter
PASCAGOULA, MISSISSIPPI, in his motel room beside the parking
lot, the door open to vent his cigarette smoke
FEBRUARY

"These bounty hunters running around with these leather outfits on?
You never wear leather. I didn't even wear a leather belt back then.
Because a bullet penetrates leather, it sets up an infection and it kills
you. Ain't no second chance. So these people you see running around
wearing leather and all that shit? You wear silk. That way if you get
hit, the shrapnel don't go everywhere. You always wear a silk shirt."

> *"It takes some fighting skills?"*
> *"Oh yeah, but size don't mean nothing."*
> *"So if somebody jumps me, what's the best first move?"*
> *"Kick 'em in the balls."*

Chapter Fifteen

"All you're really doing is reading a book, just with your feet."

A brass band was howling when she walked inside the packed bar. She was dressed up like a sexy peacock because it was Mardi Gras. I didn't have a costume. I was just the guy who was walking across America. My high school friend Steph had introduced us a few days earlier. It seemed quite likely that something was going to happen between us, and it did, as soon as she walked through the door that night. Neither of us said anything, we just looked at each other for a second and then started making out, like we were animals or gods. I was gone.

It hit me then just how alone I'd been for so many months now, and how lonely. Before, I hadn't really let myself feel the full extent of that loneliness. It would've been too much, so instead I walked in a kind of denial, pretending it didn't bother me that I'd pretty much eliminated romantic intimacy from my life. I got quite good at pretending, until I saw her. People coursed around us, dancing and shouting, but she was the only one I noticed. Her lips. Her eyes. Her long brown hair. *Oh God.* She took my hand, led me deep into the crowd, and we danced on the sound waves of blaring trumpets and sliding trombones and a massive thumping tuba. Even in the wildness of it, though, and the joy, I realized I was setting myself up for a good deal of pain. She was flying out of New Orleans the next day, and I'd be leaving soon, too, and the loneliness would probably be worse than ever.

Later that night, we lay together on an inflatable mattress in the kitchen. Steph had a bunch of other friends in town for Mardi Gras, and all the rooms were taken. The two of us didn't talk much. We hardly knew each other, and anyway, if we got to know each other too well it might just be harder to say good-bye. At three in the morning, her cab honked outside. She kissed me one more time and walked out the door. I couldn't fall back asleep. I couldn't stop thinking about her, and how I'd probably never see her again, and how much it was going to suck to get back on the road. Maybe I'd just stay in New Orleans. It'd be easier than going out alone.

Before I began walking, I'd read something in *Letters to a Young Poet* about sex that had made me pause.

> Sex is difficult; yes. But those tasks that have been entrusted to us *are* difficult; almost everything serious is difficult; and everything is serious. If you just recognize this and manage, out of yourself, out of your *own* talent and nature, out of your *own* experience and childhood and strength, to achieve a wholly individual relation to sex (one that is not influenced by convention and custom), then you will no longer have to be afraid of losing yourself and becoming unworthy of your dearest possession.

I had no idea what Rilke was talking about, which made me curious. What was it like to know yourself in such a way that you couldn't lose yourself no matter how close you got to another, to know yourself such that you wouldn't *want* to get lost? I'd never loved like that before. I fell hard for a long-haired surfer in college, a fierce and beautiful wild woman, but I'd loved her to lose myself, to get lost in the experience, and surely that wasn't love at all. Edward Sharpe and the Magnetic Zeros had just put out that song

"Home," and she and I would sing it to each other. "Home, let me come home / home is wherever I'm with you." When we broke up, this definition of home seemed much less romantic, suddenly, even a bit problematic. I realized that if I outsourced my experience of home to a lover, then I'd be homeless without her. It created a kind of existential neediness. But I'd thought that *was* love, the process of giving myself to someone else, entrusting to them my sense of belonging, my anchor. I didn't think it was enough to belong just as I was, on my own. Home had to be *with* someone else. The alternative was too frightening to consider. It felt so empty.

Giving myself away to someone else, placing the burden of my happiness on a lover's heart, that was also a surreptitious form of possessing them, manipulation. It would make them feel terribly guilty about leaving me, so maybe they wouldn't leave. *Home is wherever I'm with you, and you don't want me to be homeless, do you? So come everywhere with me, and, whatever you do, never ever leave.* It's almost a tyrannical kind of love, which isn't love at all, like Gollum and his obsession with the ring. *You are the precious, not I. You are my peace and my purpose. Home is wherever I'm with you, and wherever I'm not is alien and wrong and wretched.* I heard that Gollum voice inside me after the breakup, and I wanted it exorcised immediately. Only one way to do it: a full-on immersion into the void of my aloneness.

"There is only *one* solitude," Rilke wrote,

> and it is vast, heavy, difficult to bear, and almost everyone has hours when he would gladly exchange it for any kind of sociability, however trivial or cheap, for the tiniest outward agreement with the first person who comes along, the most unworthy . . . But perhaps these are the very hours

during which solitude grows; for its growing is painful as the growing of boys and sad as the beginning of spring.

"Home, let me come home, home is wherever I'm with you." I'd tried singing it to myself a couple times on the road. I wanted to believe it, but it just felt so lame, serenading myself like that. Whitman wasn't ashamed to do it. "I celebrate myself," he wrote, the very first line in "Song of Myself"—"I celebrate myself, and sing myself." I felt I had to try, to reach a place where I could rest at ease in that one solitude, celebrate myself and not feel like a sad fool doing it. Maybe that place was just a mirage, and Whitman a narcissistic madman, and Rilke a delusional recluse hell-bent on justifying his isolation, but I had to see for myself. So I decided I'd try abstinence on my walk, and it had been going just fine, but my resolve had shattered when I met the sexy peacock in New Orleans, just like that. When she left, I got so swirled up in neediness and disproportionate longing that I could almost hear Rilke telling me I had much more work to do. It made me wonder if I should've listened more to Whitman when it came to the subject of sex specifically. He was all, "Urge and urge and urge, / Always the procreant urge of the world."

There was still another week of Mardi Gras parties to distract me from the thought of her. The rest of us went out every night for the parades, where I tried to forget. I learned there was one thing I was supposed to desire above all else at these parades: beads. The masked people in the floats had these beads. I had to convince them to throw me some, no matter the cost. One night, the parade was backed up and there was a massive two-story float parked right in front of me. It was the Krewe of Muses. They were known for throwing out shoes—highly valuable Mardi Gras treasure, almost more coveted than the Krewe of Zulu's painted coconuts. "Shoe! Shoe! Shoe! Shoe!" we all chanted. Nothing. Finally, locking eyes with one of the shoe-throwers, I started pointing at an adorable little girl propped up on her mother's shoulders right next to me. "For her!" I screamed. "For her!" Suddenly a pair of stuffed shoes—something you'd hang from the rearview mirror—was sailing through the air. I reached up a hand and got it. But someone else did, too. We both heaved against each other, and I let out a very primal, very unnecessary roar, and the string holding the shoes together snapped. I had a shoe. I had a shoe! I dangled it in front of a friend and we both screamed in triumph, the precious trophy in our hands at last.

Minutes later, when I came to and realized I was jealously guarding a rearview mirror ornament, I gave the prize to the little girl's mother. I felt guilty. That was the general sentiment at the end of each night, walking past work crews scrubbing the streets clean of vomit and beer, piling all the leftover beads into mountains, throwing away all the forgotten Muses shoes.

New Orleans was a wasteland—totally wasted and terribly wasteful—but still, it cast a hypnotic spell on me. My walk had been many things so far, enlightening and heartbreaking and everything in between, but it hadn't really been fun. At the parades, I was having fun again. Playing. The bass drums of marching bands beat a battle rhythm into the night with the rat-tat-tat snares and the trumpets blaring and the tubas bumping away. Bagpipers sang to the high moon. Humans flowed through the streets like fleshy rivers. Men were women and women were shirtless, one of them swinging a giant rubber dildo like a lasso. Stone-faced evangelists trolled Bourbon Street shouting, "Turn or burn!" and the floats rolled down the streets for miles: a jester and Barack Obama, a bare-chested goddess and an alligator. The bass drums boomed through all of this, the heartbeat of the parade echoing my own.

* * *

I'd thought that New Orleans might be the finish line of my walk, but when Mardi Gras was over there was nothing keeping me there anymore. I dreaded getting back on the road, but I was also a little curious. I wanted to see what would happen out west. I'd begun to think of the desert as a crucible for some kind of ultimate epiphany: if it didn't happen walking across a desert, it probably wouldn't happen anywhere. What would be forged in that heat, and catalyzed? What would melt away? If I didn't keep walking, I'd live the rest of my life wondering what if, and I didn't want to wonder. I wanted to know.

I was watching the Academy Awards when I finally decided to keep walking. Half-listening to Meryl Streep's acceptance speech, I thought of the sun in the Mojave Desert. What would that be like in August when I got there, if I got there? *The Artist* was cleaning up Oscars, and I imagined the silence of the naked expanse. I imagined my thirst and my burned skin, and what the solitude might do to my mind. Sitting on the couch in front of the TV, which was now flashing a post-awards commentary complete with speculations about the celebrity after-parties, I felt both terrified and relieved to know I'd be on the road again soon.

Right before I left, I saw a graffiti mural with a John Muir quotation: WILDERNESS BEGINS IN THE MIND. Soon I'd be deep in that wilderness, out west, on the road, with fewer distractions than ever to keep me hidden from whatever lay waiting inside.

It was raining lightly the morning I finally hoisted on my pack. It felt like a breakup, and I wept for hours. The people in the cars that passed must've thought it was pretty funny, but I didn't. After almost five months on the road, the solitude still crushed me some days. I wondered if it ever wouldn't.

Normally I'd call my mom if I really needed a pep talk, but this time I called Dad. He told me he believed in me, and that he was proud of me, and that the sorrow would pass. It felt good to confide in him. I realized I hadn't asked him for advice in years, and that was part of why our relationship felt so frozen. It couldn't go anywhere without some level of trust on my part. Could I trust him enough to include him in the real stuff of my life, the stuff beyond obligatory holiday visits? In that moment, I felt I could. But maybe it was just a moment.

"I love you," he said before we hung up.

"I love you, too, Dad."

"Thank you," he replied. He always said thank you now whenever I told him I loved him, perhaps because I hadn't said it for years after the divorce. *Thank you.* Every time I heard it, my defenses dropped for an instant and I got to see some of his humanness. He wasn't some deviant, heartless bastard, which was how I'd seen him in the immediate aftermath of the breakup. He was just another human being who wanted to be loved, and was grateful for that love whenever it came. "Thank you," he'd tell me on the phone, and I'd feel it, too, grateful that we could say that to one another, even if the love felt complicated sometimes.

I kept walking, his voice in my ears, and that gratitude continued to grow. My dad was alive and present, just a phone call away, and suddenly that seemed like an incredible gift. As a teenager, lost in my own pain, I'd thought it would've been easier if he'd just died, and I saw now how terribly wrong I'd been about that. I imagined what he might be like as an old man many years from now, and then I imagined his death. Soon, I was a sobbing mess on the side of the highway again. I couldn't seem to avoid it that day. Crying was a lot like vomiting: there came a point when it simply had to happen, and I always felt much better after.

* * *

At the end of that day I was on Highway 90 again, surrounded by the bayou twenty miles west of New Orleans. There wasn't a dry place to camp, but before I could panic I stumbled across Pier 90 Bar and Marina. A man called Big George owned the property. He said I could pitch my tent under the overhang of his trailer to get out of the February rain.

The bar itself was topped by a mosaic of polished stone slabs. Everything else was wooden and well worn—the ceiling, the floor, the walls. It looked like mahogany or oak; I couldn't quite tell in the dim light. There was a pool table in the back, and a jukebox playing Lenny Kravitz.

"You moving in or something?" the bartender said when I first walked in, nodding at my backpack. There were some regulars sitting at the end of the bar, a bunch of Cajun guys, and they invited me to join them. I remembered for the first time that day why I'd left New Orleans to keep walking.

One of the regulars, a guy named Richard, kept buying me beers. I'd never walked with a hangover before and I wanted to keep it that way. "You can't tell a Cajun to stop drinking," Richard said when I told him I might be done for the night. "You want another?"

"I don't know," I said. "I probably shouldn't."

"Yes or no. Be decisive."

"No, sir."

"Go ahead and get him another one, Christy." Another beer was placed in front of me.

When I finally made it outside, the rain had cleared. A lamppost light cast a pale white pall on the bayou. Past the light, the swamp was moving and alive. Ancient cypress trees loomed, and the behemoth branches of live oaks writhed in decadal slow motion.

Underneath the black water swam a cosmos of creatures, every one of them hungry, every one of them searching. I shivered inside. It felt like a phrase Whitman had written in *Leaves of Grass*: "A contact of something unseen."

I looked into this darkness for a long time, pleased, just like the night I spent in Diane's barn outside of Royston, Georgia. It came so unexpectedly, this wonder and satisfaction. I couldn't figure it out. There was something about being filthy, exhausted, and alone in this strange place far from home, something about bearing sole witness to the swamp at midnight, and about the patter of the rain in the dark and the diffusion of electric light on the trees. Whatever it was, it was something good. Whitman was definitely on to it: "Press close bare-bosomed night! Press close magnetic nourishing night! / Night of south winds! Night of large few stars! / Still nodding night! Mad naked summer night!" It was that kind of night indeed, a night of inexplicable exclamation points.

I slept well, and woke up without a hangover.

"Coffee's ready," Big George said from inside the trailer. "Hand me your mug, there's not much room in here."

Peeking through the door, I could see he barely fit. He squeezed through the door frame with our steaming drinks, the front steps squealing under his immensity. He had a dog named Goat, and Goat came out, too. It was instant coffee, and somehow it went well with the morning mist pouring slowly from the swamp. We drank together, mostly in silence. Big George's mug was lost somewhere in his massive hand. "Look at them Cajun hands," one of the regulars had said the night before. "Those are 'gator-hunting, 'coon-hunting, fishing, drinking Cajun hands." They were swollen with work and calloused so hard they were smooth. When the coffee was finished, Big George shook my hand with both of them.

"You know," he said, "all you're really doing is reading a book, just with your feet." He gave me four soft tangerines and an alligator tooth. "Keep your eyes open. Keep your mind open."

I hadn't expected such profound parting words. All told, Big George and I had spent no more than twenty minutes together, so I knew very little about the man. I knew he was a big white guy. I knew he lived in a dilapidated trailer. I knew he owned a dive bar and that he ate alligators. When we said good-bye, though, I realized I didn't know enough.

Back on Highway 90, I thought more about what he'd said. *All you're really doing is reading a book, just with your feet.* It had something to do with paying attention, looking for the messages in the text, the connections. It was a new kind of walking: read-walking, when I could see the words of this infinite book in their spectacular abundance and intricacy. I could never read-walk for long because the strength of my attention couldn't match the magnitude of the book. I was a tiny speck navigating the expanse of a continent. I would only ever walk one narrow, finite thread of it—just a paragraph of the book, or less. I was nothing.

Walking mile after mile, however, and state after state, I began to notice a paradox: the infinite was in the infinitesimal—all the details, the details within the details. Maybe it wasn't a loss, then, to never read the whole book. Maybe it was all right here.

From the pavement of Highway 90, the swamp ran out on all sides, far and deep. Everything was wet from the previous day's rain. It wasn't long before my shoulders were screaming and my feet threatening to kill me, but the reading was rich. Three horses galloped over a grassy field. A brown, sun-wrinkled man sat on two orange milk crates drinking beer from a Styrofoam cup. An old billboard for a suburban utopia told me to live my dreams. At that particular moment, I didn't need the reminder.

CHRIS, *contractor and lay missionary*
NEW ORLEANS, LOUISIANA, sitting together in his work van
parked on Canal Street
FEBRUARY, an early spring

"*Up until two years ago, I was a criminal and a drug addict. I was walking in that at a very young age, eight years old. I almost had an experience when I was sixteen where I was going to go to jail for murder because I got so angry with somebody. I beat them with a padlock to the face and knocked their teeth out. Crushed their face. Left them in the street for dead. I didn't have no control, and I didn't want to have control.*

"*Two years ago I went to this Bible college that He sent me to, and I went to sleep one night, and I woke up and I was never the same. God had changed my life. He told me I had a purpose and a calling: 'You need to repent. There's people dying. Get up and stop being lazy.' I woke up in the morning and I wept before the Lord and repented, and ever since then, when I knew I had a purpose, it changed me.*

"*It's my job to love. It kills everything. It breaks down walls. It penetrates hearts and minds. It softens people. Love. If you can just love people, even when they come against you, you just love them and it softens them. It doesn't matter who they are. This is it. I don't know what you believe, so what I'm saying to you is this: the only way I can do it is with the Lord, Jesus Christ. He says, 'Forgive. Unless you forgive, you will not be forgiven.' So do you want to be forgiven? Yes, I do. So guess what? I'm going to forgive. And out of that comes love.*

"*I don't hold the grudges that I used to hold with nobody. I don't bring up the past. It might come up and I say, 'No. It's not gonna come up because I'm not gonna be held in bondage in my mind to unforgiveness and walk around here bitter or not be able to help others.' Because if I hold onto the unforgiveness with one person, it affects everybody else I come into contact with. It's a prison. You walk around and you're in a prison in your mind. And guess what comes with it? Fear. And then it turns into pride, anger, resentment, bitterness, murder. Fear is the root. It's fear.*

"*It's not gonna happen. It's not gonna bring me back to the place where I was before Christ. I'm not gonna let it. It's love or fear. It's how bad do you want to be free? That's the bottom line. Do you want to be free in your conscience and your mind? Do you want to walk around with a pure heart and a pure mind? Do you want to please the Lord who created you? That's it. It's do you or do you not?*"

Chapter Sixteen

"It'd make you want to drop everything and go back home."

The roads of southern Louisiana were some of the most visually delicious to walk. Ranges of lime green sugarcane combed the low blue sky. The watery rows of rice fields sparkled with noon-light, punctuated by the orange-buoy tops of crawfish traps. I passed a rundown sugar mill, and a barn full of frogs, and a diner called Fat Mama's. All the clouds billowed like Buddha bellies, and the flattened carcasses of turtles and snakes spackled the roads.

I'd never seen so many shades of green as I saw in southern Louisiana, but a dusty dead-gray often smothered all color: the shipyards, the oil rigs, the rusted mountains of scrap metal. In the wake of all this, there were the strip clubs—the Yellow Rose, Temptations, housed in glorified shacks—for the men who worked in those places.

This was the squelching heart of Cajun country, soaked through by the biggest swamp in America, the Atchafalaya Basin. The towns were tangled up in the liquid knots of rivers and bayous and lakes. From above, the land looked like spongy bone, porous. Walking on the road through this swamp was like traveling through a strange and lethal world in an unbreakable tunnel of translucent glass: I wouldn't get hurt, but I also wouldn't see much. I could only wonder what it was really like in there.

I met one guy, Dean Wilson, who'd lived alone for months in a far corner of the swamp. He was my age at the time, he said, while preparing us a dinner of braised rabbit in his kitchen. Living in the swamp had suited him well because he liked animals better than people. He'd been planning on living with an indigenous tribe in the Amazon, but when he came to Louisiana to train for a life in the jungle, he liked it so much he stayed. He'd been very afraid only once while living in the swamp. It was night. He was bullfrog hunting with a friend and the motor broke down. They had to slip into the water and pull the boat behind them. With his flashlight, Dean could see alligators everywhere, and cottonmouths, too, which went crazy under the light. Tugging the boat behind him, he flipped the snakes away with his cane knife, careful to shine the light away. He watched the shining eyes of alligators in front of him sink to the bottom, and seconds later he'd feel their wake against his ankles as they swam by.

"Wilderness begins in the mind," John Muir said, via the graffiti in New Orleans, and I came to think of the swamp as my mind. There were so many creatures inside: the fear of death, the grief around my family, the longing for home, the suspicion that I was somehow not enough. I conjured up Dean, flipping away the cottonmouths, continuing calmly as the alligators slid by. *Breathe. Go slowly. You will only survive if you breathe and go slowly.* The creatures would come and go, sometimes without my even knowing it. Even the joys and delights. I had so much uninterrupted time with all these creatures on the road. I came to know many of them well. Some just required acceptance. Others demanded a specific set of actions— *Don't shine light on the cottonmouths at night*—little tricks that would keep me safe in the mind swamp. I had to know how to live with these things. I had to know how to hunt them when necessary.

Alligator garfish, for example, those saw-toothed monstrosities of the deep. A young guy named Ollie Ware told me how to hunt an alligator garfish. He said you can't use nylon string to catch it. You have to use cable, because when you hook one it'll fight, and since they grow upward of twelve feet long, this is not a fight you can take lightly. When it bites, you work the cable, pulling and pulling. It'll tire, and when it comes up alongside the boat, you have to aim well and shoot it directly in the head. Do not hesitate. Whatever happens, you can't let it get ahold of you; it has a mouth full of barbs that will tear you wide open. After the kill, you'll have to cut it up with a chainsaw. You'll have to gut it and fillet it and pick it clean. And then you eat it. You feast. You do it in order to live on and continue.

My alligator garfish was probably the feeling that I was not enough. Not enough to bring my family together again. Not enough to finally forgive Dad. Not enough to simply accept who I already was, instead of trying to become someone else, someone who actually knew himself and loved himself, someone who had walked across America, proven his worth. Not enough to give something meaningful back to the world. When I didn't hunt down that alligator garfish and shoot it directly in the head, the walk that day would get quite ugly. Swamp-walking.

Ollie Ware, the garfish hunter, spent an hour by the fire in his backyard telling me stories about growing up in the swamp. He lived in the little town of Franklin. I'd met some of his friends a few miles back east, and they'd pointed me his way. He agreed to put me up. Ollie was my age, and he was a father. His baby boy was one, born a week before Ollie's twenty-second birthday.

"Tell you what," he said by the fire, "that was the best early birthday present I could've had."

Ollie and the baby's mother were no longer together. Ollie had him on the weekends. He was a mechanic. He had a chin-strap

beard and tattoos. He didn't smile much, and he didn't use his
eyebrows much, either. Before we started talking about his son, I'd
assumed he was much more stoic than he actually turned out to be.
He gushed over his child.

"When you first found out about the baby, what did you feel?"
I asked.

"Oh, I was happy," he said. "I was happy. One day she came
home from the doctor—they did blood work—and they called us
two days later and were like, 'She's pregnant,' and I'm like, 'This is
awesome.' It just wasn't even like, 'Oh, shit,' or, 'Oh, what do I do?' It
was just, 'This is awesome.'"

"You were there when he was born, right?"

"Oh, yeah. I stayed by her side the whole time."

"So, what was it like when he was born?"

"Pretty awesome. I asked the doctor if I could cut her open.
Doctor said I wasn't sterile. Told him I could wash up real quick, but
he wouldn't let me. I have pictures of all that. If you want I could
show you. He didn't cry. He just looked at me the whole time."

I asked if he was ever afraid—of having a son at this age, of
being a father. I asked because I assumed I would be.

"Honestly, no. Take it day by day. It's different and weird, but
you adapt. I can't say nothing bad about it. I don't regret nothing. I
love my little boy and I always will. If you had to find out right now
you had a kid, it'd make you want to drop everything and go back
home."

It was a glimpse at a part of myself that I wasn't sure was actually there. I'd never seen it in me, that capacity for unconditional
selflessness, especially on the road. I wasn't walking with anyone. I
wasn't taking care of anyone. It was easy to get lost in my own little
head. *If you had to find out right now you had a kid, it'd make you
want to drop everything and go back home.* I almost wanted that, to be

bound to something so important that it would tear me away from even this, this walk that was becoming my life. But I still couldn't quite imagine it, that kind of selflessness. For me, it was theoretical. For Ollie, it was reality. *I love my little boy and I always will.*

"It's not how I want to spend my life," I said rather abruptly.

"Doing what?" Ollie said.

"Living alone. Wandering, searching, traveling. I love it all, but in the end it feels a little bit empty."

"It is," Ollie said, "but you know, after you done walked this whole way, and met the different people, at the end, it's going to make you a different person. You're not going to be who you are today. Is it going to make you better? Worse? Yes. No. Maybe. But let's say you run into about five more people who's doing parent shit like me—single fathers, single mothers. Everything that everybody tells you, it might help you out to become this person. A better father, a better husband, whatever. I hope you become someone way better for it. I hope you succeed in everything what's going on. I hope a lot of people can help you along the way. I hope you meet more people. I hope you have a safe journey. I hope something really good comes out of it."

We were two young men, twenty-three years old. I was walking. He was raising a child. I saw something of myself in him, something I hadn't found yet. I hope he saw something of himself in me, too.

PAUL FITCH, *civil servant*
FRANKLIN, LOUISIANA, *in his kitchen after a dinner of home-made crawfish étouffée*
MARCH, *perfect walking weather almost every day*

"I didn't close myself off to anything, and at one point I couldn't get enough of anything. I experienced everything I could experience, because I wanted to see what it was like and to say that I did it. Most of it was wonderful. Some of it wasn't. But it's all learning. It makes me who I am today, which I'm glad of, because I love me. I'm very content with who I am. And I did not always love myself. I didn't know myself when I was younger. So I'm very happy about that, about knowing myself."

"How did you get to that point?"

"It was like, one day the thought just struck me that, just because people say X, Y, Z is so does not mean it's so. It's a simple thought, but it was just an awestruck moment. Like the day I realized that I don't have to finish a book just because I started reading it. That had never occurred to me before. 'You don't have to finish this.' And one day I said, 'This book is crap,' and I just put it down, and I said, 'Oh, wow.'

"This is so simple, and almost trite, but there was another thunderbolt for me: When I was living in New Orleans, my friends and I became surrogate grandchildren to this older couple who were just a real hoot, and they took good care of us, and the guy was in his seventies and he said, 'Baby, let me tell you something.' I said, 'What?' He said, 'No matter where you are, no matter what you're doing, if you're

not having a good time, walk the fuck out. Just walk the fuck out.' And I was like, 'Oh, wow.' That really struck me, that just because I'm somewhere and I'm miserable, I don't have to sit there. I can just leave, and that had never dawned on me before, because for years and years and years I was a people pleaser. I was always in this regimented pattern of: This is what you do. This is what's expected. This is how you behave. So that has stood me in good stead. If I'm not enjoying myself, I just walk out."

Chapter Seventeen

"Gotta stretch it out and make it last."

I crossed into Texas near Beaumont on I-10, taking a bridge that bounced with the weight of the trucks. A big sign with the Texas state flag read,

WELCOME TO TEXAS
DRIVE FRIENDLY—THE TEXAS WAY

There was another sign, a green mile marker indicating the distance to New Mexico: 880. I tried not to freak out while I did the math. At three miles an hour, it would take me almost three hundred hours to cross Texas. That was two months or so. I was in the big leagues now. This was no Maryland.

Nothing had really changed, though, now that I was in Texas. I was still walking, nice and slow. The slowness demanded an acceptance of the fact that most transformations seemed to happen at that same glacial rate. The highway was an aberrant stream of time jacked up to fast-forward. Nothing else went that fast. "Must be patient," I wrote in my journal. I was tired of running after all the questions. I figured I might as well relax into them instead. It was April. Six months on the road had shown me that coming of age was a constant process. Unlike walking across America, there was no ocean where it all ended. There was always something new to learn.

The people continued to teach me, and so did the solitude, especially on the nights I camped. The stillness and the silence were the sternest of all my teachers, and the most powerful. They didn't bother me as much as they had back east. Sometimes, I actually quite enjoyed them.

"Love your solitude," Rilke said to me one night in my tent, from *Letters to a Young Poet*, "and try to sing out with the pain it causes you." Ever the champion of solitude, Rilke always hammered this one home to the young poet without mercy: "For ultimately, and precisely in the deepest and most important matters, we are unspeakably alone." Sometimes his thoughts on the importance of solitude seemed to be nothing more than the rationalizations of a very lonely man. But, more and more, they were making sense to me.

> Those who are near you are far away, you write, and this shows that the space around you is beginning to grow vast. And if what is near you is far away, then your vastness is already among the stars and is very great; be happy about your growth, in which of course you can't take anyone with you.

He might be proud of me, I thought, if he could see me now, camped out in the dirt behind a gas station in the middle of nowhere.

Human company, though, was the necessary counterweight to the aloneness, a place to breathe when the solitude became suffocating. That company could be abrasive and abhorrent, but sometimes it was better than nothing. Like Rick, outside Houston.

"Hey, there's a Hooters, man. Let's grab some titty and run like hell."

I didn't really want to be walking with Rick. He was filthy. He seemed a little unstable. He said things like, "Let's grab some titty and run like hell." I'd been wading through the commercial sprawl north of Houston when I saw him in front of me. He was walking at just the wrong pace: too slow to stay ahead, too fast to pass. When I was a few feet behind him, I said hello. He recoiled.

"You scared me for a second there," he said. "I saw you a ways back. Thought you turned, though." He spoke in a low voice. His skin was tanned and wrinkled from the sun. The teeth that he still had were also browned. His boots were separating from their soles and he had a backpack, the kind a kid would wear to school. I asked him where he was coming from.

"Downtown Houston," he said. "Been walking since eleven last night. Trying to hitch a ride to Dallas but ain't nobody picked me up yet. Fuckin' Houston people."

I found this hard to believe, not that he hadn't been picked up, but that he was on course to complete a double marathon by the day's end. It was noon and almost forty miles from downtown Houston. And on top of that it was humid and hot, and he hadn't slept. Rick was either an athletic beast or a liar.

We shook hands, guardedly. It seemed neither one of us really wanted the company. We passed a mile or so in silence.

"Downtown Houston's a long way from here," I said eventually. "That's a crazy walk, man."

"Oh, I been walking all my life," he said. "Hell, I walked from El Paso to Abilene one time, almost all the way. Wasn't even planning on it. Nobody stopped to pick me up then, either, so I ended up walking it. Hot as a bitch out there, too."

I suspected Rick was a liar after all. You don't just walk from El Paso to Abilene by accident. That's 450 miles of bleak and brutal country. Unprepared, it could be deadly.

"Went to the doctor a few years back, and he said, 'Rick, you're about the healthiest man your age I know.' I said to him, 'Well, Doc, if you did as much walking as I do, you would be, too.' Hey, you have any smokes on you, man?"

Interstate 45 ran through a frenetic mess of car dealerships, fast food chains, and furniture stores. An orgy of malls spawned together, multiplying and spilling out over a land that was otherwise probably beautiful. Rick and I were on a frontage road that paralleled the interstate, and a steady flow of traffic passed us by. The people in their cars were looking at us. I wondered what they were thinking.

"Do people ever look at you?" I asked Rick. "You know, like they're afraid or something?"

"Oh, quite a bit," he said. We walked in silence some more, and then I asked him if he had any family. He said no. "Wife died in eighty-six and I been on the road ever since." We didn't talk about family anymore after that.

Soon enough, we passed the Hooters, and Rick offered his suggestion.

"It could be fun. And hell, I could use some titty. You probably could, too, with all that walking. Makes me remember these two broads who picked me up one time in New Mexico. We stayed in a hotel and I fucked the shit out of them for a week. And then both of them left. One got homesick and one got herself another man. So I was out on the road thumbing again."

Not twenty-four hours before Rick, an unlikely stroke of serendipity had found me sitting in the office of former president George H. W. Bush. One of my mom's childhood friends knew him and had told his staff about me. They had invited me to stop in and say hello when I passed through Houston. It was bizarre to be in the presence of such an influential man, having just been walking on the side of a highway. Again, I felt a bit like Forrest Gump, as I had in Selma. We only had fifteen minutes together—far too brief to dig into much of anything—but I did manage to ask him for advice. He answered simply: "Go for it." It was sound counsel, I thought, but I had to assume it didn't apply to Rick's titty schemes. They were a strange coupling, President Bush and Rick. But there it was: they were coupled together by the string of my footsteps, a former president and a man who slept on flattened cardboard boxes under bridges because someone had stolen his tent. I suppose they both altered the course of history in their own ways, big and small.

Rick was hurting. He didn't say it, but I could tell, because he stayed on the grass to spare his feet the concrete. If he'd been walking for twelve hours and forty miles as he claimed, he'd probably been hurting since sunrise. I guessed it was the worst inside his feet. That's how it always went for me: it sometimes felt like swarms of ant-size rats gnawing their way out. Rick slowed. I slowed with him. When he stopped to rest, I did, too. A chafing but not wholly unpleasant partnership seemed to have taken shape. We were sitting on a mown strip of lawn outside a mall with an ancient Grecian aesthetic. Faux-marble columns pretended to support the storefronts, and toga-robed goddesses danced on three-story pedestals. I assumed all of it was hollow. Rick eyed a pond next to us. A dozen fountainheads sprayed rockets of water into the air. The prefabricated rock walls glistened.

"You know, if I jumped in there to wash off they'd probably throw me in jail," Rick said, picking up a half-smoked cigarette next to him, and a bank receipt. He lit the cigarette and held up the receipt.

"If this fell into the wrong hands, they could empty the entire account," he said. "That's why I rip these apart when I find them." He tore the receipt into pieces. The glaze-eyed goddesses stared down at us from their pedestals.

"There was one time I found thirty-five hundred dollars in cash wrapped up in a brown paper bag. I thought it was a beer or something. I found a hotel and said, 'I'm staying here for a week,' which I did. It was a damn good hotel, too."

Eventually Rick and I resumed our northward trudge. It wasn't long before I could see my turn up ahead. I quickened. Friends were waiting for me, Josh and Tina Hubert. We would have fish tacos that night, and play music together, and I'd get a shower and a bed, and this put the spurs in me. I flew faster because I just wanted to get there, get off the road, get away from all the staring eyes in the passing cars. By the time I made it to the turn, Rick was far behind. He walked alone against a rushing backdrop, the only human being in the world, it seemed.

Before he got to me, he picked something up off the ground and stuffed it in his pocket. When he reached the intersection, I asked him what it was.

"Dollar bill," he said.

"Nice, man. You should get something from the dollar menu at that McDonald's over there."

"No, I'll wait till dinner, when I'm really hungry," Rick said. "Gotta stretch it out and make it last. But I'll go in there to get some water and rest my feet."

The light turned green and we split for the first time in three hours. After we'd both taken a couple steps, we looked back at each other and reached out our hands simultaneously, he his left, I my right, and we held tight for a second.

"Good luck, man," I said.

"I'll see you around," he replied, and then we both went back into our solitude.

JOSHUA TERZIU, young father of two, and a self-described "mathmagician and thought physician," with his wife, Laura
LAKE CHARLES, LOUISIANA, on a floor of pillows in their closed-in front porch, a calm wind through the windows
MARCH, getting hotter

"For me, reverence goes beyond understanding that there's a sacredness to everything. It goes beyond knowing that there's divine everywhere. Having reverence is acting in every breath with full faith that everything around you is conscious and is affected by all the movements you make. So if you move real quick, you're kind of disturbing the surroundings if you're not necessarily being mindful. Or if you're just kind of doing shit, you know, just doing things, 'I like to do this, I'm gonna fuckin' do it, no matter what, no one's gonna tell me what to do.' That's not necessarily having reverence because there is a living being surrounding you that's very delicate, even though it's strong and eternal. It's very delicate. It's like a dandelion. As soon as you start spitting shit off, it's not going to be there in its fullness because it's a delicate dandelion, a living flower being. So having reverence is understanding that you're walking around nothing but dandelions, and even if you whisper too hard they may just fall over.

"And reverence is also knowing that everyone has a divine take on things, and you gotta be listening for it. It means the next person in your experience is another version of divinity having something very real to say to you, and if you're open to the blessing of what they're bringing in the unique moment, you're going to draw that out of *them, no matter what they think they're going through. When you wield reality, like, wield it in your breath and in your action, then you demand it in the people that come into your experience. They can't help but reflect this back to you, even if they are zooboobaba bad guy, because that's what you're putting out there unconditionally, even to him who is the booboobaka, or whatever name we put to the boogeyman. You love him as he gets closer and he has to transcend and transform."*

Chapter Eighteen

"This is from me, and of me, but it is not me."

I bought a baby stroller outside Austin, Texas. My baby was my back-pack, and I couldn't carry it anymore. It was torturing me. In the mornings, it was fine. I loved it at first—the loaded sway behind me, the waist-strap embrace around my hips. The world was so beautiful in the mornings: the steer pastures, the pine forests, the post oaks dripping their dewy nighttime dreams. But at noon the sun raged, and the backpack got grumpy, then mean. It weighed me down, and made the humid heat intolerable. I couldn't feel anything but my own boiling brain. My bones burned. Every gas station was a Garden of Eden. I'd stumble inside, drop my backpack on the floor, and bask in the AC. But I always had to go back out into the purgatory again. This was why-walking, when I couldn't stop thinking, *Why am I doing this? Why bother? Why, God, oh, why?*

It was serendipity and selfishness that landed me the stroller. Toward the end of one day's walk outside Brenham, a young guy named Peter McMinn pulled over and invited me to stay at his family's ranch. He'd thru-hiked the Appalachian Trail the year before—a walking colleague—and there was an REI sale in town the next morning. Peter was going to camp out that night to be one of the first shoppers inside. I joined him, but not without some hesitation. I wasn't thrilled about the idea of sleeping in a mall parking lot, just on principle. That was for the Taser-wielding Black Friday types, those full-grown adults you see every November on the news clobbering one another over a Barbie doll. It's always midnight in these news reports, and people are pouring into the stores like they're running from zombies. They *are* the zombies, hungry for human blood, almost literally. People have gotten shot at these sales, and stabbed, and trampled. People have died. Camping outside REI, I was the zombie now. The next morning, we all rushed through the doors. I found two high-end strollers, both marked down to one hundred dollars. Right behind me came a mother with a toddler on her hip. We each grabbed one; good thing there were two or else it might've gotten ugly. At the checkout line a young couple asked me if I'd surrender the stroller. I'd taken the last one, and they couldn't afford the normal price, and they had a real-life baby they had to take care of. I said no, because I was a monster. The Texas heat will do that to you. Malls might, too.

The stroller came with a name: BOB. The letters were emblazoned across its sun shield, an acronym for "beast of burden." With Bob, walking was easy. I could see everything again, especially the wildflowers. They'd erupted, and they could not contain themselves, a visible symphony of sound. Soft pinks cooed sleepily and softer lavenders whispered secrets, barely inaudible. Scarlets and sapphires yowled, and yellows warbled a duet with the violets. Over all of this, a burning desert orange nailed the glass-shattering high note, the soprano queen of this opera. "I hear the chorus," Whitman wrote, "it is a grand-opera ... this indeed is music!" If their silent song wasn't enough, the flowers had names that read like the ingredients of a witch's potion. I looked them up later: baby's breath and bastard cabbage, prairie paintbrush and Indian blanket, winecup and goat-foot-morning-glory and goldeneye phlox.

Among the flowers the butterflies danced, drinking deep with their straw tongues. They might've been on the path of some great migration, but they all seemed to float aimlessly around me. Did they feel their fragility? Were they aware of their own audacity, flying on the highway? The cars batted hundreds of them to the ground, where they fluttered on the asphalt in delicate paroxysms of death. The ants always found them and carried them away. I would swerve Bob to avoid these funeral processions.

The flowers brought more than just the butterflies, though. People flocked to the highways of the Hill Country for the bluebonnets, the grand empress of the whole affair, and for once I wasn't the only human being outside a car. People wanted to smell the bluebonnets, and touch them, and walk among them. The people were lovelier than the flowers themselves, wandering around enchanted like children. It looked like they were seeing the world for the first time: curious but hesitant, uncertain but excited. A father took photographs of his daughter submerged in the azure sea, her face floating on the petals. A family waded through the flowery waters. Everybody breathed the blue for a moment or two and then got back in their cars and drove on.

Most of the miles were calm and effortless with Bob, and now that I'd walked more than halfway across America, I felt a certain familiarity with how the whole thing worked. At lunchtime, I'd find a hidden spot to eat, where I was the only one in the world who knew exactly where I was. Near the village of Ledbetter, I found the perfect bridge. Underneath: the sweet shade cooled me, the brown stream flowed, the silence. I ate a peanut butter and jelly sandwich on pita bread and some dried apricots, while the ants gorged themselves on a mountain of fallen jelly. Whitman came out to join me. I turned to a random page: "Do you suspect death?" he wrote. A little light reading for lunch today.

If I were to suspect death I should die now,
Do you think I could walk pleasantly and well-suited
   toward annihilation?
Pleasantly and well-suited I walk,
Whither I walk I cannot define, but I know it is good,
The whole universe indicates that it is good.

Something to chew on for a while, if the Snickers bars weren't enough.

The land slowly became what I'd always imagined the west to be. The ground was dry and calloused with granite and limestone. Juniper and dwarf mesquite pockmarked the fields, and prickly pear cactus clawed itself out from below. As I walked, the lush kingdom of the Gulf bowed, step by step, to the savanna. Barefoot country was no more, but even still, the wildflowers weren't all gone yet, and the butterflies still danced and drank, and sometimes I couldn't tell which was which, so that when a camouflaged butterfly took flight it looked like a flower was flying on its own petal wings.

At dusk one night, I saw a billboard advertising the world's best burgers at a general store a mile away in the village of Andice. It was out of my way, but it seemed worth the walk. In the store, an ornery old man named Sonny stood guard behind the counter. A chalkboard menu advertised smoked brisket sandwiches, chicken-fried steaks, rodeo burgers, and pulled pork tacos: surely this was the west.

I'd just finished my brisket sandwich when a young woman walked in to buy two cases of Keystone Light. "Dad's having a crawfish boil," she said to Sonny. "Gotta resupply."

"Why don't you take this young man over there with you," Sonny said. "He's hungry. He walked two thousand miles to get here."

"No, that's all right," I said. "You don't have to invite me to your party."

"Come on, man," she said. Her name was Meghan. "Let's go. We'll get you fed, and maybe a little drunk, too."

Andice was a tiny town, and the party was just across the street. Strands of golden lights traced the house against the dark. A group of men played washers in the front yard, a game kind of like horseshoes. Everyone else sat on picnic benches and lawn chairs, eating and drinking. Country music played. Meghan's father, Greg, got me a heaping plate of crawfish. He was a tall, lanky man with an impressive Fu Manchu mustache and a camouflage button-down. He declared, right on the spot, that'd I'd be staying with them that night. He was tipsy. After handing me a beer, he took me into his house to show me his taxidermy collection: deer heads, boar heads, turkeys frozen in flight, a raging bobcat under the TV. He pointed out a sign on the bathroom door that read, YOU KNOW YOU'RE A REDNECK IF YOU HAVE A DEER MOUNTED IN YOUR BATHROOM.

"Go ahead," he said, "take a look." I peeked inside. From above the toilet, the glassy eyes of an eight-point buck stared back at me, one of its prongs sheathed by a roll of toilet paper.

Greg went by Wey. He also called everybody else Wey. He called me Walking Wey, and then Walkawey, and everybody else called me Walkabout. With a surname like Forsthoefel, I'd received my fair share of nicknames in school: Forest Quaffle, Forest Awful, Four Hot Waffles. I didn't mind, but none of them really felt like me. It was strange, then, to feel so deftly named by the Alexanders, this family of self-proclaimed rednecks who'd known me for less than an hour. It was like they'd constructed a space for me to live among them, my own home within theirs, my new name. Walkabout. It felt expansive, liberating. Four Hot Waffles just didn't have the same effect.

Wey's son, Mitchell, was about my age. He was a massive banyan of a man, bearded and stone-faced. He gave me two more names: Silly Fucker and Fuckin' Nut. I rather liked them, too. If I hadn't, though, I wouldn't have made a big deal out of it. You tread lightly around a man of that size.

At midnight, a boar hog showed up. The two men who'd shot it grabbed its hind legs and slid it from the bed of the pickup, dumping it on the dirt. Tiny insects scuttled across its hairy black skin. The hog lay on the ground while one of the men hooked up a heavy gambrel from the garage ceiling where the hog would hang upside down, legs splayed. Two little children kicked it where it lay. Mitchell placed a Keystone Light at its mouth, so it appeared to be drinking. I took several pictures of this, and suddenly it didn't seem so different from the tormenting of a passed-out drunkard—the giggling abusers, the frenzy of photography. It was like I was back in college.

Then, the hog was hung and the butchering began. I'd never seen anything like it. I found it deeply unsettling to witness the methodical disassembly of an organism that just moments before had been living. It was so close to us, we who were still alive, and that made me think about my death once again, and about the mystery of my birth. The hog's blood spilled into a big plastic bucket, splashing onto the ground. The iron that made the blood red had once been a part of the core of a star somewhere far away, a star long dead at this point. My own blood was red for the very same reason. I wouldn't be alive if the star hadn't died, if I didn't have the remnants of its heart running through my veins. Right now, I could see this liquid stardust pouring from the hog, and I could smell it, and even touch it if I wanted to. But I didn't want to. I just wanted to throw up.

The butcher nicked the gut during the disembowelment. The sound of deflation was audible. In seconds, the stench was everywhere, a pervasive ether of feces. When it hit the back of my throat I could almost taste it.

"Goddamnit, Scotty. I heard that sombitch, too."

"Fuckin' Scotty don't know how to skin a pig."

"Knife was too big."

"Y'all must've run that sombitch for a while." The longer the hog ran, they explained, the more it stank—the adrenaline. Humans weren't so different. I'd learned that from Simon, the ex-Marine at the homeless shelter in South Carolina. "If you don't rinse 'em good, you'll smell it in the frying pan. But he'll make good sausage. Damn good sausage. We're gonna pack you a lunch, Walkabout."

The blood flowed, spilling onto anyone who got close. Their hands were red. "His nuts are looking good right now. Y'all probably don't eat too many nuts up there, do you?"

I said we didn't.

"Man, I guarantee you that's probably the first time he's ever been asked that in his life."

"Yeah, well, cow nuts? We fry them."

"Are they any good?"

"Oh, hell yeah. Taste like chicken. And it don't look like a nut when you eat it."

I asked if the hogs were dangerous.

"Only if you mess with them. Then they'll fuck with you, and you ain't gonna outrun them. Those fuckin' jaws? They'll chomp through bone like nothing else."

After the butchery and before bed, Mitchell asked me to go inside with him. He took out a large semiautomatic rifle and sat next to me on the couch. He removed the magazine, and then placed the weapon in my lap. It was very heavy.

"It's just to make sure you're not a serial killer," he said. "You don't want to know how many guns we have in this house. So don't kill me in my sleep tonight, because I'll kill you right back." He and his wife, Lacy, lived in the house with their baby son. I promised him I wouldn't kill anybody, and he took his heavy gun back and put it away. I'd quite forgotten about this version of American manhood—the masculinity of intimidation and metal, the manliness of grunt swagger. I couldn't totally blame Mitchell, though. His wife and baby would be sleeping under the same roof with a stranger that night. I'd probably be nervous, too.

When we all woke up alive the next morning, it was raining. Wey invited me to stay, and Mitchell said he would cook me steak that night. He might've felt bad about threatening to kill me just a few hours earlier. Mitchell and I were the same age, but I kind of felt like a kid around him. I'd felt the same way around Ollie Ware, too, back in Louisiana, hearing him talk about his little boy. It was so humbling, and almost embarrassing, to be around young men my age who, in some ways, felt so much further ahead in life than I was.

One of my best high school friends was now a father, too. He and his wife—Lark and Izzy Mason—lived in Abilene, a few weeks down the road. They put me up for a week when I passed through. Staying with them, I saw just how much growing up I still had ahead of me. I'd left home in order to catalyze a coming-of-age, but sometimes it seemed like I was just putting it off. Was I walking away from adulthood or toward it?

It was so good to see Lark, a beloved face from my previous life. He'd been a wild-man at boarding school, the big-hearted goof who would do anything to make someone laugh, even if it meant smashing into a brick wall full-speed on a bike. We would sneak out of our dorm at night to go climb roofs—the gym roof, the arts center roof, the roof of the main Hogwarts-like building. Now, Lark had a baby, and he was working three jobs and finishing college. By all accounts, he'd grown up. He'd had to.

One night in Abilene, late, Lark and I hopped the fence of an abandoned coal factory nearby and climbed up a gutter to the roof, just like old times. We sat together and watched the city twinkle in the night. I'd brought my recorder because I wanted to interview him. I wanted to know how he'd changed, and what he'd learned. He and his wife astonished me—the way Izzy spent nearly every hour with her little boy, the way Lark swaddled him with such confidence. The endurance of that. The surrender. The image of this young family triggered a kind of fearful longing in me. Strange, to desire something so much you become afraid to pursue it, because what if you tried as hard as you could but it still wasn't enough? Or what if you finally found it, only to find next that it wasn't what you'd dreamed it would be? What if it all fell apart one summer morning without any warning whatsoever?

"In high school, my happiness was coming from me, and it left me kind of empty," Lark said when we made it to the roof. "This was all I was, and I got a single-faceted kind of outlook on life. And so for my wife and for my son, it's been interesting to see that it's not just momentary. It's not something that you can do and walk away from. It never ends. You have to keep giving and keep giving. Before it was something I thought I should do. I wanted to give to people, but there was a point at which I stopped because I had no more to give. And now I've realized there's always more to give."

"Are you ever afraid? Like, you won't be able to do it?"

"For me, it's these overbearing fears that I won't be able to give them the life they deserve because of mistakes I might make. I fear that I'm going to work and work and work, and never be able to give enough to them. At first I had this whole vision of this sad life working at, you know, Whataburger or something like that, coming home smelling like French fries and my son is a jerk because he has no father to parent him. I think it just comes about because the stress builds up inside of me. Turning in papers late, rushing to my job but still getting there late, working my tail off but coming up short at the end of the month, having to wait until next month to pay the bills. It's just hard, man, you know?"

The truth was, I didn't know. I had no clue.

"But it's been a magical time in my life. It's been incredible. I was about to graduate and I was so tired of not having a purpose. With the birth of a child there's clarity. You know what you have to do, and it doesn't really matter what you do to get there. I don't care what kind of job I have, to be perfectly honest with you. It doesn't matter. But I know I have to provide a home. I have to have a working car. I have to put food on the table and clothes on our backs. And I'm willing to sacrifice anything that I have to get that for Izzy and for my son."

We heard a train howl in the distance.

"Every night, I hear that train," Lark said. "It reminds me that I've always wanted to train hop. Every night that I hear it, it calls me back to adventures, when I feel frustrated about being stuck in the same place. It gives me a chance to adventure."

"Has your sense of adventure changed at all," I asked, "now that you have a son?" He was quiet for a long time.

"I don't know. It's difficult to think of it like that, because most adventures I've willingly gone into, in my past life, and this was one that came upon me. But I guess as we've been going, it has. It has all the same characteristics, where you have time lapses, where you don't realize where you are and you lose yourself in the moment. And there are frustrations, and there are setbacks, and then there's such great joy at other moments, and true peace. I feel like adventures need all those things. It's different. But, I've always thought that where you are not so much decides your mood as you do, so anything can be an adventure."

It was past midnight, and we still wanted to climb the towering smokestack above us, but before I turned off my recorder I asked him what it had been like to be there for the birth, to meet his son for the first time.

"After he was born I got to hold him. It's unreal. I was just like, 'Wow, this is my son, but I don't really understand what this is,' if that makes sense. It's like a dream, or right when you first wake up, when you still have a sleep fog around you, and you're walking out into a forest and seeing these shapes kind of emerge. You'll see the edge of a tree or the side of a building, maybe a glimpse of a rock, but you don't really know what you're looking at. And I don't know if I ever really will. Maybe that's what another human being is. When you try to understand somebody, you can hold them, but you can never truly understand. You can't ever get inside them. And looking at my son, I guess I was kind of feeling that. That this is mine, but it's not. This is from me, and of me, but it is not me. It's really fun. It's been really crazy, raising this little boy. There are still days when I look at him and I still have that foggy vision, and I think I will throughout my life. 'I can hold you, and I can make you laugh and all that, but I don't control you, and I don't own you.' It's like nothing else in all the world. He's beautiful. For the first three hours of every day all he does is smile."

GALE, grandmother, gas station attendant, member of Star Ranch nudist club
McDADE, TEXAS, in the back of the gas station on a work break
MAY

"*My granddaughters, they were nine and eleven when they started going out there, and we just had this sit-down talk about what it means, that it's not something sexual, just because you're running around without clothes on. It's just because you enjoy the freedom of being nude. That was five years ago. They grew up as teenagers being there. They have a lot more self-confidence. They're happier with their bodies. They see things differently. I don't think they see nudity as being sexual like a lot of people do. Because it's not. Not at our club, anyway. We're a family club.*"

"*Do you remember the very first time you went out there and took off the clothes?*"

"*Well, yeah. You're very self-conscious, regardless. If you're not used to being nude in front of people you're gonna be self-conscious. But I think it slips away pretty quick for most people. You realize nobody pays any attention to it. Once the clothes come away it's kind of hard to hide behind anything, or pretend to be anything. What you see is what you get. It's kind of a freedom out there. I think it helped my self-image. People can be beautiful no matter what they look like, and you're not necessarily judged, because we have all sizes, shapes, colors, everything. Everybody's equal. So that's the biggest thing. Are we all crazy? No. We're normal, for what we do. Just like other people think they're normal. It's normal for us. I think if people are opposed to it, they don't understand it.*"

Chapter Nineteen

"You'll know when."

I kept getting all these glimpses into what my life could become someday. Each person offered something a little different, the young and the old alike. Each family reflected a possibility I'd never seen before. I was privy to snapshots of the human experience in these brief moments, seeing what these people had learned and become by walking the walk of their lives. Some were at the beginning. Some were nearing the end. All of them were their own unique wellspring of valuable information.

But I also began to see that there was a limit to the usefulness of all the listening, this daily search for answers outside myself, in others. Rilke reprimanded me on this during a lunch break one afternoon in a culvert by the highway. "You are looking outside," he wrote to the young poet, "and that is what you should most avoid right now. No one can advise you or help you—no one. There is only one thing you should do. Go into yourself." It made me wonder about the very premise of my trek—walking to listen. All the interviews, the conversations: was there a point at which they became more distracting than instructive? Evasive of my own process? So many people, so much talk; all this seeking outside, and the inside might become a kind of empty receptacle for the lives of everybody else.

Whitman was with Rilke on this one:

You shall no longer take things at second or third hand . . .
    nor look through the eyes of the dead . . . nor feed on the
    spectres in books,
You shall not look through my eyes either, nor take things
    from me,
You shall listen to all sides and filter them from yourself.

When I left home, I'd hoped that the story-gathering and advice-harvesting would become a reliable way of navigating my own existence, but I hadn't seen the potential pitfalls, the ways in which the listening could become a crutch, a way of avoiding the responsibility of experiencing it for myself. Theory was far less threatening than reality, and taking things at second or third hand was a way to keep everything theoretical, keep me out of the story, a detached observer. The logic was seductive: if I could meet enough people and hear about how *they* did it, perhaps that'd be sufficient, a kind of living by proxy. That way, I wouldn't have to pay the price that most of these life lessons cost. I'd be so full of vicariously learned wisdom that no pain could touch me. I would outsmart it.

After about half a year on the road, however, I was beginning to see that no amount of listening would spare me. There wasn't a formula for how to live my life, because my life had never been lived before. I would stumble and fall, like any child learning to walk. I would break, too, and have to rebuild. There was just no way around it, the formula-lessness of my life, and the more I tried to get around it, the less alive I'd be. *Go into yourself.* That embrace, that full immersion, had something to do with finding the courage to actually feel, to meet everything that came upon me with intimacy, without shying away. No more trying to do it right. No more trying to live it the way somebody else lived it. Just feel. Embrace. Immerse. *Filter them from yourself.*

But still, I couldn't quite let go of the possibility that there might be an easier way, some outside teacher who would do the work for me, revealing the secrets of how to achieve a skillful passage through this life. There was such solace in looking outward, like a child expecting to be carried the rest of the way home. But maybe that was a part of coming of age: discovering what it means to look inward, and then trusting yourself enough to actually do it.

I kept trudging northwestward across Texas. Jerald and Nena Wilson lived in the little town of Novice, not far from Lark and Izzy in Abilene. They'd driven by me on a farm-to-market road, and then Nena had come back a few minutes later. Without even asking me my name, she'd offered to put me up. It reminded me of Willie and Bernadette Verrett outside Sulphur, Louisiana. When they pulled over, all Willie had said was: "Would you like to refresh yourself at our house?" He didn't even bother with hello, and it didn't matter that they had seven children, all of whom were peeking out at me through the van's windows. I told Nena she'd just made my day, maybe even my week, and that I'd get to their house soon. She drove off, and the invitation lingered in her wake. It had an almost narcotic effect. My feet didn't hurt so much anymore. They'd been torn to shreds that day by a new pair of hiking sandals apparently made of steel wool. Instead of the pain, I saw the surrounding fields erupting in yellow: buttercup, goldeneye, sleeping daisy, prairie broomweed. Everything was laughing with yellow. I rode this current all the way to the Wilsons', where Nena had prepared a saltwater footbath for me and a bowl of vanilla ice cream. I almost swooned.

Nena wore eyeglasses and kept her white hair cropped short. She was a soft grandmother, the kind of soft that was perfectly suited for hugging. She made me sit while she cooked dinner: venison steaks and deviled eggs and mashed potatoes and gravy. It was so much better than the Uncle Ben's I'd been planning on. When Jerald got home from baling straw, we all sat down at the table.

During the blessing, I noticed Jerald's hands, and then I couldn't stop staring. His shirtsleeves were rolled up, and the forearms were bloodless and pale, but the hands were as brown as the earth they worked. His fingernails looked as hard as stone, caulked tight with soil. The soil had melded with coagulated blood to scab up two gashes just below the right pointer knuckle. In his palms, the lines were cut with such clarity that a palm reader would've needed just a second to know everything. I couldn't stop myself from mentioning them. I asked if I could take some pictures. Jerald seemed amused, and maybe a little bashful, looking at his hands as if noticing them for the first time.

"I've always enjoyed work," he said. "You can join me tomorrow if you want to see how it goes."

At the table, I learned that Nena was as quick to cry as Jerald was to laugh.

"I can't help it," she said. "And especially since I've been saved, I think I've been more tender to cry than what I was before. These are tears of joy. I don't know that I can explain it any way except that it's just an overflow of the goodness of God. There may be tears of sorrow, too, but generally it's just a joyful expression. And it just flows freely from me. It's not a bad thing. It's a good thing. I think it shows there's not a hard shell around your spirit."

Jerald was tender, too, and a good listener. "I don't know, I guess I've always just been friendly to speak to people," he said. "I've always liked people. Just to listen to people talk. I guess I've realized over the years, the less talking you do, people will tell you more of their life experience. I guess that's kind of what I've contributed to."

The next day we rose early, around sunrise. Over breakfast, Jerald got a call from his grandson, who'd already been working long enough for the round baler to break. Our rations had to be rushed—the coffee swigged, the biscuits inhaled. We drove to the wheat fields in Jerald's pickup, passing the yellow flower seas and a lazy pump jack rocking like a seesaw Sisyphus. In the driver's seat next to me, Jerald was wearing a pinstripe button-down shirt and jeans. The jeans were one of at least five pairs he wore for work, probably on rotation throughout the week. I'd seen the other four in the backyard hanging from a clothesline, indigo and black. When the breeze blew, they all floated slantwise together in unison.

Jerald had worked the field with the combine a few days earlier. As he turned off the road and ran the pickup into the field, I saw the cut straw laid out across the land in long, golden windrows that followed the field's curves like the whorls of ridges on fingertips.

"I like threshing with the combine," Jerald said. "That's enjoyable to me, just watching it cut, and it gathers it in. And you can just see it gathering it, going through the machine, and the trash goes out the back and the clean grain goes into the tank. I feel like it's an accomplishment, to watch it do that. To me, the combine, watching it, whenever it cuts it off—" and out of nowhere Jerald choked up. He had to pause. "It's just like God wants to do with His children, wants to just wrap His arms around us and bring us to Him. That's what it reminds me of."

Grandfather and grandson conferred over the broken round baler. The problem had to do with the netting. It wasn't wrapping the straw tightly enough, so the bales were spat out loose. Jerald explained it to me, pointing out the drive sprockets and leaf springs, the pivots and tension arms. I didn't understand a thing. To me, the baler was an enigma. I'd stand the same chance of fixing it as I would successfully piloting a spaceship to the Moon. But Jerald knew, and his hands worked over the tractor's engine and then to the back of the baler. He reached under a lip to fiddle with something. Satisfied with his adjustment, he climbed up into the tractor and started driving down a windrow, and the bales rolled out the back as tight as could be.

Jerald knew the machinery of his work so well. My work, for now, was walking, and I still knew so little about how the body did it, even just what went into a single stride. I looked it up on online later, and I patched together a ragged understanding. First, there was the inception of the desire to move, and this happened somewhere in the motor cortex, whatever that was. The motor neuron— or neurons?—traveled across an interlacing grid of white matter that was tens of thousands of miles long. This white matter was fed by capillaries that were in turn fed by veins and arteries, and these, too, stretched out tens of thousands of miles, channeling an astronomical amount of blood over any given lifetime. And then what? Muscles twitched, tendons held fast, bones lifted, all made possible by the elasticity of skin and the padding of flesh and the exquisite miracle of balance. And then I was walking, even as the Earth was spinning at however many miles an hour—hundreds? thousands?— the Solar System hurtling around and around, the galaxy firing off into God knows where. In truth, I had no idea what was going on. It was just going on.

"I feel like if I just sit down or retire, I feel like maybe I'll waste away," Jerald said back at the house as the afternoon fell to evening.

"As long as I feel good, and my health is still good, I just like to be busy and be working. It's wonderful to be able to do it. I know there'll come a time when I can't. Something'll happen. Maybe a disease or a crippling effect to the body. There'll be a time. It'll come. And I'll know when to quit."

Nena was sitting on the couch across from us, and she said, "Hmm," in a way that suggested this was probably a contentious topic between them. Earlier, when Jerald hadn't joined us yet in the living room, she'd hinted at her own feelings around aging.

"I've always asked the Lord to let us have a long life together," she'd said, "and really, I don't know, I think sometimes that it might be easier to just go ahead and die. I get tired sometimes. At this age, sometimes you feel like you don't have anything to live for. When I got married, I had kids right away. Five of them in ten years. And you were busy, busy, busy for twenty years, until they were all gone from home. And you think that's your life, having those kids and taking care of them, raising them, teaching them, training them. But when they're all gone, sometimes you get to thinking, 'What am I here for?' I need something to keep me knowing a reason why I'm here. So, I'm not sure what keeps me going."

It made me wonder, as I seemed to wonder in some way every day, what lay ahead. Nena was in her seventies and she was still asking the same questions I was asking now.

"'Hmm?' What do you mean, 'Hmm?'" Jerald said in the living room.

"Maybe it'll just be a time whenever your mind says it's time to quit. We won't have to have a disease."

Jerald laughed, and looked at me. "Well, you know, you get to be seventy-seven, eighty years old, things happen to your body. It'll be . . ." and he paused here. "You'll know when."

I asked him what he'd do when he finally did sit down and retire.

"Oh, I don't know," he said. "I've always liked pottery."

I'd been walking for about six months when my mom decided it was finally time to see her oldest son again. Since I wasn't finished walking yet, she flew out to meet me. Her plane landed in Austin, so she and her friend Leslie had to drive out and pick me up off the highway. The sight of a car pulling over on the shoulder in front of me wasn't unusual: people often stopped to see what I was doing, or to make sure I wasn't pushing a baby in Bob. It was strange, however, to see my mom get out. She ran to give me a big hug, laughing at the sight of her son pushing a baby stroller on the side of the highway. We looked at each other as if for the first time.

"Are you still here?" she seemed to be saying with her eyes. "Who have you become? Who is my son now?"

We drove two hours to Austin—a three day walk—and we spent a week catching up, resting. We were at a café one afternoon when she told me she thought I had indeed changed.

"You seem more yourself," she said, "like you're at home with yourself. You've been calling me less, you know."

"I know," I said. "I'm sorry."

"No, no, it's okay. At the beginning I could tell you were calling me because you needed it. It was for you. But now when you call me, it's more for me. You've just really settled into this walk."

I felt that way much of the time. Not always, but often. More and more, the walking was like a well-trodden path back into a kind of sanctuary, where no one else could come with me, even if I wished they could. I was realizing that the aloneness wasn't going to kill me after all, kind of like an astronaut taking off her helmet on an alien planet only to find that she didn't need it, she could breathe there just fine, the atmosphere was made to support her, and she was made to thrive in it. Sometimes the aloneness was nothing short of wondrous, just abiding in it, regardless of where I happened to be in the outside world—under a bridge, or on the side of the interstate, or tucked away in the mesquite trees. I was learning to trust it.

Even as a toddler, the alien planet of solitude had a gravitational pull on me. I would seek it out, even at the cost of occasional loneliness. When I was two or three years old, I disappeared behind the Christmas tree for hours, sending my parents into a panic. A few years later, I started climbing trees to get there, finding quiet nooks in the air where there was nothing but the bark and the wind and the birds. I took to the trees again in college, at night in the farm fields and the forests, in stands of pine on top of hills glowing with snow and moon, on a mountaintop nestled snugly in a crook of an evergreen's crown. I could breathe there again. I could find whatever I'd lost that day.

But solitude had always just been an alien planet I'd go to visit once in a while. When I started walking, it was as if I'd chosen to accept that planet as my home. Hearing Mom's words made me remember just how unbearably lonely and frayed I'd often felt in the early months of my walk and, in some ways, for years. In Texas, even though I felt more at home in myself, that loneliness hadn't disappeared. Perhaps it was an effect of the lingering longing to love someone in a way that would dissolve me, merge my planet with theirs. But this was an impossible wish. Each one of us was stuck on our own planet—we each *were* our own planet—and any attempt to squash two planets together would result not in a new planet, but in a catastrophic collision in the cosmos. It was like Rilke wrote:

> Loving does not at first mean merging, surrendering, and
> uniting with another person (for what would a union be of

two people who are unclarified, unfinished, and still inco-
herent——?), it is a high inducement for the individual to
ripen, to become something in himself, to become world, to
become world in himself for the sake of another person; it
is a great, demanding claim on him, something that chooses
him and calls him to vast distances.

I felt as if Rilke were speaking directly to my most private
experience, the baffling process of attempting to understand this
longing inside me. There was just no hiding from the guy.

Only in this sense, as the task of working on themselves ('to
hearken and to hammer day and night'), may young people
use the love that is given to them. Merging and surren-
dering and every kind of communion is not for them (who
must still, for a long, long time, save and gather themselves); it is the ultimate, is perhaps that for which human
lives are as yet barely large enough. But this is what
young people are so often and so disastrously wrong in
doing: they (who by their very nature are impatient) fling
themselves at one another when love takes hold of them,
they scatter themselves, just as they are, in all their messi-
ness, disorder, bewilderment . . . And so each of them loses
himself for the sake of the other person, and loses the
other, and many others who still wanted to come. And
loses vast distances and possibilities . . . in exchange for an
unfruitful confusion, out of which nothing can come; nothing
but a bit of disgust, disappointment, and poverty, and the
escape into one of the many conventions that have been put
up in great numbers like public shelters on this most
dangerous road.

Two planets shattering themselves by trying to be one, catastrophic collisions in the cosmos. Better to be like binary stars, two celestial bodies orbiting around a common center, existing on their own together. Looking up into the night sky with your naked eyes, binary stars appear to be a single point of light, but they are in fact two separate entities, connected by the space between them, not divided by it. What holds them together? I'm no astronomer. Wikipedia tells me that some binary stars take less than an hour to orbit each other fully, and some take a few days. Others take hundreds of thousands of years to complete a single round, untold lifetimes to come full circle. It also tells me that if they are close enough, binary stars can actually exchange mass, a transference that can bring their evolution to stages they wouldn't have been able to attain on their own.

I knew *how* to float through the cosmos on my own, how to walk in solitude and even enjoy it, but I couldn't stop myself from wondering what it'd be like to do it with another. Perhaps we were already orbiting each other, getting pulled closer each day by the momentum of our unwitting choices, in which case there was no need to wonder what it'd be like, because it already was. No need to fear, either. It reminded me of what Whitman wrote of the night: "I know not how I came of you, and I know not where I go with you . . . but I know I came well and shall go well."

One night in the boondocks outside Merkel, Texas, I camped in the yard of a run-down mariachi radio station, where the music floated out of the open basement into the twilight, and I thought how sweet it might've been to be there with a lover, to weave our way through the tires and the chickens and the piles of trash, hand in hand, dancing to the sound of the guitarrón, twirling in circles around the ever-moving center between us. I could get up and dance on my own, I supposed—but really though?

It seemed a bit more possible that I might be able to trust someone else enough to love them someday, now that I was falling into a deeper trust of myself on the road. I felt changed, too, by the fact that so many people had trusted me during these months, over and over again, by taking me into their homes. I felt bigger in some way, more expansive, like maybe there'd be enough room in my life that it could accommodate someone else, too, without contracting in fear—trusting my own aloneness, trusting theirs, trusting the space between us.

After a week in Austin, Mom dropped me off where she had picked me up. The day was gray, and it was strange to say good-bye again, and sad. I got homesick trudging down the side of the highway, but after a few miles the walking brought me home again, and Texas continued.

"I tramp a perpetual journey," Whitman wrote. He must've walked across the Lone Star state. It just wouldn't end. The fire ants marched, and the trees shrank, and the dirt took on a tinge of orange. It was the bastion of the Baptists, the buckle of the Bible Belt. One guy gave me a hand-crank radio; I didn't use it much but when I did, the airwaves sang the songs of that land: country and mariachi, evangelists and Rush Limbaugh.

So many of the little villages seemed to be dying. Their streets were devoid of any movement at all. The storefronts were cracked and peeling, and the weeds grew tall. Some store owners didn't even bother staffing their shops. The salvage store in Santa Anna had a sign with the following instructions for potential customers:

STOP
LOOK

SEE
SOMETHING
CALL ME

It was very evident that these towns revolved around high school football. There were bumper stickers everywhere, and one magnificent stadium rising from the ashes of an otherwise desiccated village. The local newspapers revealed whose territory I was walking through on any given day: Eagles' country, Badgers' country, Lions' country. It was spring, so I never saw a game, but I did notice a front-page article in one newspaper. The writer scolded a coach for his recent decision to change the color of the band's uniform to black, because this was Dragons' country, and green would've been a better color for the Dragons. He could comment on the subject with authority, he wrote, because he'd been a Dragon his whole life.

I knew from cross-country flights that these plains looked like a patchwork quilt from the sky—cornfields, wheat fields, cotton fields, pasture—but from the ground it was just dirt stretching out into an eternal horizon. All across the land, pump jacks sprayed the sweet stink of natural gas into the wind. The freight trains rolled by, and when I waved they blew their horns hello. I could sing as loud as I liked in this emptiness, and often I did. The only other sounds were the rushing of the road, the soft slapping of my soles on the asphalt, and Bob's squeaking. His load was so heavy. It was in the nineties each afternoon, and I was averaging about twenty-five miles a day.

I'd been in Texas for almost two months when I finally made it to the panhandle, and a man named Mel Jack pulled over one afternoon. He was a trucker who hauled milk from New Mexico to Louisiana. I'd been walking his trucking route for a few days, and he'd become curious about me. Finally, he decided to stop. I saw the truck slow down as it passed me going in the other direction, and seconds later I heard the sound of a man's voice muffled in the wind. "Sir! Sir! Excuse me, sir!" I looked back. The truck was parked on the shoulder, its cylindrical tank buffed silver. A man was walking toward me, waving an arm in the air. "Sir! Wait!"

Mel wore a classic trucker's mustache, and he had an immense globe of a belly: it swelled against an orange polo shirt that was baggy at the sleeves. Two Gatorades were cradled in the arm that wasn't waving. When he caught up to me, Mel explained that he'd seen me a couple times and wanted to know what I was doing. "And I thought you might want a cold drink," he said, giving me the Gatorades. He spoke excitedly, stuttering over his words. When I told him I was walking across the country, Mel got even more excited.

"Well, you'll be walking my route until you get to Clovis, so whenever I pass you, you can count on a cold drink, because I have a fridge in the truck." He asked if I liked popcorn. We walked over to the truck's cab, and Mel climbed up, leaving the door hanging open. A giant teddy bear was buckled into the passenger seat. Mel climbed back down and gave me a sleeve of popcorn, saying good luck and I'll see you again soon. When he drove away I started walking again, and it felt like I was watching a fantastic movie—I had the popcorn and everything.

Mel tracked me for a week. On two separate occasions he stopped ahead of me at gas stations to let them know I was coming. He told them he'd pay for whatever I wanted. The last time I saw him, he pulled over on the shoulder again, blatting his horn hello. He got out and handed me something he called a Bubba cooler. It looked like a pony keg.

"I went to Wal-Mart and got this for you," he said. "With the hottest leg of your journey coming up, I want you to have a cold drink whenever you need it." We shook hands good-bye and we promised to keep in touch, but I knew we'd probably never see each other again. He drove away, and when I knelt down to tie the cooler to Bob, a fit of sobbing hit me like a rogue wave. Until that instant, I'd had no idea it was bothering me so much, but it was, this bone-deep dread that I'd be outmatched by the desert, that I didn't have it in me to make it across and survive. It was so close, and the temperatures were rising, but now I had a Bubba cooler that would keep my water cold. Now I had Mel Jack walking with me.

KENNETH, *a trucker and a former prison guard*
SNYDER, TEXAS, *a few miles outside of town at a rest stop by the highway*
MAY

"*Did you have any weird days or scary experiences when you were a prison guard?*"

"*Every day was weird and scary, man. You see things in there you don't see out here. The shit that happens in there stays in there. You don't hear about it. It stays there. Killings and stabbings and rapes. It never leaves. Like there was this one kid, twenty years old, and he got transferred to us from another facility—raped by five guys on his first night. They tore out his rectum and now he's shitting out a bag for the rest of his life.*"

"*Did working there change your perspective on humanity?*"

"*Yes. For a while I did see the prisoners as less than human. In there, all they know is the streets so I thought you gotta give them the streets. But that ain't fixing nothing, man. It used to be called the Texas Department of Corrections, but they changed the name because they ain't correcting nothing. Now it's the Texas Department of Criminal Justice.*"

Chapter Twenty

"Take a good look."

If you're ever walking from Las Vegas, New Mexico, to Santa Fe on I-25, you should know that you might not be alone. There's a man, I was told, who spends his days walking back and forth between the two cities, sixty miles each way. He travels with six suitcases. He'll drag two ahead for a good stretch, and then he'll set those down and go back for another two, and then he'll do it again for the final pair. Back and forth, back and forth. He continues this until he reaches the end, and then he turns around and does it again. It's anybody's guess as to what's inside the suitcases: tribes of mice, bricks of gold, transcripts of his interviews with God. His reasoning, if there is any, is also largely unknown. He's crazy, or enlightened, or both. We never met on the road to Santa Fe, so I don't have any idea.

I did meet Daniel and Raymond on I-25, though, two Latino boys who'd just graduated from high school near Albuquerque. They were on a pilgrimage to Las Vegas, New Mexico, celebrating. Daniel was wearing a new pair of cowboy boots—blisters—and Raymond had on a baseball cap dashingly cocked to the right. They hadn't slept in seventy-two hours, but when I took their picture they both smiled and flashed thumbs-up signs without a hint of irony. It seemed they couldn't believe they'd made it this far.

"We graduated!" Daniel said. "We're free! We're single! Well, kind of single. I got my chick back at home waiting for me."

They had so much to tell me, so much they wanted me to know. We stayed there for a while, three walkers on the interstate, and they recounted all the highlights. "I feel like I've touched God out here," Daniel said.

Thunderclouds were growing in the north, and I told the boys they might want to get off the highway so they could find some shelter. They dismissed the idea. They were wizard-walking, when internal faith somehow determines external reality, magically. Nothing could throw them off.

"We're not gonna get slammed with that today," Raymond said. "We only have twenty miles left. We almost made it. We'll get there. We'll get there as long as we keep thinking we'll get there."

I saw myself in the boys, my Pennsylvania self: the wild exuberance of starting something utterly unfamiliar. It'd been nearly eight months now, and a few hundred miles short of three thousand. I'd made it to New Mexico. I was about to turn twenty-four.

"Damn, look at his calves, man," Daniel said. "I know you've been out here way longer than us because of those things."

I kept doubting it, but something in me really was changing, something beyond the circumference of my calf muscles. I kind of felt like a grown-up around these boys; like a man, maybe. At least for a second. It got me thinking about my dad again.

I didn't remember much of my life from before my parents' separation. At first, it wasn't because I couldn't remember, but because I didn't care to. Memories have to be cared for, though, if they are to survive, and remembering is the only way to care for them. After I'd neglected them for long enough, my memories must've taken the hint and realized they weren't particularly wanted. Most of them decided to move on, make room for something else. Now, I just couldn't remember much from that time, even if I cared to. I hadn't lost them all, though. Some still lingered, stubbornly believing in their own worthiness. My first memory of Dad is from quite early, when I was three and he took me to the circus. We were sitting in the bleachers, maybe seven feet off the ground, and there was a little boy next to me. At the end of one of the acts this little boy pushed me backward and I fell to the ground. I'm underneath the bleachers on the wet, filthy concrete, and it's very dark. I look up to see Dad. He's lowering his sweater down to me so I can grab it and get hoisted up, but it's just beyond my grasp. Even if I could get it, I wouldn't be able to hold on. We're both trying so hard to reach each other, but it's not enough. The memory ends there.

From what I do remember of my childhood, I know that it was mostly a happy one, full of wonder. Gnomes lived hidden underground; fairies frolicked among the flowers, just out of sight. Before my sister was born, I'd spend hours playing outside, taken by the butterflies that sometimes landed on my shoulders, and then when Caitlin came, we'd make jungles out of all the houseplants by collecting them in one room, and we'd cushion the hallway with pillows, get a good running start, and try flying.

Despite the troubles they would eventually face, my parents created a very loving home for my siblings and me, in all of the apartments and houses we inhabited. They also created a rich environment for us: our kitchen was a revolving door for guests and friends, wherever we happened to be living. All manner of people sat at our table: Catholic priests and Hare Krishnas, activists and shamans, midwives and academics, journalists and artists. As a child, I got to hear all these conversations, and although I often didn't understand what was being said, I witnessed so many different forms of human communion.

I recently asked Dad what he remembers of the two of us from those early years.

"Well, you know I was there when you learned how to ride a bike, right?"

We were in the back alley of one of our apartments in Chicago. The memory begins in the middle of the ride. He's got his hands on the handlebars, running to keep up, and I'm rolling, rolling, and then softly he lets go without my even knowing it. I only realize I'm on my own when I hear him laughing and cheering a few feet behind me, and then his voice fades as I ride on, leaving him slowly behind.

"And I'd take you and Caitlin and Luke to the movies. That was kind of my thing, the movies. Just some time to have fun, you know, let your hair down."

We had to leave the house whenever Mom had a massage client, and that was when we spent most of our time with him. He'd take us to the movies or we'd go get Italian ices, sometimes both. With Dad, it was all about play. Mom was the one who insisted on keeping the TV in the closet, only to be taken out on very special occasions. Meanwhile, Dad took us out to the movies.

It's strange remembering those afternoons we had with Dad, knowing what I know now: that he was, in fact, very depressed, and that my mother was also suffering, and that the close-knit family I thought we had was mostly a facade. Reflecting back, it's hard not to see my parents' relationship as a toxic failure, which would make me the product of a toxic failure, perhaps even the catalyst of that toxicity. It's dramatic to put it that way, maybe, but it's a dramatic place, the subconscious mind. The whisper that's so easy to dismiss at the superficial level, but sticks somewhere deeper down: *If they hadn't had me, maybe it would've been better for them.* Perhaps this is why I don't have many memories of that time.

It's also why I preferred to focus on other peoples' lives in the conversations I had on the road. I didn't share much about my past with most people. Better to listen. That way, I wouldn't have to reenter the brokenness from which I came. And I wouldn't have to look at my own role in perpetuating that brokenness by my bitterness and shame, by my reluctance to accepting the reality of it. In deflecting the spotlight to others, I could hide from the task of sharing who I really was, my own story. In some interviews, I would actually shut off the recorder if the conversation turned to me, and then flip it back on when I was able to corral the attention back toward them. I would rationalize it to myself: *No need to waste any tape on my stuff. No one needs to hear this part.*

"Turn the lens on yourself," my professor told me when I was writing my senior thesis. It was some of the best advice I'd ever received—although I didn't know it at the time—because that type of inquiry, that unflinching gaze inward, that willingness to see whatever might be there and start working with it, that was the first step toward peace. "Not I, not any one else can travel that road for you," Whitman wrote. "You must travel it for yourself." How could I, though, if I couldn't stand to take a look in the mirror?

There was a moment in New Mexico when I realized, if only for a few seconds, that accepting my own story was the only way I was ever going to find peace, otherwise I'd be wandering forever, searching for an impossible something else.

I was in the Cerrillos Hills outside Santa Fe when a man in a cowboy hat pulled over in his pickup truck. He had a British accent and a big smile, and he said his wife had passed me earlier and wanted him to go investigate. They lived just down the road, and after chatting for a few minutes he said I could spend the night with them.

Archie Tew and Alexis Higginbotham were both in their early sixties. Their adobe house was tucked away in the scrubby hills far from the road, shielded by cedar trees. They had a fishpond in the back, and horses, a few dogs, and a gigantic tortoise. She was an artist, he a transformational consultant, and they were both meditators and yoga practitioners. They had a big Buddha statue in the kitchen, and Indian art, and immediately I felt at home. It was like a New Mexican version of my mom's house.

After a shower, I joined them out on the back porch and I interviewed them, asking for advice. They had such a calmness about them, a sense of peace and belonging, and I wanted that.

At dusk, Archie prepared dinner while Alexis and I continued to chat in the kitchen. He kept taking trips out to the porch to set the table, and by the time everything was ready, night had fallen. Alexis and I followed him outside, but when I saw the table I was confused. It was set as if for a feast, and the chair in the middle was a kind of throne. Flowers and candles surrounded the plate, and right in the center of the place setting, facing the throne, was a mirror.

"That's your seat," Archie said. "Take a good look."

I was shocked. I sat down, my reflection staring back at me, and for a few seconds, before the self-consciousness of my ego scrambled up the purity of the message—*Don't look at yourself in the mirror, you fucking narcissist!*—I understood what Archie was saying. It was simple: *I* was what I was looking for, not someone else, some teacher or lover or friend, some epic epiphany. Not some other version of myself, either. Just me, exactly as I was seeing myself now. There was nothing inside me to fix or get rid of. Nothing to add. "I exist as I am, that is enough," Whitman wrote. He had been saying it all along, and then some:

Why what have you thought of yourself?
Is it you then that thought yourself less?

Is it you that thought the President greater than you? or the
rich better off than you? or the educated wiser than you?
Because you are greasy or pimpled—or that you was once
drunk, or a thief, or diseased, or rheumatic, or a prostitute—
or are so now—or from frivolity or impotence—or that
you are no scholar, and never saw your name in print . . . do
you give in that you are any less immortal?

I sat in the throne at the feast, understanding, for a moment,
that it was only by knowing myself as worthy that I could cleanly
reflect back the worthiness of others, as Archie was doing for me
now, as Whitman has done for millions. I realized that so many of
my interactions had a subtle agenda: looking for affirmation,
seeking myself in everyone else, hoping someone might give me
the crown of acceptance. But I had to accept myself, and until I
finally did, I'd always feel unacceptable, no matter how many
crowns I was given. And the only way to do it was to sit down and
take a good look in the mirror, until the mirror wasn't necessary
anymore. *Turn the lens on yourself.*

And then we started eating and admiring the stars, and the
significance of the lesson began to fade. I'd have to learn it again
many more times. I'm still learning it five years later. Apparently
it's a long walk to peace.

ARCHIE TEW, *transformational consultant*
THE CERRILLOS HILLS, NEW MEXICO, *out on his back porch*
over a rolling expanse of golden dirt, cedar, and sagebrush
JUNE

"I was a little middle-class English boy that was told, 'No, you can't go to drama school because you're not mature enough yet. Go and grow up.' That's what they said to me. 'Go and grow up.' So I said, 'I'll go to Africa and be in the Peace Corps. That's what I'll do.' The thing is, I never knew how I was going to grow up. I didn't know what was going to come at me."

"So what's the gorilla story?"

"Well, we were looking for gorillas so we went into Rwanda. Never seen any before. The gorillas, when they live in dense jungle they create tunnels through the underbrush, and we had to go down the tunnels. I was told that if we ever confronted a gorilla, that you can't run. They said, 'You make a face and you stand as tall as you can and you just go "GAAAA!"' And I thought, 'Well, that's not going to happen because we're not going to see any damn gorillas anyway.'

"So we're going down these alleyways in the jungle and sure enough, of course, I meet a gorilla. The gorilla comes towards me— huge, HUGE, hunking thing walking right towards me. In the moment I'm going, 'Okay, so this is it, right? Either I do it or I don't.' And it was intense because the gorilla saw me and it just grew big like this, and then he started his, 'HHUUHH!' and then I just stood there like some clown and went, 'HAAAAA!' It was funny, because he went like,

'Huh?' It was almost like he was saying, 'I got it. You know how to communicate with me. You're actually doing the right thing. That's cool. All right, I'll let you go.'

"Here's the deal on this, for me: Once you really understand the true authentic power you have, there's no need to prove it. There's no need to say, 'I need to kill you to show you how strong I am.' The only reason we kill or we hurt is out of fear. But if you have knowledge of your own power, if you have knowledge of your intrinsic self, and who you are, and you have nothing to prove, then there's no reason to hurt. All you can do is love. That's what I learned from the animals. That gorilla knew it had power over me. It knew it could kill me, but there was no need to prove it to me. And by the way, I wasn't even threatening it. My pathetic attempt at trying to show him that I was something stronger than I was? I knew in his head he was going, 'You look like a complete nutcase, but cool, I'm going away, because I can do you and you wouldn't even know it.' Because there was no reason he had to walk away."

Chapter Twenty-One

"These days are gone."

My high school friend Tolly came to walk with me for three days outside Albuquerque through the Pueblo Indian reservations. We had been paired as roommates for our freshman year at boarding school. His parents had separated that summer, just like mine had, and so we'd grown very close. Tolly knew me so well he could make me laugh on command, effortlessly. When he flew out to meet me, he'd just graduated from college, unsure of what was next. He was taller than I was now, and bigger, but he was also a tenderfoot, so he had a hard time keeping up. We traveled about sixty-five miles in three days. Watching him adjust to the discomforts, I realized I wasn't as clueless as I used to be. I was a little more patient, a little more tolerant of the pain and the filth, the slowness and the unknown.

I'd never walked through reservation land before, however, and that made me nervous. Were non-natives allowed? I didn't know anything about tribal law, and I was worried we might get arrested. Tolly would probably love that, as it would give him excellent fodder for complaining.

Walking together, I felt a bit like a babysitter. I carried Tolly's backpack for him, and I made sure he had enough water. After walking for eight months, I'd forgotten how hard it could be. At the end of the first day we'd only walked seventeen miles but Tolly was dying. We reached a gas station and he collapsed on the cement, his face chalk white. He said he was on the verge of throwing up, which I took as the perfect opportunity to shoot a video for our friends back home.

"Tolly, what's going on?"

"Not much. Fucking terrorist over here made me walk for-fucking-ever."

"Tell me what happened today."

"Well, my feet fell off. So, other than that, yeah. To all you saying seventeen miles isn't bad? It's not. But on the fucking highway it's awful. And it's a fucking hundred degrees out. Terrorist plans. Terrorist idea."

"So what's the plan for the rest of the night, Tolly?"

"The plan is to go get fat at the local gas station, and then to dress my wounds, which are plentiful, and then to pass the fuck out. Well, after pillow talk. There will be much pillow talk."

We got permission from a Pueblo police officer to camp out on the side of the highway. He didn't seem to think it was a big deal, which made me feel a little better about crossing the rest of the reservation. Tolly and I snuggled up in my tent, almost on top of each other. Our pillow talk that night was just like it used to be, and I drifted to sleep chuckling, amazed by the experience of friendship, how its changes in form do not change its nature, that fundamental magnetism that brought you both together before you even knew anything about each other.

At the end of the second day, Tolly was on the brink of physical and psychological collapse. We made it to an overpass after twenty-three miles, where we finally stopped. Tolly sat down, making a weird squealing sound when he hit the gravel. I shot another video.

"What just happened?"

"Sitting down. That's what just happened. I just sat down and it was one of the greatest efforts of my life."

"What happened today?"

"Today we walked twenty-three miles, which is six more than yesterday. And it felt like six more. I'm going to have to amputate."

"Tolly brought *cotton* socks . . ."

"Go fuck yourself, these socks are great."

". . . And he brought *cotton* underwear."

"It's not like it's the fucking Arctic, all right? There's no water anywhere. It's just fine."

". . . Tolly also blew half a dozen tires on my stroller today . . ."

". . . Minus half a dozen."

". . . And he broke the entire zipper of my tent . . ."

"Well, yeah. That's true. I did do that."

"What else did you do? He ruined me. Tolly ruined me."

"I did way worse stuff. I just can't remember right now."

"So what's the plan for tomorrow, Tolly?"

"The plan for tomorrow is to walk three miles. Stuff our faces. Walk another three. Stuff them some more. Then walk the rest of, what, the nine miles to a casino and lie out in the pool and be fat and sleep in beds and probably pass out before we even gamble. That's the plan. It's a beautiful plan. Flawless. Yeah, there was nothing in between the last place and here. Not a gas station. Nothing. There were two bridges, which provided the only shade we had all day, and we stopped under those. But right now, the place we made it to, there still hasn't been anything. So tomorrow, finally, there's going to be a gas station that serves breakfast apparently. That's three miles away, and then three miles after that there's a Dairy Queen, and I'm going to get a banana split and a large fucking Blizzard and I don't care what anyone thinks."

"Any parting words?"

"I have at least five goat-heads in my ass. Good-bye."

The goat-heads were everywhere. They were these hard, spiny burs from a plant called puncture vine, perfectly designed by evolution to destroy inflatable stroller tires. Bob didn't stand a chance.

Before we could set up the tent, a pickup truck pulled off the road and stopped right next to us. An elderly man and woman got out, offering us a grocery bag full of grilled corn and fruit—leftovers from a ceremony, they said. Their names were Pat and Jan Dyea, and they were a part of the Laguna Pueblo tribe. I explained what I was doing, and told them how Tolly was here to keep me company for a bit. I could feel Tolly watching the entire interaction unfold, absorbing it—one of his first encounters with people on the road—and after just a few minutes Pat said we could spend the night at their place. I was thrilled, because now Tolly would get to experience it, too: the kindness of strangers, the remarkable intimacy of spending an evening sharing with one another.

The Dyeas' house was nestled at the bottom of a bloodred mesa, dripping with gypsum. Outside: lava rocks and cedar trees, sagebrush and tumbleweeds, swallows flying through the sepia light of sunset. Lightning kept striking in the distance, and then a rainbow bloomed on the horizon. We walked inside, the Miami Heat battling the Oklahoma City Thunder in the NBA finals on TV—small potatoes, compared to the scene outside.

"You should bring the La-Z-Boy out there and watch the real show," Jan said. "And you can see the highway from here, too, just barely. That's what my parents used to do, used to pull out two chairs and just sit there and count the trucks."

We all sat down at the table, where Jan laid out some more leftovers. Both she and Pat put aside a few spoonfuls of their food, which remained untouched. "It's for the spirits," Pat explained. "It's inviting them in to eat, and us saying thank you."

Jan told us that Pat was a dancer in their ceremonies throughout the year. Most of these were closed to outsiders, non-natives. The dancers would go for hours, often in the high heat. "I love watching him dance," Jan said, rubbing his back. It was a form of prayer for all people, she said, and an expression of gratitude.

"When we have our doings," Pat said, "that's what we sacrifice ourselves for. For the people. It doesn't matter the color. It's just for everybody. And you always put yourself last, at the end. You put the people, the land, the animals first. In our ceremonies, that's how it is. You lose sleep. It's hot. You're sweaty. Ugh! Sometimes you feel like you just want to get out. But if you really are sincere, all this doesn't take effect or bother you until it's over. Then you realize the tiredness.

"Just like for you, at the end of the day, you're tired. But if you put these things into prayer, it's gonna mean a lot more for what you're doing, instead of just walking. As you're walking you can say, 'This is for them. I'm doing this for you. I'm sacrificing myself for you people, so you can have a better life.' Something like that, it would be good. Because you're out there walking and it's a lot! It takes a lot out of you. You're thirsty. You're hot. You're sweating. That's really something. That's sacrificing for people. I know you started out not thinking of that in mind, but now, from here to California, use that. Just to pray for somebody. Anybody. Because prayer does a lot for all of us. We have to keep praying. I think that's the greatest thing we can do for each others, is pray for each others."

I'd unwittingly done that a few times already, dedicate a certain day's walk to a particular person. It lent a different kind of richness to the miles, and it coupled my pain with a purpose greater than myself. Even if that coupling was just imagined, it did have an effect. I often felt stronger on those walks, more committed, and sometimes the recipients were very moved. I gave twenty-three miles to one woman in Louisiana after she shared a very painful story from her past, and she was so touched that she told the local newspaper about it. "I couldn't believe someone would do that for anyone," she said. "God sent him our way for a reason. I'm just still wowed." It was such a small thing for me to do, but far more often than not, I'd forget to make these dedications and just get lost in my own little walk. I told Pat I'd try to remember more often. He took off one of his seashell bracelets and gave it to me.

"I use that in ceremonies," he said. "When you go home you'll have to tell everyone you got that from a great Indian chief."

"You're in the Parrot clan, right?" I said—he'd told me earlier. "I'll say that Chief Parrot gave it to me. Chief Flying Parrot."

"More like Chief Lying Parrot," he said. Jan laughed and rubbed his back again.

Tolly and I shot one more video for our friends before he left. It was the night before my birthday, and we were staying in a casino—Tolly's treat. Toward the end of the video, I asked him what he'd learned from the road, and he dropped his standard sarcasm for a second.

"I decided I was here 'walking to share,' that is, share Andrew's experience, and I learned a lot. I see why he's doing this. You know, it's as much for other people as it is for him. So, yeah, it was special to do this. Really glad I came out."

It was the same sincere voice I often heard in our pillow talk. His parting words, however, on how he felt about finishing up his stint as a pedestrian on the highway were as salty as ever: "The walking is over for me. Forever. I'll never walk again. It's a dry casino here, but as far as I know they still serve soda so I will be getting drunk off that . . . And if you ever see a semi truck, blow it up. That's about all I have to say about those."

Tolly got a ride back to Albuquerque the next day. It was my birthday. I spent it walking alone on I-40. After traveling with a buddy for a few days, I'd forgotten how to do it on my own. I relapsed into angst and loneliness, projecting all my fear onto the wind. It was whooshing right into me, absolutely relentless. At first I spoke gently to it, like I was cajoling an infant. "Shh, you don't have to blow so hard." When that didn't work, I tried reason. "Come on, you must be exhausted. You should take a break." I tried charming it. I tried trickery. But the wind didn't give a shit about me. Finally, I started screaming. I had no control.

"Do not go gentle into that New Mexican headwind," Dylan Thomas could've written. "Rage, rage against that bastard." It didn't have quite the same ring to it, but it shared a certain spirit. The headwind really wasn't so different from death after all: inexorable and indifferent. That was my birthday gift from the road, the reminder that I'd be dead someday. By this point I'd really started to fixate on death, so anything might remind me of it, or seem like an omen. When Bob blew another tire, a million quivering nerve ribbons unraveled inside.

When I got to Grants that night, I was jittery and hollow. I booked myself a room at a Motel 6, bought some chips and salsa at a gas station, and watched *Titanic* on TV. It was not the delicious kind of solitude, not at all. It was the kind of solitude that made me want to give up.

I had to snap myself out of it, or else I might never leave the motel. *Titanic* wasn't helping. I shut it off and got out my laptop to listen to an interview I'd done with an old cowboy preacher in Melrose, New Mexico, not far from Texas. His name was Otho Rogers, and he was the most natural-born storyteller I'd ever met. He and his wife, Kay, had taken me in after some friends passed me on. They fed me green chile stew and biscuits, and Otho spun yarns in his living room about all the cowboying he'd done. But now, depressed in the Motel 6, it was his talk about aging and death that I wanted to hear, for some perspective. I found the interview and fast-forwarded to the best part.

"You were saying before that you can't do some of the things you used to be able to do?" I heard myself say in the recording. Weird, to hear my voice, so comfortable in that living room with good human company. If I were to speak aloud now, it would sound different.

"Oh, yeah, and it breaks my heart, too," Otho said. "To put your foot up in a stirrup and just step up on a horse? I can't do that anymore. And it's embarrassing to go lead a horse to a fence and get up on the fence and then get on the horse. I hate to give up my independence thataway. Dependent upon a fence to get me on a horse. That's dumb.

"I was satisfied doing what I did, because I always tried to be the best hand in the pasture or the best hand in the pen. I could do the work. I could pick sick cattle and I could doctor them. But as far as wishing I could do it again, sure I do. I wish I didn't get old. I wish my body would do what I tell it to."

"The reason I ask is because, you know, God willing I'll be there someday, too, an old man . . ."

"I understand. So get all the best you can out of your youth— your strength, your body, and your mind. While you got the time. Because it hadn't been, I don't know, the day before yesterday or something that I was in my twenties. It just goes by. Whenever you're young and you're waiting to get sixteen to get your driver's license, the years go by kind of like high-line poles. And then you get that, and you get out and you go to work and all that stuff, and then they get a little faster. They get like fence posts. Pretty soon, you get up to sixty-five years old, and things change in your life so much so drastically, of putting your feet where you want them and your body where it needs to be, it's gone. And time goes by like . . . like cross ties on a railroad track. Just chh, chh, chh, chh, chh. These days are gone. So while you got it, use it. Your mind. Your strength. Your agility. Use it.

"Yeah, if I could call back forty years . . . I'm looking forward to going to heaven, and I wouldn't want to go through all my youth again, but I miss what I could do. I miss it. If I got ten more years in me that'll be plenty. I'll be eighty-three. I don't want to live past eighty-three. I don't want to be where somebody would have to take care of me, or lead me around, or I'm slobbering on my belly in a rest home somewhere from a stroke. I'd rather a horse fall on me and break my neck. I really would.

"You come back through here ten years from now, I may be around and I may not. If I ain't, it's all right. I've had a good life. You're what, twenty-three? Seventy-three looks pretty old. That's fifty years difference, son. Fifty years makes a lot of difference. But I relate. I can remember twenty-three."

I was now twenty-four. I could walk thirty-five miles in a day, sleep it off, and then start it up again the next morning. My body had no problem with that, and most of the time my mind didn't, either. But the years were already going by like fence posts, and I believed Otho when he said they'd only get faster. The walk was speeding up, too. I was almost in Arizona. Soon, I might even make it to the Pacific. I felt considerable ambivalence about that, the end of my walk. Actually, ambivalence might not be strong enough. Sometimes I felt outright dread at the prospect of the end. Because during the past couple months I had, in a half-literal sense, come to think of the walk as my life, and of the end of the walk as a kind of death. In my rational mind I knew I wasn't going to die when I stopped walking. But during my many hours of solitude, that's how it started to feel: like I was facing death, trudging toward it, even. And wasn't I? Weren't we all? At the same time, it didn't seem possible that I'd actually get there, that it would ever really end— my walk, or my life.

In any case, after listening to Otho that night, it didn't seem so sad to be spending my birthday alone in a Motel 6. It was actually kind of funny. On the metric of existential angst, it was a paltry joke compared to what Otho was thinking about these days.

ALEXIS HIGGINBOTHAM, *artist*
THE CERRILLOS HILLS, NEW MEXICO, *in her kitchen*
JUNE

"There's the genuine person that you are that's free of artifice, free of thinking about what you think is the appropriate way to present yourself. The you that is not self-conscious about the way you look. That only exists in fragments, because trying to maintain your true self is really hard when people are constantly telling you that you're not good enough. So, those moments when you can be your true self, those split-second moments when your judgment voice doesn't come in, your presumption voice, your regret voice, or any of those voices—they don't enter into the picture. It's, 'I am experiencing a genuine moment that's not colored by anything.' I think you know what I'm talking about. Those are those moments when you're on the road, and you're trucking down, and it's just you and your feet. You're not anyone's son, cousin, brother. It's just you. That moment where you're not trying to impress anyone, you're not trying to fool yourself. It's just those brief glimpses of just being your genuine self. For me, that has been my life's goal, to be as true to myself as I can be."

Chapter Twenty-Two

"He's very happy being a rock."

Walking in the desert of Arizona emptied me, a simple blankness impossible to describe using words, which fill rather than empty. The heat melted tons of bullshit from my mind. The dry drained the swamps inside. The sky seemed to lend its own expanse for the unfolding of my own. There was no escape from the nothingness: no trees to hide me, no buildings to break the wind, nobody to carry me. My feet gathered grit throughout the day, and when I took off my sandals at the end I had a film of salt covering them, covering all of me. My skin cracked, not unlike the earth, and I turned an even darker shade of brown, just like the rest of this place. I was burning like everything else here, too, an aura on the road shimmering in heat. "There's nothing out here," lots of people said— thunderheads appearing from nothing, green-silver sagebrush growing from nothing, wind blowing from nothing, and I, too, born out of the same. "Is today nothing?" Whitman wrote, "Is the beginningless past nothing? / If the future is nothing they are just as surely nothing." Lots of nothing in Arizona. Or maybe it was boundless, infinite everything.

I stopped journaling so much, and my blog entries slowed. I recorded fewer interviews. I shot fewer photographs. Remembering everything became secondary to just living it. I sat under one overpass for a few hours, hidden, watching the cars flow by. Another day, under a different overpass, a man named George stopped and said,

"I'm living life. I'm old, so I figure what the hell, why not? I sing in the car and I dance around everywhere. I do it so I'm not so sad." I'd spot prairie dogs in the distance scampering over their underground homes, and I'd watch them for a while, silent and still.

Today, when I forget what I've learned and the questions start itching all over me again, I try to get back to the blankness of Arizona, the space in between the words. The kind of walking I fell into there was called beauty-walking, I discovered later, in the Navajo Nation: it was a state of clarified connection, after my body and mind had been so exhausted that there wasn't much strength left to hold up the heavy misperception of being a barricaded individual existing on his own, that burdensome belief that I was an isolated self, somehow separate from everything else. Atlas finally collapsing under the globe. Beauty-walking. It was quite like what that elderly walker Jerry Priddy called the white time. *You can't see anything and you're not aware of anything, and it's going on around you. It don't amount to a whole lot, but the sum total is it's a beautiful experience when you get through. It clears your head. You're there.* Beauty-walking, I was just there, without interpretation or analysis, without imposition or manipulation, and that felt a bit like not being there at all. Not being there at all, it was impossible for me to be against anything, even the headwinds. I was with everything. Beauty-walking was one of my absolute favorites. Whenever it came, all I could say was thank you.

Before reaching the Navajo reservation, I'd accidentally traced the route of the Long Walk across New Mexico. In the winter of 1864, the United States government forced thousands of Navajo people to march more than four hundred miles to a relocation camp outside Fort Sumner. I couldn't imagine the pain, just couldn't see it. It was too great to see, too different from my own experience. I'd enjoyed walking those miles, but I was young and it was summer and no one was making me do it. Grandmothers and grandfathers suffered the Long Walk in the freezing cold, and children and pregnant women. There were no highways to make the miles easier. There were no gas stations where they could buy ice cream sandwiches. There were, however, American soldiers who might shoot them if they fell behind. Hundreds died, God knows how gruesomely. I tried to imagine these scenes on the road, but the dissonance between their past and my present was far too vast. I saw only the unspeaking land. It shared nothing of what it knew, and so I could only wonder what it thought about us humans, having watched us for millennia, about how terribly we've always treated one another. "Dumb animals," the land might say, shaking its head if it had one. "Really fucking dumb."

I'd never heard of the Long Walk before—we didn't cover it in any of my American History classes—and as I prepared to cross into the Navajo Nation I realized I knew next to nothing about the tribe. I hadn't had any problems on the Pueblo reservation, but maybe Navajo people were different. I was a white man: the White Man. The people who'd driven the Navajo like cattle across the cold high desert looked just like I did. Routes 264 and 89 ran more than two hundred miles across Navajo and Hopi land. It'd be better than walking on I-40, but still, I was concerned my white face might be an unwelcome sight.

In the Navajo Nation, the land was living. A kind of sentience stirred in the stands of piñon pine and juniper. The rock especially appeared to be alive, watching me walk, listening to my footsteps. Looking out at the horizon, it filled up half the frame. The other half was sky.

The sky, here and everywhere, seemed outside of time, immeasurable, but the rock in this place was deep within time, the recorder of antiquity. There was sandstone from the Cretaceous, limestone from the Permian, Pliocene basalt, and Jurassic mudstone, all of it harboring a planetful of memory. Here in the Holocene Era, I was walking on asphalt made of petroleum, which was made of things that had once been alive: zooplankton and algae. I was walking on the labors of time, the shape-shifting flux. In it, I felt I was nothing, a tiny zooplankton destined, perhaps, to become a particle in the highways of tomorrow's apex species. It was hard to escape the fact of my insignificance in that bare expanse, and the terrible brevity of my turn here. There was a kind of beauty in that brevity, though: that existence, mine and the world's, would be exactly like this for just one quick blink, never to take this form again.

Ten miles from Window Rock, the small capital city of the Navajo Nation, James and Chris Paisano pulled over on the highway to give me a grocery bag of Snickers bars. I hadn't expected this at all. Back in Gallup, New Mexico, before I crossed into the reservation and Arizona, I'd been warned about walking on Highway 264 because of all the drunk drivers. One Latino guy told me that diluted hairspray was a popular drink among some Navajo people. They called it "ocean water," he said, and they drank mouthwash, too. This kind of talk had fed my fear, but as soon as I got to the reservation, I met James and Chris. They said they'd seen me a week earlier outside Albuquerque, slogging along on I-40, and seeing me again here, just a few miles from their home, they figured I could probably use some candy. I spent the next eighteen hours with them.

James was in his seventies. He wore eyeglasses with the slightest yellow tint. He was forthcoming and frank, and spoke with calm enthusiasm about most things. His son Chris was in his forties but seemed younger, the way he laughed so easily, his levity. They both practiced a traditional form of Navajo spirituality that was slowly getting forgotten, they said, as the generations passed.

Chris had just moved back to the reservation from Washington, D.C., in order to live with his father because his mother had died recently. James missed her. He was lonely. He and Rhoda had been married for forty-seven years, together for fifty-five.

"We were never really separated," James told me later that night. "We were always together. We had a good life. I really enjoyed her. I miss her very, very much. It's difficult even now because it's only been a year and a few months, but I'm glad Chris is out here with me."

Chris and James chatted with me on the roadside for a while. I still had a couple hours to Window Rock, but I didn't want the conversation to end.

"I should probably hit the road," I said eventually, "but I'll be in town tonight and I'd love to talk some more."

A few hours later, the Paisanos met me in Window Rock. The town's name came from a giant red rock formation with a dramatic hole in the middle of it. Chris and James treated me to dinner at the Quality Inn—Navajo tacos—and then they took me for a ride into the back canyons off the highway, where James had grown up. He pointed out the cliffs he used to climb as a kid and the little hiding places he'd find among the rocks. Cows roamed the roads in front of us, and stray dogs, and the riverbanks were thick with cedar and elm, cottonwood and Russian olive. We drove up into the mountains where the ponderosa pines took over, and where James and Rhoda used to gather piñon nuts before she died.

"Why can't we pick piñons by shaking the tree?" Chris said to me later, explaining the traditional Navajo perspective. "It's easier to do that. Well, we don't do it because bears do it. A bear is a very powerful being, so you're sort of insulting a bear by doing what bears do. And because of that, you harm yourself."

Sometimes Chris and James spoke to each other in Navajo, a beautiful language that also seemed impossible, at once guttural and punctuated by glottal stops, but at the same time smooth. To me, it sounded like a mix of French, Arabic, and Mandarin. I couldn't pronounce anything right.

We cruised back down onto the plains where James had hunted prairie dogs as a young man. The hunters would gather together after they'd killed their share of the prey. They'd burn off the fur, bury the carcasses, build a fire over the grave, and then they'd have roasted prairie dog. We drove on, the chapters of James's life narrating the landscape around us: two nearby mountains called the King and the Queen. A stone arch where the medicine men used to gather to perform ceremonies. A canyon where his grandmother's grandmother's grandmother's mother had lived.

His knowledge of place, and of his place within that place, dizzied me. He knew, down to the specific canyon, where he'd come from and where he'd been, and all of it informed where he was now, driving over it and through it and calling it by its many names. I didn't have that kind of intimate knowledge about my ancestral origins, nor about any place in the world, and that never used to bother me; but hearing James describe his home, seeing how completely he belonged here, I felt that absence as a loss, as if I'd been orphaned long ago but only just realized it.

I rode in the backseat of the pickup truck, listening and seeing quite differently than I would have if I'd been on my own.

"It's going to be hard for you," James said at one point, about what it would be like to return home, "because you've seen so many other things which will probably change you. They say you can never go back to being who you were before. Hopefully when something like this happens to us, we become better people, not going the other direction. Hopefully all the good things you've seen, you'll adapt that into your personal life as you grow older and older. And hopefully you'll take the lessons of talking to people and you'll be a very, very good person. A lot of times that's hard to do, because there are so many distractions."

"I think also a lot of the lessons that you've learned probably won't make sense until you're older," Chris said, driving the pickup. "I think that's one thing I've learned, getting older. I'm not saying I've learned everything or I'm wise or whatever, but I do know, hopefully, that I've become much smarter than I was when I was in my twenties. I'm like, 'Oh, you were stupid.'" He laughed. "But now I've learned a little bit better."

The Paisanos lived in a little house just outside the village of Fort Defiance, a few miles north of Window Rock and Highway 264. Chris drove us there, and when we arrived and stepped outside, the quiet was overwhelming. It was bone dry, but Chris still kept a garden. His corn wasn't as high as it ought to be, because of the drought, but his prayers for rain were answered that night. The sky opened up lightly at twilight, and James said I could spend the night in their living room if I wanted.

We sat together there that night, the front door cracked open because of the heat. I interviewed James and Chris. It was here that I realized just how deeply James was still grieving his wife. If I didn't ask questions that took the conversation elsewhere, she was all he talked about.

"She collected mice. Oh, she was a little mouse lover! Not real mice. The little figurines. She has boxes and boxes. She loved bags, purses, and mice. She liked to go to casinos. One thing I liked to do with her when we were traveling: 'Rhoda, have you ever been this way?' 'No.' 'Let's go!' 'Okay!' We'd just take off and drive someplace. Just go, go, go. We'd get there when we'd get there. I just wish my wife was here so we could go out and enjoy these things."

"It's something that's hard for me to imagine," I said to James, sitting next to him on the couch, "only being twenty-four. It's something I . . . Yeah, how do you move on? How do you heal?"

"Tell you the truth, I haven't yet," he said. "It's just a matter of day after day after day. I try to keep busy doing these things around the house here."

"It's interesting to think that at any point in life there can be new beginnings," I said. I was trying to find some kind of silver lining. I didn't know how to witness his grief and just let it be. "You have no choice but to have a new beginning now, and in some way, I think that's kind of exciting, almost. With any beginning there's an ending, and that's sad, of course, but—"

James interrupted me, laughing a little bit.

"I haven't gotten to that point, 'something exciting,' but I'm keeping busy, and Chris is planting out here, and slowly we're coming to the point where I guess you might say there might be a new beginning. But it hasn't really started yet, because I still miss my wife. It's really hard. It's kind of hard to go out somewhere and talk to people. Maybe people consider me more reserved now than I was before, because everywhere we went, we went together. I imagine she didn't want to go. She still had her whole life, her family, her home, everything. I don't think she wanted to. I don't think anybody that dies wants to, but we don't know that either, because when it happens, we're still over here on this side. So, the living part of you just has to keep on going."

I shut up about new beginnings after that.

There was one more question I wanted to ask before we all went to sleep. I'd started seeing a phrase written on signs and stickers in the outer orbit of the Navajo reservation: *Hózhó náhásdlíí'*. I'd seen it translated as "Walk in beauty." I asked Chris what it meant.

"*Hózhó* is one of those words that's really difficult to translate," he said. "It's not 'beauty' as in something that's pretty. It's really a condition in your mind. It's like yin and yang. It's when everything that you are, you *are* balance. Everything is the way it's supposed to be. There's a right amount of rain. There's enough snow. It's not too cold. In your mind you're not thinking horrible thoughts. You're living your life in the way that you're supposed to be, that the good Lord, the Creator had meant you to be, who you're supposed to be. And that's what *hózhó* is. It is the ultimate goal of what Navajo people strive for. It's what all of our Navajo ceremonies are for, to get back to *hózhó*, to get to that place where you are content and alive and balanced with yourself and everything around you. And it's something I struggle with every day."

He laughed here, at himself, at his struggle, and James jumped in:

"With you right now, it would be like you have shoes to walk in, your body's strong, and you have a goal that you want to go to and you're happy going there. And when you get there you're saying, 'Oh, this feels so good. This is so nice.' You might not have anything to own, but you, yourself, are feeling well. You, yourself, you're walking in balance. You're walking in happiness. Maybe sometimes you feel that way when you're walking. You look around you, everything's happy. You might not have enough to drink. Your shoes might be worn out. But you, yourself, inside of you, you're feeling well, and you're happy. That's what *hózhó* is.

"Everything on this earth is like us," he continued. "It has a life. It has a being. Even a rock. A rock is what it's supposed to be. He might've fallen off another bigger rock, but he's a rock, and he's very happy being a rock. He's in *hózhó*, because *he is what he's supposed to be.* Whether he disappears today or stays forever, he's a rock and he loves it. Everything has a way of saying, 'This is what I am and I belong to the earth.' We can think and we can talk and everything else, but we are also a part of that. Everything depends on something else. This little rock? He depends on the big rock where he fell from. And he's giving shelter to the ant down there. An ant is an ant. He's happy being what he is, because he has shelter, he has food, and he has a home, and he has a way, and he's an ant, and that's what he is. He's happy. He's *hózhó*."

"If you know why things are," Chris said, "and if you know how to respect the things that are outside you, then you can walk *hózhó* because you know the rules. You know where to go. You know how to travel in life. You recognize there's something larger than you out there, and you respect it. And we're trying to reach that. That's *hózhó*. And it's a struggle, like I said. I haven't reached it yet."

I wish I'd asked the Paisanos a few more questions: How does a rock know he's a rock, and how does he then know how to be a rock? How can I say, "This is what I am," if I'm not exactly sure? How am I supposed to know "why things are"? How does my uncertainty change the way I belong? How do I find the beauty way if I've lost it? Will I ever really walk in beauty? Am I walking in beauty right now?

Later, I took out Rilke to see what he might have to say about it. He just threw it back at me, as always:

> There is no one anywhere who can answer for you those questions and feelings which, in their depths, have a life of their own; for even the most articulate people are unable to help, since what words point to is so very delicate, is almost unsayable.

Whitman had a verse for this, too: "All architecture is what you do to it when you look upon it; / Did you think it was in the white or gray stone? or the lines of the arches and cornices?"

All right, all right, I thought, *I get it, I get it: the answers are mine to see for myself.* But still, they seemed so elusive. They seemed to be outside somewhere, in the architecture, certainly not in my own vision, and since everything outside was constantly changing, the answers were like the shape-shifting skin walkers that were said to haunt the hills of the Navajo Nation. The skin walkers could transform into whatever they wanted: coyotes and foxes, eagles and owls. They could even transform into a specific person, if that person looked one dead in the eyes. Skin walkers could not be caught. It seemed the answers were no different: shape-shifters transforming with each new moment, just barely out of reach. If only I could get one to look me dead in the eyes.

James and Chris prayed for me the next morning at dawn. Their people used to do what I was doing, they said. They'd be walking with me now. Chris sprinkled corn pollen into the wind as an offering to "the good Lord, the Creator," murmuring Navajo words I didn't understand. He gave me a medicine pouch he'd made for me, for protection, and then they both dropped me off where they'd picked me up.

"We'll see you soon," James said after we hugged good-bye. They were going to meet me down the road in a few days and take me to a Hopi ceremony.

I was walking west on Highway 264 through Window Rock when I saw a man up ahead, also walking west. He was wearing skateboard shoes and a polo shirt striped purple and black. His dark hair fell down to his shoulders, Jesus-style. He had a backpack. I didn't think anything of it until I pulled up alongside him and saw that he, too, was a young white kid. This surprised me, as I hadn't seen a single white face since entering the reservation.

"What's going on, man?" I said.

"Oh, hi," he said. His build was slight, almost a child's. From his cracked lips, I would've guessed he'd been walking for a long time, but his skin suggested otherwise; it was blanched a bloodless white. He was carrying a single gallon of water, half-empty. This, too, told me he was just beginning; if he'd known what he was doing, he'd have a full gallon, even two. The desert didn't forgive poor planning.

I asked him why he was walking, and he said he'd just gotten off the bus from Austin, and that he was heading to the Hopi reservation.

"But why?" I asked.

"Because I'm delusional," he said, after a pause. At this, a rapid-fire succession of scenes flashed through my mind, predictions of what was going to happen in the next few miles. None of them looked good. The kid didn't appear to be delusional, though. He seemed to be quite normal, and I told him that.

"Yeah, it's a long story, man," he said.

"Well, I'm walking to listen." I showed him my sign.

"Basically, I think I'm the messiah," he said. "There are these Hopi prophecies that say a leader will come, the great white brother or something, and I think it's me. I'm not a bleeding heart or anything, or a savior. Just a leader."

We were coming up on a gas station. James and Chris had called a Navajo radio crew to let them know I was walking through the reservation, and two reporters had come to interview me. They were waiting in the parking lot where the kid and I met them. The kid went into the gas station to fill up on water, and then he came back out and joined us. There was nothing to do about it: He was walking west. I was walking west. We were going to walk together.

"It must be kind of arrogant or egotistical," the kid continued once we were on the road again. Window Rock was slowly disappearing behind us. "It has to be. I know that. But I'm pretty sure I'm the one. I don't normally tell people about this, though. I don't like to, because they think I'm crazy."

The kid was from a big family of half-brothers, half-sisters, and step-siblings. He'd gone to art school, hoping to study graffiti, but he'd left after a while. No one knew he was out here. He was fresh off the bus. He had no sunscreen. He wasn't carrying enough water. And, to top it off, he was walking straight into the desert convinced he was the great white brother. It wasn't a good way to make friends, and he was going to need friends if he wanted to survive.

"It feels like all of my interactions are so selfish," the kid said. I bit and asked why. "Because I know someday I'm going to have to enslave and master all y'all, so it's selfish of me to just be with you and pretend like nothing's gonna happen. I don't know if I'll be able to do it, though. Have you ever read Psalm One Hundred Ten? I don't know if I could do that." The kid got out a Bible later on and flipped to the passage. One excerpt stood out: "The Lord is at your right hand; he will shatter kings on the day of his wrath. He will execute judgment among the nations; filling them with corpses; He will shatter chiefs over the wide earth."

"Yeah, that'd be tough, man," I said. "Glad it's not me." We were far into the outskirts of Window Rock now, slowly heading up into the ponderosa pines of a low mountain. It was just the two of us.

"Hey, what's your name again?" he asked me. "I have a hard time remembering names. I had to ask a girl her name twenty or thirty times at this party once. Eventually she stopped telling me and just glared at me. It was pretty embarrassing. I was a little drunk and high, so, you know."

We kept walking, and talking. Savior complex aside, the kid was quite normal. I actually enjoyed the conversation when we weren't discussing his future plans, so I spoke to him that way, as if there were nothing wrong.

"Well, I'm glad you're on the road," I said at one point. "It'll teach you a lot. You'll learn more than you ever would've thought."

"Yeah, people say that," he said. "But I have my mission. I have my calling. Maybe that's sad, but it is what it is."

The day's hike was going to be a twenty-eight-miler for me. Ray Tsosie, the director of the Navajo radio station, had offered to put me up when I reached Ganado, the next town over. There was no way I was going to miss out on that. There was also no way I was going to stay with the kid. I didn't want people to think I was his disciple or something. I told him I had to get going, that I was walking across America alone.

"What, you're just gonna speed up?" he said. It was a good point. How do you leave someone in the dust when you're both walking? The good-bye would be extended over several awkward minutes. But the kid had no idea how hard it was to walk on the highway with a backpack in the summer heat of Arizona. At that point, I'd earned my calluses, and I had Bob to carry my stuff. I knew how to be on the road, and my feet knew how to walk. He wouldn't be able to keep up.

"Pretty much," I said. "I'm sorry, man." I gave him one of my gallons of water, and a vogesite stone, too. We exchanged e-mail addresses. I hugged him and called him my friend, because it seemed like maybe that's all he was looking for, not a following.

"Before you leave, I have to ask you, do you always wear that shirt?" I was wearing a red, sweat-wicking T-shirt that I'd picked up at a Wal-Mart in New Orleans. The backpack had torn my first shirt to shreds.

"Yeah, but I have another one in my pack if you need an extra."

"No, it's just that . . ." and he paused here for a second, and tilted his head, and smiled. "It's funny. Because in the prophecy, it says the messiah will stand out. He'll be really conspicuous." He pointed to Bob and the neon yellow WALKING TO LISTEN sign lashed like a sail to the sun cover. "And it also says he'll be coming from the east and dressed in red." He nodded at my shirt.

"I don't know about that, man," I said.

"Maybe you're the one in the prophecy. Maybe this is all just a big joke on me."

"No, man," I said. "I wouldn't say that." I wished him good luck, and told him to stay in touch. The good-bye had to be amicable. I didn't want the kid to snap.

"Yeah, stay in touch," he said. "Back home I don't really have that many friends, so, stay in touch."

I've thought a lot about this kid over the past four years. What was he actually looking for? And how different were the two of us, really? Maybe he thought he was the messiah, but I think he just wanted to be seen, recognized as an integral part of the world's unfolding story, included in it, loved. I wasn't free of that same desire. Who was? At the root of it, perhaps the kid wasn't crazy at all. He believed in his greatness; there was no insanity in that, no inherent problem. He just misinterpreted the mystery of it, to think that he, alone, was the messenger of God. In truth, I was, too. Everyone was. The past eight months had begun to convince me of that, and Whitman had, as well:

I hear and behold God in every object, yet I understand
   God not in the least,
Nor do I understand who there can be more wonderful
   than myself.

Why should I wish to see God better than this day?
I see something of God each hour of the twenty-four, and
   each moment then,
In the faces of men and women I see God, and in my own
   face in the glass . . .

I saw the kid again the next day at dusk in Steamboat; he'd
hitched a ride. He was sunburnt, and he'd picked up another gallon
of water. Someone had taken him in the night before, but he was on
his own now. Even the Mormon missionaries had turned him away.
He told me that the translation of the town's Navajo name was
"burden," and that he felt that way, burdened. He wasn't so sure
why he'd come out here anymore. He was starting to think he
might be crazy after all.

"If I'm not the messiah, maybe I should just kill myself," he
said.

We spoke of *hózhó*, the beauty way. What was it? How do you
find it?

"I don't know, but I think I might be walking the ugly
way."

I asked him if he missed anybody back home, friends or family.

"No. But you know what I do miss, man? I miss my childhood.
It's gonna sound corny, but everything was magical back then."
Here, the kid wept.

I had another invitation to stay with a family that night. When
I went to leave, the kid asked if he could join me. I said no, leaving

him there on the side of the road. I still feel the shame of that years later—the curt rejection, my inability to receive him as so many others had received me. That God needed help, and this God refused.

TERRAN LOVEWAVE, astrologer
SANTA FE, NEW MEXICO, in his office at his house
JUNE

"We're deluded. We're asleep. It looks like we're awake right here. Mary's sewing. Barry's sitting. You're recording. It looks like we're awake, but if we're only using eight percent of our brain, and we only have ten percent of most of our DNA switched on, we are—pardon my expression—fucking asleep.

"The real issue isn't about which philosophy to believe, but that there's an opportunity to wake up in the midst of the dream. So if you've ever been dreaming in the middle of the night, and let's say a dinosaur walks by and you go, 'Wait, that's strange. Maybe this is a dream,' and in your dream you wake up—lucid dreaming—then you can do whatever you want. You have absolute freedom. There's something about waking up that frees us, but we're sound asleep, and the biggest hype is to make us believe we're awake when really we're sleeping. If you have a bad dream at night, one that you don't like, you can control it by waking up. And this is a weird dream right now."

Chapter Twenty-Three

"We've been waiting for you."

KTNN, the Navajo radio station, put it out on the airwaves that I was walking through the reservation. Lots of people must've heard it. The cars kept stopping for me. At one point, I was given more food and water than Bob could carry. I kept track of these episodes: Al Spencer spotted me on 264 and brought me a Burger King lunch. Nate and Elizabeth pulled over to give me a baked chicken dinner. A truck full of construction workers loaded me up with bottled water. Anderson and Christine cooked me fajitas and then kept me company on the roadside while I ate. A van pulled over and the family inside passed me some burritos from Taco Bell. Duane and Leona Melvin took me in for a snack. Billy Curling gave me cash at a gas station. Kelly Baste gave me three dollars. Outside Ganado, Ray and Darlene Tsosie took me in. Outside Steamboat, Sarah and Irving Curtis took me in. In Shongopavi, Joseph and Janice Day took me in. In Hotevilla, Ramson and Jessica Lomatewama took me in. In The Gap, Jason and Gwynn Secody took me in. In Bitter Springs, Marjorie Tsosie and Keith Lane took me in. In Tuba City, Rodney and Crystal Yazzie took me in, and gave me an extra key to their home to keep for whenever I returned.

Before entering the Navajo and Hopi reservations, I'd been worried for my safety. As I approached the western border, however, I didn't want to leave. I'd slipped into a vein of *hózhó* somehow. There was no end to the beauty. It seemed to reinforce itself and attract itself, and I got to be the witness. The goodness of people wasn't so shocking anymore—it was natural. What was shocking, however, was the juxtaposition of this goodness to all the suffering that surrounded it.

Rodney Yazzie, the man who gave me the key to his home, was a police officer in Tuba City, a dirt-swept town where horses ran through the streets. Rodney and his wife, Crystal, were a young, soft-spoken couple. Folks from a few towns east had passed me along to them, and they let me stay for a couple days to rest. One afternoon, Rodney took me on a ride-along in his cruiser. I sat shotgun as he responded to calls: a guy at a gas station picking fights with the tourists, an out-of-towner suspected of running drugs, a young woman who'd attempted suicide by overdosing, a box full of abandoned kittens. There was also one of the town drunks, a guy named Henry. Henry was middle-aged, and he lived with his mother, who was in her nineties. When the radio crackled with instructions to go pick him up, Rodney didn't seem surprised. We navigated through a neighborhood of small suburban homes with dusty front yards, and when we arrived at the house Rodney got out to assist. I stayed in the front seat of the SUV, watching everything from behind the glass.

The officers escorted Henry to the ambulance almost lovingly. This was a routine, and everyone knew how it went, including Henry. He liked going to the hospital, Rodney told me on the drive over. Was it for the attention? For the touch of a nurse's hand on his forehead? The whole ordeal was almost like a parade, riding in the ambulance with the lights flashing and the siren singing. He shuffled across the dirt with a kind of clubfoot, and his hand lay against his belly, as if in a sling. He was muttering and waving his good arm like a malfunctioning robot. The paramedics helped him onto the stretcher, and he asked for oxygen, but they didn't give it to him.

Rodney had mentioned earlier that Henry had once drunk so much that it had triggered a seizure; he'd been outside, and it had been hours before someone found him "cooking in the sun." He picked fights with his brother. Both of them would be in jail that night, apparently.

"I'll get to go to sleep early tonight," Rodney told me their mother said as the ambulance took Henry away. When Henry wasn't in jail and didn't come home, she'd drive around Tuba City looking for him. She'd find him, and bring him back. If he'd soiled himself, she would bathe him. Then, she'd put him to sleep.

In the two short weeks I'd spent walking through the Navajo Nation, I'd been given so much. I felt I belonged, even though the place wasn't my home. I felt I was important, even though I was just walking. This made me wonder about Henry. Did he ever get what I got, over and over again, every day?

If everyone was, at some point in their lives, the guest of honor at a full-blown feast prepared for them by complete strangers, we'd all be much better off. It's utterly humbling. It makes you fall in love, makes you want to spend your whole life throwing full-blown feasts for people you don't even know. I had it done for me in Jeddito, an island of Navajo land in the Hopi reservation. I'd met Arlena Gomez and her stout, wizened grandmother, Lily, forty miles back east at a gas station. I'd stopped there to get an iced tea, and the two of them had approached me, asking if I was the guy they'd heard about on the radio. We had talked for a while, and before they left Lily had said something to Arlena in Navajo.

"She wants to cook for you," Arlena translated. We exchanged numbers, and Arlena said they'd be waiting for me when I made it to Jeddito.

Two days later, I walked down 264 where a valley swept up into the sky. The land was desolate, a void that muted all sound, not that there was much sound to begin with, just the slow trickle of pickup trucks hauling drums of water. Lily lived on the other side of 264, miles from the highway up on top of a mesa. She and Arlena didn't want to make me walk there, so they'd set up a big party tent on the roadside. I saw it in the distance as I came down the mountain. Through the hazy heat, I could make out a bunch of pickup trucks parked next to the tent, and tables under the tent, and lawn chairs. Getting closer still, I could see people. Lots of people. When I finally made it, they all greeted me warmly.

"It took you long enough," one woman laughed. "We've been waiting for you."

The tables were the picture of abundance: big pots of mutton stew, Navajo fry bread, blue corn mush wrapped in corn husks, cupcakes, cold iced tea. Arlena and Lily had been cooking since the late morning, and the neighbors had joined them around noon, and it was five o'clock by the time I finally arrived. As I shook hands and learned names, it hit me that these people had spent the whole day preparing for this moment, my arrival. It was the kind of gift that felt too big to receive. It was given unconditionally, which only made me want to give it back more, or give it away elsewhere, just give. To be recognized like that, and celebrated, by people who didn't even know me—what if Henry in Tuba City could've had this, or the deluded kid who thought he was the messiah? What if all of us had this? What would that America look like?

Two of the neighbors cornered me. Melissa and Angelita Blake were sisters, somewhere in their thirties. They were a part of the Navajo Many Goat clan, they told me. They were as uproarious as their mother, Monita, was placid. Melissa taught elementary school. Although she had no children of her own, she had a motherly inclination.

"I'm the one that has to take care of everyone," she said later. "I play more of a mommy role than anything else sometimes." Melissa was the rising matriarch of the family. Angelita, a bit slighter than her sister and a bit older, had been weakened by an ongoing battle with lupus. She couldn't work because of the illness, and so she focused on healing and taking care of her sixteen-year-old son. Both women lived off the reservation, but they visited often. Monita had grown up here. Their grandmother, Fannie, still lived up on the mesa, hidden from the highway by the meandering dirt roads and the mazes of cedar. She had not come to the feast.

When I asked the Blake sisters if it'd be okay to camp on the roadside that night, they protested.

"You can come with us," Melissa said. "We'll drive you up and then drop you off right here again. It's no problem. Yeah, you're coming with us. We're going to steal you from Arlena. You better be careful. You might never come back."

"We're home wreckers," Angelita said, teasing me. "The Many Goat women always get what they want."

"How could I resist?" I said, and she hooted with laughter. It felt good, just to laugh with someone else. There hadn't been enough laughing over the past nine months on the road. Most of the laughing I'd done, I'd done alone, in pseudo-delirium at the end of the walking day. Kind of like Whitman, giggling madly in the night: "I am the everlaughing . . . it is new moon and twilight."

We struck the party tent before the sun got too low, and broke down all the tables and chairs and loaded them into the pickups. Then, I threw Bob into the bed of the Blakes' truck, and we started up the mesa, careening into potholes and ruts carved deep into the dirt road.

"What's Grandma gonna say when she sees we brought home a white man?" Melissa said. Angelita giggled.

I knew it was a joke, but still, it made me uncomfortable. One branch of my maternal ancestors had been pioneers. They traveled west in wagons, settling in Minnesota. One of them, a farmer named William Duggan Sr., joined a unit of volunteers from Minneapolis to fight in the 1862 Sioux Uprising, which ended in the largest mass execution in American history—the hanging of thirty-eight Sioux captives. What else had my ancestors done? How else had they been a part of the story of violence and retribution that seems to be the ongoing story of humanity? What stories had Grandma Fannie grown up hearing? Who were her ancestors? What would it be like for the two of us to meet here today, our respective histories propelling us into one another? Would we connect? Would we collide? Melissa and Angelita talked about her with a reverence that bordered on fear. She was very strict, they said, very austere. She practiced the old ways. She woke up every day before sunrise to pray, and she was well versed in plants and their medicinal uses. She'd been sent to an Indian boarding school as a girl so she knew some English, but she chose not to use it, not around me at least, except once, right before I left.

We pulled into the family compound. The ground was hard-packed dirt. Cedar and juniper grew in thick walls of green. The kitchen hut sat at the center of the compound's solar system, and several weathered structures orbited around it: a few houses, a hogan for ceremonies, a corral with horses, a pen with sheep, an outhouse. There were no lights, no telephone wires, no water heaters or septic tanks. Sometimes, when the kids wanted to watch TV, the sound of a generator hummed in the air.

Grandma Fannie didn't acknowledge me. She wore glasses, and her hair was thin and gray. She moved slowly, but not in a frail way. Melissa said Grandma didn't mind me being there, just that she was embarrassed about all the stray dogs. I wasn't sure whether to believe her or not.

Melissa and Angelita wanted to show me around before it got dark. We walked west toward the sunset. After just a couple hundred yards, the land dropped off into an abyss, flattening out into an expanse of rippling plains—breathtaking, the sound of breath taken. Tall rock formations sliced through the plains like shark fins through water, and at the far end of the valley the rock walls rose again. It was a vast bowl of glistening gold filled to the brim with gloaming.

Melissa told me to look at the ground. There were shards of pottery everywhere. "Anasazi," she said—a Navajo term referring to the Ancestral Puebloan people who mysteriously disappeared from the area sometime around the thirteenth century. She urged me to take one, so I did, and the women began talking excitedly in Navajo.

"What?" I said. "What's going on?"

"It's just that it's against the rules for us," Melissa explained. They were laughing. "We've always been told it's forbidden. We're not supposed to touch anything or take anything, but we don't know what would happen if we did."

"What, so I'm like your guinea pig?" I said.

"Yeah, but don't worry because you're not a Navajo so the rules are different for you."

"Are you sure the rules are different for me?"

"We're pretty sure."

"But what if they aren't different?"

"You'll probably be fine," she said, and they laughed and said some more things in Navajo. I put the shard back on the ground, whispering my apologies.

We followed the lip of the cliff until it ended in a rock wall rising up even higher into the sky. There was a shallow cave in the rock with a stone wall built up about three feet. The women told me it was an abandoned dwelling, the Old Ones again.

"Go ahead," Melissa said. "Go in."

"Why?"

"We want to see what'll happen," she said, barely able to suppress her laughter.

"Yeah right," I said. "Ladies first." Melissa hooted again.

On the way back, they showed me a foot-size depression stamped into the sandstone. Yet another sign of the Old Ones, Melissa told me. The place was primordial, strewn with clues to the past left by those who'd preceded us. Maybe they were still around, these Old Ones. Some people still saw them, Melissa said. They were little, apparently, and they had tails.

Navajo country was saturated with legends like this, stories of invisible deities and supernatural beings. There were the *diyin diné'e*, the Holy People, said to live within the bounds of the Four Sacred Mountains. What about them? Maybe they were watching us right now, just as we were watching the sunset. And then there were the skin walkers to consider, and the *ye'ibeshichai*, the ineffable entities believed to inhabit the bodies of masked dancers in ceremonies. Just a few days later I would see the *ye'ibeshichai* myself, with James and Chris Paisano from Window Rock; they took me to a ceremony called the Cross-Legged Kachina dance on the Hopi reservation. It was open to outsiders, but photographs were not allowed. Even writing about it was not allowed, so I'll just say that if you ever find yourself standing on the rooftops of an ancient village staring down into the dusty plaza at the dance, listening to the sound of a single beating drum, and of stomping feet, and of men chanting into a vast desert-scape rushing out into nothingness all around you, you might shed the presumption that you know the ins and outs of how everything works, and you might start thinking twice about skin walkers and *ye'ibeshichai* and the *diyin diné'e*.

When we got back to the compound, I asked Melissa what it meant to live the way her grandmother lived. What did that entail? I brought out my recorder, and at first it made her nervous.

"First of all, family is very important to them," she said, of the old folks, "because without their family they wouldn't be able to do some of the common chores they'd normally do. There's more hands to go get the wood, or go get the water, or herd sheep. They measure their wealth or success based on their family, their live- stock, and their happiness. So it's just really different compared to, 'What is your salary? How big is your house? What kind of car do you drive?' I came back and forth. It was nice to be exposed to the traditional culture, but then also to go back to the white men's version of life."

"What's it like for you to switch back and forth?" I asked.

"I like the fact that I can go back and forth. When I come here I really like it, but also when I go home I really like it, because then I have those amenities, like the TV, and having the bathroom inside, and having the grocery store down the road and not having to drive far.

"I came from a strict family where my grandparents were medicine people. They helped people and cured people. So that's what I saw and was exposed to, but when I got older I just wanted to know how everybody else functioned in the world. So we went to a Muslim church, or whatever you call it. And then we went to Catholics and learned about the Vatican and how they do stuff. And then we also learned about Mormons, and Seventh-Day Adventists, and Baptists. We wanted to learn a lot more rather than be secluded.

And I think our curiosity is what led us to do a lot of these things for ourselves, and try to figure out our culture. Not to justify it, but to have a better respect and understanding of it."

We were sitting together outside the kitchen hut, all the women and I. Melissa mentioned that most of the older women had been sent to Indian boarding schools when they were young. I'd heard about these schools before. Most had been established by Christian missionaries, and over the course of a century or so, tens of thousands of native children had been enrolled in these schools. Most of these institutions had disparaged indigenous culture and forbidden its expressions—native names, language, dress, ritual. I asked Monita about her experience.

"I had to go," she said. "It was good. I liked it. At home, my mother would make us do everything—haul water, get wood. Going back to school, it was nice. You didn't have to do all that."

"They had to choose what faith they wanted," Melissa interjected. "They didn't offer traditional. They had a number of churches they could choose from. She told me a story where one church would do movies and popcorn, and another church would do ice cream, and that's how they'd choose their religion."

"So which one had the best?" I asked Monita.

"I went to the Baptist church."

"What were they giving out?"

"Popcorn."

"One of the best stories my mom used to tell me was about hippies in the sixties," Melissa went on, laughing. Monita shook her head. "The kids were scared because they weren't exposed to a lot of things, so a lot of them had fear towards other people and other things, and one of those things was hippies. Someone would start a rumor and that rumor would spread, and they said that hippies were bad people, and that they would kill people. So, in the middle of the night when they saw a Volkswagen van they would run and hide out in the middle of nowhere and sleep there! Without their shoes!"

We all visited like this for a long time. I didn't want it to end, but one by one the women went off to their homes. When the conversation outside the kitchen hut lulled, the silence was such that I could hear the families murmuring behind the walls. The stars were impossibly bright and ancient.

After a while, Grandma Fannie said something in Navajo and left us, too.

"She gets up early," Angelita said. "She gets up at four."

"Sometimes three."

"So she's the matriarch, huh?" I said.

"Yep," Melissa said. "She's the boss. She got kind of irritated with us because we brought you home."

My heart sank. "Really?"

"Just kidding! She's all like, 'What are you guys doing?' And we said, 'We're gonna take him home to show him some of the stuff,' and then she said, 'Okay.' I think she's just a little shy. Or maybe a little embarrassed. She's embarrassed because usually there's no dogs around, and she likes to chase the dogs away. She's mean. Not mean in a bad way, but very strict. She has high expectations."

Slowly, the silences in the conversation grew longer and longer.

"The moonlight," Melissa said, "that's what we use as the light. We can stay up and talk, but we don't have the ability to go and turn on a TV, so a lot of this stuff is oral entertainment, talking about stuff in our personal life or referring back to what happened when we were little, or Grandma telling us a story about the old days."

"We talk because there's nothing else to do," Angelita said. "We'll just lie there and talk about stupid stuff. We just talk and talk until we fall asleep."

And we did. Monita, Melissa, and Angelita were staying in a little two-room house. They'd set up a cot for me in one room, and the three women slept in the adjacent room. We left the door open so we could keep talking. I drifted in and out of sleep, and the two sisters teased me, and Monita laughed, and it was all like a lullaby. I thought about Grandma Fannie again, and what it must be like for her to have me here.

"She's gotten a lot better," Melissa had said earlier, "between me and my cousins and stuff. We're more open and I think the older ones just get used to it. My mom's gotten used to it because I make her try new things. I know that sometimes people can be more critical towards other people, and I try not to because you never know what those people are going through. You never know what they're supposed to do. Everybody has their own plan and everybody has their own thing they're trying to achieve in life, or they're trying to find what they're supposed to do. And sometimes you guide them, but you can only do so much."

My camera gave me the excuse to make eye contact with Grandma Fannie twice. I didn't know how else to connect with her. She was up early to pray, and in the shallow waters of my dawn-sleep I heard the thwacking of her ax splitting logs for the fire. By the time I finally got out of bed, all the women were in the kitchen hut, laughing and chatting in Navajo. Monita was making homemade tortillas on the stove. Melissa was brewing coffee. Aunt Claudina was scrambling eggs and frying Spam. The radio crackled over the conversation, informing us that Tom Cruise and Katie Holmes were filing for divorce—astonishing to remember that people cared about such things. I took a photograph of this happy scene from the very back corner of the kitchen. At the center of the image is

Grandma Fannie. Her eyes, looking straight at me as I took the photo, are not unkind, but they're not smiling, either.

In the second photograph, a sheep is lying on the dirt, its legs trussed in yellow twine, neck on a wooden plank. It was for the medicine man, a part of the payment for Angelita's healing ceremony. I'd gone down to the sheep pen with Claudina and Melissa, and had offered to wrangle it myself, but they'd just laughed at me. Claudina roped it on the first cast. She bound it, and one of the uncles lifted it into the bed of the truck. Its eyes were so wide. Nobody wanted to be the one to kill it, so Grandma had to do it, and I took the photograph right before she did. In the image, she's standing over the sheep. You can't see the knife, because her left arm is in midswing behind her back. I was squatting, so she's looking down, over her glasses and, again, right into the camera. I snapped the photo in the seconds before she drew the knife across the sheep's throat. Monita caught the blood in a big bowl, and the bowl filled up. We all winced and looked away, except for Grandma, who seemed to know how this would go, and accepted it. The sheep was utterly silent as it died. It didn't take more than a few moments, then it relaxed, and we relaxed, too, our own deaths forgotten again. Grandma walked away after a few curt instructions as to how she wanted the butchering done.

I stayed with the family for several days, and it was only right before I left that I was convinced Grandma didn't resent me. I gave her one of my vogesite pebbles as an offering of gratitude.

"Thank you, my son," she said in English.

Later, Melissa texted me and said that Grandma had cried when I left. I'd been a bit choked up myself. The family compound had become a kind of home, like Marian and Herb Furman's Homeplace in Alabama, and I didn't want to leave, but at the same time I couldn't stay. I spent the whole day walking in that contradiction.

PAT DYEA, Laguna ceremonial dancer, grandfather
MESITA, NEW MEXICO, in his living room after dinner
JUNE

"*There are things in your life when you go through, it's bad. Just like when my first wife passed away. I was hurting. I was mad at the Creator and everything else. When that happened to me, then I knew what it was like to be in that situation, somebody telling you, 'Have faith,' and it doesn't even make sense to you anymore. When people commit suicide, I used to say, 'Oh, they're not man enough or woman enough to handle life.' It's so easy to say those things, but when you're in that situation, oh man, it's bad. You're all by yourself. There's nobody, even though you have kids or relatives, but nobody comes to see you or talk to you, and that's when I was trying to take my life. So, then I knew what it was like to be in that situation, where it's so easy to commit suicide. It's so easy to think that way because the evil one is right there telling you, 'Go ahead, go ahead.' All these negative things come into being, where it makes you feel like nobody cares.*"

"*What was it that finally brought you out?*"

"*I wanted to die so bad. Every morning I used to get up and say, 'One more day closer to death.' Then I was telling my brother, and he said, 'Why don't you say this instead of saying that: One more day closer to healing.' So I started saying that. And at first it didn't mean nothing. I was just saying it just to say it. But as it went along, it started to have a meaning.*

"Those are the things that, if people can realize what an individual is going through, especially at a time of death ... Because when they're gone they're gone, man, and it's something that you don't want to go through, but we all have to go through because we're all headed that way, no matter what. But a lot of times people don't even see what you're going through. So those are the things that we have to see."

Chapter Twenty-Four

"What's your idea of the perfect life?"

In Nevada, the heat hovered in puddles over the highway, blurring everything together. I had to walk at night, but in some ways the desert was finest at night. I was like an alien floating in the cosmos. The big rigs were spaceships, studded with golden lights, their high beams halving the void. Before dawn, when it was neither dark nor light, I confused boulders for cows, saltbush for mule deer. These metamorphoses happened over and over again. Everything seemed to be something other than itself. Maybe a skin walker had followed me from Navajo country. Maybe I was just hallucinating.

In the daytime, sleep didn't happen much because sleep is impossible in the fires of hell, so at night I would dream-walk almost every mile. There were eyes in the abyss surrounding me, but that was no dream. I'd see them glowing green when I shone my headlamp into the darkness off the road.

Everything had gone a little strange after leaving the Navajo Nation a few weeks before I crossed into Nevada. That first night off the reservation, I camped on a cliff above the Colorado River, a few miles northeast of the Grand Canyon. It was raining lightly, pitch dark, and I was lying in my tent when a powerful urge to dance filled me suddenly, like a bizarre stranger in the night barging through the door without knocking. The urge wasn't so much to dance, really, as it was to just go crazy. Berserk. Let myself snap after holding it together all this way. *Fuck it*, I thought. I stepped outside, blasted some dubstep in my earbuds, and gave over to it, sweat blending with rain, gone, lost, disappeared. "O Christ!" Whitman howled, "My fit is mastering me!" Just a few bounds away, the raindrops fell into the far depths of the canyon. I could fall, too. I could. But I wouldn't. Not now, not yet, not like that. At the height of my frenzy, two orbs of light appeared across the chasm, and they began gliding toward me. I froze. Maybe I'd summoned them. They passed unhurried through the dark as if on a sea of liquid velvet, closer and closer through the silence and the smell of sage, swelling in size until the two lights split into four—a pair of cars. *Enough. Time to rest. Time to sleep.*

The end of the walk wasn't far away now, and I was still looking for some kind of vision, some conclusive transformative moment. I'd reached the desert, the place where it was supposed to happen, but it was just hot, and miserable more often than not, and I was exhausted. Even if there had been some kind of divine lightning bolt I probably wouldn't have seen it because I was so sleepy. "I'm pretty tired," Forrest Gump had said in the moment of his desert epiphany. There was no hidden meaning there for his followers, no coded message. He was just tired. That was it.

"Know that you know already," a mystical Cajun man named Joshua Terziu had told me back in Louisiana. "I don't have to tell you that you know. You don't tell a tree how to be a tree, and you don't tell a transcender that they should transcend. It's obvious that they will. Because that's the nature of the growth of the human experience. We're in a constant state of overcoming. So it's all about understanding and getting acclimated to that process."

His words made more sense when I made it to the desert. *We're in a constant state of overcoming.* That meant there was no end to it, no divine lightning bolt that would strike me in some far-off place if only I could just get there. There was only the slow process of overcoming, one moment to the next, one step after the other. *So it's all about understanding and getting acclimated to that process.* This realization was both liberating and devastating at the same time. On the one hand, it meant that I'd already arrived, and that I'd been there all along. The beginning and the end were the same thing. There was only the process, the walk, and it was always happening now. On the other hand, it meant there was no finish line. I'd be walking for the rest of my life, and that sounded completely exhausting. And then there was eternity to consider.

I found that Rilke had some thoughts on this in his letters. What Joshua Terziu called a "transcender," Rilke called an "artist":

> Being an artist means: not numbering and counting, but ripening like a tree, which doesn't force its sap, and stands confidently in the storms of spring, not afraid that afterward summer may not come. It does come. But it comes only to those who are patient, who are there as if eternity lay before them, so unconcernedly silent and vast.

The spring had passed and the summer had come, at long last, but as far as I could tell the summer was nothing but hot, hotter than the devil's asshole in the innermost circle of hell. The storms of spring were sweet compared to this.

Passing the Grand Canyon, a relentless rush of RVs clogged the highways. Their sides bulged out into the shoulder, threatening to kill me dozens of times each day. It was a stark contrast to walking Highway 264 through the Navajo Nation, where no more than a handful of cars had gone by every hour. Now, the traffic seemed truly murderous.

Before I got to Nevada, I had to make a detour around the Grand Canyon. It would take me right through Zion National Park in southern Utah. Outside Zion, I met a young couple from Quebec—Jean-Sébastien Babin and Cristelle Arsenault. They were spending a year traveling around the world together in their maroon Westfalia van. We ran into one another at a coffee shop in Kanab, and they invited me to explore the park with them for the next few days. I took them up on it, because I was tired of walking, tired of saying good-bye, tired of myself, and sick of the mystery, too, sick of the goddamn questions. I was done. Every time I looked at my map, a little part of me would panic. I was going to walk across the Mojave Desert, and probably Death Valley, and then the Sierra Nevada Mountains, six hundred miles to the coast. It was the last thing I wanted to do, and at the same time I couldn't imagine doing anything else.

Hanging out with Jean-Sébastien and Cristelle was a respite from the whole thing. The three of us spent the next two days climbing up cliffs and hiking down canyons. I watched them a little jealously. Sometimes, they'd give me their camera and I'd take a photograph of the two of them. Then, I'd give my camera to Cristelle, and she'd take a photograph of me by myself. They slept together in the belly of the van. I slept in the popup section above them, alone. I just wanted to touch someone. It had been so long that even just the thought of it was electrifying. Whitman knew the feeling: "To touch my person to someone else's is about as much as I can stand." Just to hold another, and be held. My God! All the months of monkish celibacy suddenly seemed completely insane. A piercing flash of doubt: *What have I done to myself? Why am I doing this?*

I turned to Rilke again—the second time that week—illuminating his words with my flashlight.

For one human being to love another human being: that is
perhaps the most difficult task that has been entrusted to
us, the ultimate task, the final test and proof, the work for
which all other work is merely preparation. That is why
young people, who are beginners in everything, are not yet
capable of love: it is something they must learn. With their
whole being, with all their forces, gathered around their
solitary, anxious, upward-beating heart, they must learn to
love. But learning-time is always a long, secluded time, and
therefore loving, for a long time ahead and far on into life,
is——: solitude, a heightened and deepened kind of aloneness for the person who loves.

Lying in my sleeping bag above the Canadian lovers, I tried to
sink into my solitude, learn from it, use it as preparation for the
ultimate task, the final test and proof, but it just felt lonely and kind
of pointless.

We were sitting around a campfire the next night when Jean-
Sébastien asked me a question. "Tell me, Andrew, what's your idea
of the perfect life? Your perfect life?"

I thought about how grim I'd felt since leaving the Navajo
Nation, and I tried to imagine my perfect life. Surely it wasn't this.
How could perfection include loneliness and longing, filth and
exhaustion, whispers of despair? It seemed there were countless
other potential versions of this life that'd be so much better. I could
spend hours fantasizing about them, wondering what that perfection might look like someday, wishing it would come soon. I could
spend my entire life that way, wondering, wishing. It'd be so easy. It
was, in fact, the inevitable result of believing that perfection was
anything other than what already was. "This minute that comes to
me over the past decillions," Whitman wrote, "There is no better

than it and now." If I couldn't find perfection in this, then what made me think I'd be able to find it tomorrow, next month, or two decades from now? Peace had to be an inner perspective, not a specific and temperamental set of external conditions. The fire cackled, lighting up Jean-Sébastien and Cristelle in hues of yellow and orange, and I realized that this was my perfect life. It had to be.

"I must be living it," I said, and then told them about my recent state of mind, the longing to be somewhere else, doing something else, with someone else. I was so close to quitting.

"Maybe that yearning is a part of the perfect life," Jean-Sébastien said. "Maybe desires for future things aren't imperfections. Maybe they're a part of the perfection."

The next day, Jean-Sébastien and Cristelle dropped me off where they'd picked me up and waved good-bye. I slept under a bridge that night, trying to remember what we'd discussed around the fire not twenty-four hours earlier, struggling to believe any of it.

I made it to the eastern gates of Zion at sunset the next day. Inside the park, I'd heard there was a one-mile tunnel that ran straight through a mountain—no walkers allowed. I didn't want to hitch a ride, so I decided I'd walk it at night. Wisps of mist wavered like pale candle flames over the road, visible only in the instant before I passed through them. Where the clouds parted above, stars shone like luminous fields of cotton. They were the kind of stars that made me snort and shake my head, the kind of stars that raised the deafening roar of infinity. I was almost certainly the only human being awake in the park that night. I was, quite possibly, the last human being alive in the world.

I wound through Zion on the rose-colored road. The surrounding darkness shrouded everything, and so I walked as if in a womb, blind and floating. If it weren't for the road, my constant reference, up might've been down and down up. Nothing was visible: not the mountains of sandstone, dunes of deserts past; not the mudstone cliffs left by long-lost seas, or the arches and their yawning mouths of sky. I was walking through a grand hallway of the gods and I couldn't see a damn thing. I'd seen some of it before with Jean-Sébastien and Cristelle, so I knew what I was missing. It was all lost, walking in the dark.

And then, the heat lightning would flash, and for an instant I'd see everything.

I arrived at the mile-long tunnel and began to sprint, pushing my baby stroller. It had taken a year to build that tunnel. I ran it in six minutes, without incident. On the other side I lay down, my chest raging, and watched the sunrise wash out the stars. I wanted to sleep, but I couldn't sleep yet. There was still a long way to walk that day.

At a diner over breakfast, I got terrible news from the outside world. There'd been another mass shooting, this one at a movie theater in Aurora, Colorado. James Holmes, a young white man my age, had walked into a midnight screening of *The Dark Knight Rises* with a shotgun, a semiautomatic rifle, and a pistol. He had thrown two canisters into the crowd, which had filled the room with smoky gas, and then had started shooting, as if he were in the movie that was playing on the screen behind him. He'd injured seventy people. He'd killed twelve more. The nation was reeling, and now that I knew, I was, too.

It was such a brutal contrast to what I'd been experiencing with people on the road for almost an entire year now—the kindness, the trust, the generosity. I wondered about James Holmes.

What if he'd been one of the people I'd met on my walk, in a diner or at a bar? What if we'd gotten into a conversation? What would he have said? Why had he done it? His face stared at me from the newspaper: hair dyed a startling neon orange, vacant doe-eyes, a glazed, almost plaintive look on his face. Who was this young man? What had he lived, inside and out, that he was capable of such evil?

The pages of his journal are publicly available online. I stumbled upon them recently, and was shocked to read the very first words on the very first page: "The Questions," it said, underlined, and then, "What is the meaning of Life? What is the meaning of death?" It could've been the first page of my journal. The image I'd had of some frothing, insane devil, a non-human, an anti-human, cracked a little when I saw such familiar questions staring back at me. I read the rest of the journal in an almost-continual shiver, not just in reaction to the demented logic Holmes used to justify mass murder, but in recognition at the existential longing for understanding that permeated every word, that must have consumed his entire consciousness. I knew that longing. I shivered, because I saw, by his madness, how there are certain questions, seemingly simple, that can lead you down very treacherous paths if you don't know why you're asking them, or how to ask them, or what you even want of their answers. *Who am I?* I saw how a question like this can be deadly when asked in isolation, without people there to support you in the asking, support you in the confusion that might arise when you stop assuming you know the answer and let go into the unknown. Finding support should be a prerequisite for the task of asking such a question, especially if your brain chemistry is whacked, but even if it isn't.

Holmes's journal depicts his process of attempting to swim deep existential waters alone. From the very start he's lost, but he does seem to want to find a way out, find an alternative path to truth that won't necessitate spilling blood: "I have spent my entire life seeking this alternative so that the questions of how to live and what to live for may be addressed." *The questions of how to live and what to live for.* The same questions I was walking with, and that every human has to confront. Human. The man was human, and he hated himself for it, it seemed. Under a section entitled "Self Diagnosis of Broken Mind" he picks himself apart: a bullet-point list of suspected ills almost twenty deep, from social anxiety to schizophrenia and nearly everything in between. In another list, "Symptoms attributed to Self Diagnosis," he catalogues his brokenness. A very abridged excerpt:

Catatonia

Excessive Fatigue

Isolationism

Avoid social interactions

Recurring return to mirror to look at appearance. Particular
  attention focused on hair styling. 10+ times a day

Concern with teeth

Concern with nose. Often drippy, a leaky faucet, requiring
  continuous wiping

Concern with ears. Cannot hear very well

Concern with eyes. Imperfect biology, had to wear glasses

Concern with cock

Inability to communicate what I want to say although I
  can understand it. Typically have an image in my mind
  but can't say images or draw them, would be nice if
  there was some form of telepathy to transfer images

Odd sense of self. View myself as divided . . . The real me
  is fighting the biological me. The real me, namely
  thinking me, does things not because I'm programmed

> to, but b/c I choose to. The latest battle I lost was
> when I finally succumbed to falling in love
> Can't fall asleep when I want to fall asleep
> Hair pulling.

Holmes wasn't unique in his brokenness—the raw self-consciousness and judgment, the fear—but maybe he did think he was alone in it. He might've found solace in Rilke, who reframed brokenness as an agent of internal transcendence, not as something that needs to be fixed.

> Why do you want to shut out of your life any uneasiness, any misery, any depression, since after all you don't know what work these conditions are doing inside you? Why do you want to persecute yourself with the question of where all this is coming from and where it is going? . . . Don't observe yourself too closely. Don't be too quick to draw conclusions from what happens to you; simply let it happen.

But I doubt Holmes ever received such advice. What if he had?

"So anyways," he concludes his scathing self-analysis, "that's my mind. It is broken. I tried to fix it. I made it my sole conviction but using something that's broken to fix itself proved insurmountable."

Perhaps he was just putting on a show in these pages, evidence that could later be used to support an insanity plea. Perhaps not. Either way, the brokenness he describes is painful to read, made only more painful by the eviscerating self-loathing. I was haunted most by his description of the universe, however. Haunted because I found it beautiful.

In one's selfish nature, we choose to view ourselves as distinct or separate from the universe. A single universe ourself, per se. This isn't correct. We are all one, unity. As such, there is no difference between life and death or spacetime. All things, actions and phenomena are not multiple ripples. Instead the universe is a single unitary preponderance of which we are each a part of. This may be unfathomable to some and result in the seeking of escapism and attempt at reductions of unity into fractured entities. To me, this unity is infinitely complex. Much more preferable is a simple system. Unity through nil.

That last line is where the beauty of this Buddhistic worldview goes haywire: annihilation was his nil, his way to experiencing unity. Facing his own death, and bringing death to others, was his deluded means to finding oneness. It was the logic of a madman, or of someone desperate to be loved.

He finishes his homegrown philosophy by writing "Why? Why? Why?" over and over again for seven and a half pages, 247 times, his childish cursive getting bigger and bigger until the why finally exhausts him and all he can do is write it just once more, taking up a page of its own. "Why?" Say why 247 times aloud to yourself to get a taste of his torment.

I'm reminded of another Whitman line: "Do you guess I have some intricate purpose? / Well I have . . . for the April rain has, and the mica on the side of a rock has." It's a kind of Zen koan, meant to stump you into just being present, into experiencing the April rain instead of analyzing it, into abiding with the mica instead of asking it why. *"Do you guess I have some intricate purpose?"* the universe asks us through the poet. What if its presence *is* its purpose? What if it's enough that it all just *is*? Maybe the seductive question of why is moot. Maybe existence isn't a puzzle that needs solving, just like rain isn't a problem that has to be fixed, or mica a code that must be cracked. "The reason why life should exist is as arbitrary as the reason why it shouldn't," Holmes wrote. But it does exist, arbitrary or not, which is reason enough to experience it. However, life as it experienced itself in James Holmes was tortured and isolated, and therefore filled with hate. So he concluded, "Life shouldn't exist."

"The message is there is no message," he wrote toward the end of the journal, in reference to the meaning behind his imminent attack, namely, that everything is meaningless. Eerily, it seems quite similar to what Whitman is saying about the April rain and the mica, and to what I understand the Buddhists say about reality: it just is, and any attempt to define that is-ness—"The message is *this*" or "The intricate purpose is *that*"—will neglect some aspect of that is-ness, or impose upon it the biases inherent in the mechanism that is doing the defining, the mind. You can't take a picture of the entire universe, just what the viewfinder can fit inside it; the camera will never capture the whole thing, and it will never produce the universe itself, only representations of the universe. Is it not the case that every interpretation of reality dreamt up by a particular mind will be constrained by that particular mind's experiences? Can reality, in its infinitude, in the fullness of its truth, ever be wholly perceived by a limited and limiting lens such as the conditioned human mind? What is a "message," anyway, or an "intricate purpose," if not just more constructions of the mind? Interpretations *of* experience, not experience itself. And yet, I have a mind, and so do you, and so does James Holmes, and these minds create perfectly unique interpretations of what's going on, day after day, year after year, always seeking the message in various ways, the intricate purpose. My stories will never quite match up with yours;

there will always be differences, subtle and vast, and even those differences will largely remain unknown. Maybe the point is to learn how to watch these stories without really believing any of them. I don't know. Maybe the point is to say I don't know.

Whitman knew how to bask in the mystery of the message-lessness, the purposelessness, delighting in that which he could not understand, and trusting it:

> The sun and stars that float in the open air ... the apple-
> shaped earth and we upon it ... surely the drift of them
> is something grand;
> I do not know what it is except that it is grand, and that it is
> happiness,
> And that the enclosing purport of us here is not a specula-
> tion, or bon-mot or reconnaissance,
> And that it is not something which by luck may turn out
> well for us, and without luck must be a failure for us,
> And not something which may yet be retracted in a certain
> contingency.

Whitman didn't know. He was content to wonder at this wondrous world. Holmes, on the other hand, did not know how to not know, and so naturally he was terrified. Without medication, he wrote: "I was fear incarnate." With medication: "Anxiety and fear disappears. No more fear, no more fear of failure. Fear of failure drove determination to improve ... and succeed in life. No fear of consequences. Primary drive reversion to hatred of mankind."

James Holmes came of age in America, this country that I walked across, my home. I can't help wondering about that coming-of-age and where it went wrong, how universal some of his questions were, how that questioning didn't have to be a destructive force in his mind, how it might've propelled him toward an act of creation if he'd been better supported in the intense process of becoming an adult. I don't know his story. Perhaps his brain was doomed from the beginning, but I think it's misguided to blame that brain alone. Because that brain was not raised in a sterile laboratory, immune from the effects of its environment. That brain was raised in a society shaped by certain conventions, beliefs, and practices, a culture that influenced the way Holmes reacted to his own existence. Nature and nurture. Nature will do what it wants, but we are the nurturers. What are we nurturing in America today? These mass shootings are not isolated incidents. Nothing is an isolated incident, arising somehow on its own, tidily contained, without a whole web of interconnected causes. Every apple grows from a tree, even the bad apples. These shootings—a macabre normality at the turn of the twenty-first century—they're symptoms of a cultural disease, painful flare-ups that, like any symptom, call attention to the fact that something is wrong inside. So what's wrong, not just with these sick boys? What's wrong with all of us, we who are living beside them?

James Holmes tried to fix himself. "Alternatives to death," he wrote. "1. Ignore the problem: If the problem or question doesn't exist then the solution is irrelevant. Didn't work. Forms of escapism tried included reading, television, and alcohol." He tried delaying the problem: "Didn't work. Pursued knowledge to increase the capacity for answering the questions with improved cognitive function." He tried pawning it off to others: "Didn't work. Everyone else didn't know the solution either." His fourth and final attempt, he writes, was love. He only lists one word to explain why love didn't work: "Hate." Love might've worked, if only he'd known how to, but no one can learn how to love on their own. We need one another for that. It might be the thing that makes us most human:

we need one another. But that's something that has to be learned, too, and taught. Tragically, James Holmes never got that lesson, even though he seemed to be looking for it.

I finished my breakfast and walked out of the diner, stunned, sickened, still sleep-deprived. A young man walking across America with his questions. Another young man sitting in prison with his. That bastard should've walked. He should've just walked, and we should've helped him, but we didn't, and he didn't, and now twelve people were dead, seventy were injured, and the whole fucking country was broken. Would America break itself even more in the years to come? Without a doubt. It was like Holmes trying to fix his own mind. *Using something that's broken to fix itself proved insur-mountable.* Holmes needed to ask for help. Or if he did, then he needed to scream for it. That morning, it seemed like America did, too, and since America was nothing if not a collection of individuals, the onus was on each of us. But maybe we already were screaming for help. Were we listening to one another? Was anyone listening at all?

By the time I reached the southern tip of Nevada a few days later I was completely strung out. Sleep deprivation is a form of torture in some godforsaken places. And the heat. My God, the heat. Before, I thought I knew it. I thought I really understood it. Texas in May had to count for something, or New Mexico in June. Surely Arizona in July was a legitimate inferno. How naïve I'd been, entering the southern reaches of the Great Basin in August, the Mojave Desert in its fiery climax. The air was a melting ocean of madness. The wind washed tidal waves right over me, and some of the waves were rogues—hotter than the rest—and my own breath would've set me on fire if my body had been just a little more flammable. By afternoon, after the sun had

had all day to vomit itself over everything, the asphalt seemed to throw fury up at me from below. My thirst was unbearable, and my sweat flowed so hard it freaked me out, though I knew it was better than no sweat at all. That would've meant dehydration, and out here, dehydration meant death.

And it was cool for that time of year, apparently. That's what they told me in Mesquite, anyway.

I'd left Mesquite around nine in the morning after a short rest at an air-conditioned McDonald's. I'd been walking since three A.M. After another ten miles or so I came across a bridge in the middle of nowhere. It was probably the only source of shade for miles, so I set up camp underneath. It was now eleven in the morning. I thought I'd be able to sleep, but it was too hot. I recorded an audio journal entry at dusk to distract myself.

"The worst of the heat I think has passed. This heat's got me thinking. It's a totally different ballgame than anything I've really had to deal with. Basically it feels dangerous. Even just sitting, you know, trying to sleep a little bit, not moving. The water's just getting sucked right out of me. And I'm drinking, drinking, and all of a sudden I'm like, 'Oh, God, do I have enough? You can get caught out here. You do not want to get caught out here. Bring more water next time.' I feel like I'm on the brink, you know? And I could either fall into a sense of calm or I could freak out. I see how the desert does what it does to people."

I sifted through my memories to pass the time. The bridge above me groaned, and all else was silent, except for the flies. The Virgin River crawled low and warm nearby, loaded with cow shit and cow piss. I took a dip anyway. I had to, because I was on fire. I called a lot of people that day, to avoid the silence. This day's solitude had a kind of malevolence to it. I talked to my grandma. She was in her condo in Michigan, probably sitting in her recliner in front of the TV where she always sat, with the newspaper on her lap. We laugh about that conversation now—how strange it was that we were talking to each other from two totally different worlds—but in the moment it wasn't funny at all.

Around eleven that night it was cool enough to start walking again, although "cool" was nothing more than a concept now, a faint dream that was slipping away too fast to remember. I packed up Bob and got on the road. It was thirty miles to the next town, and I had eight or nine hours before the sun came back to destroy me. I'd pored over my plan on Google Maps a few days earlier: take Riverside Road to I-15, walk on the interstate for a few miles, then take the exit for Carp Elgin Road, a shortcut, and follow it into the town of Overton. I didn't want to walk on I-15, especially at night, but there were no other options.

At first it was fine. Strange, to be on the interstate in the middle of the desert at night, but fine. Then, through the darkness, I could see the iridescent green of the exit sign winking in the high beam of my headlamp. Carp Elgin Road. *Thank God. The interstate's almost over.* I relaxed. I laughed a little. *What are these people thinking, anyway, driving past a guy pushing a baby carriage in the desert at midnight?* I took the exit, but right away it didn't look good. The road was an old one—pockmarked cement, potholes. There was no traffic at all. The road probably hadn't seen traffic in years.

Is this even a road? Whatever it was, it was better than the interstate. A minute or two went by, and I crossed a cattle guard. The road turned to dirt. I didn't want this road to be a dirt road. Dirt roads did not bode well in the desert at night.

It's okay. Just keep walking. You checked it on Google. It'll be fine. I didn't have any cell phone service, but I figured that wasn't too much of a problem. This wasn't an emergency; I could always return to the interstate, assuming I could find my way back, which, now that I thought about it, wasn't a given. I was getting farther away with each footstep.

"Holy shit," I said out loud, shining my headlamp around. The void devoured the words. Beyond the realm of the small circle of light, I could see nothing. I didn't want to backtrack, though. It would just add miles to an already long night's walk, and I was so tired. *When was the last time I slept?* I couldn't even remember. *It'd be so nice to sleep, just for a second.* I lay down on the dirt and closed my eyes. Just as I was drifting off, a voice started shouting inside my head, furious. *What the fuck are you doing? Get up! You know what'll happen if the sun catches you out here! This is the real-life fucking desert and it doesn't give a shit about you. Get up, right now. Get up.*

The dirt road was more of a trail at this point, and then, to my dismay, it forked in front of me. I heard the angry voice again: *Two roads diverged in a wood and I? I took the one less traveled by, and that has made all the difference, because it fucking killed me.* This was not the imagined danger I'd encountered so many times before on my walk, my own mind's fear projected onto the world outside itself. This danger felt real. I imagined the local newspaper head-line: LOST IN DESERT, MAN DIES.

"Has any one supposed it lucky to be born?" Whitman wrote in *Leaves of Grass*.

> I hasten to inform him or her it is just as lucky to die, and I
> know it.

> I pass death with the dying, and birth with the new-washed
> babe ... and am not contained between my hat and
> boots.

I'd underlined that verse when I first read it, feeling rather uncontained myself, "deathless," the way the poet described himself in another line. But that was earlier, when I wasn't out here, walking deeper and deeper into a darkness that would soon become light. And not the hopeful kind of light. Rather, the kind of light that burns and melts. The kind of light that extinguishes anything it touches. Now, the poet's words came off differently. *You know what? Fuck you, Walt Whitman. Deathless my ass.*

I took a right turn at the fork. I'd seen something like this on Google Maps: Carp Elgin Road branched off twice, and I had to go right both times. Sure enough, the trail split again. I went right. But then it split again. And again. I was getting deeper into the maze. Finally, another fork materialized in front of me and I'd had enough. It'd be better to walk thirty-five or even forty miles on the interstate than continue on this trail. But could I find my way back? I stumbled around, pushing Bob through the sandy dirt, hoping he wouldn't pop a flat, taking the turns that seemed familiar until I saw the slow stream of passing headlights in the distance indicating the highway.

I fear-walked the rest of the way to Overton, where I got a motel room and slept all day, trying to forget what had almost happened. The air-conditioned room was paradise, but I knew what was just outside the door. I couldn't ignore it, even in my sleep. Around midnight I began walking again—a new walk, a new moment—but it would not leave my head, the image of that desert trail winding into the darkness.

HAROLD TSO, *Navajo drummer, member of the Native American Church*
JEDDITO, ARIZONA, in his house the morning before an all-night peyote ceremony
JULY

"When I'm drumming, I think about the patient, what the meeting is for, what the purpose is. You think it through this song, and when you think about it, then there's a tune, this nice tune in there that makes you go day in and day out during the meeting, and it's all about your life ahead of you, about what you need, what good things that you're gonna be going through, all the good things that you're gonna get, not the bad things. We can talk to this drum and make it sound good, make everything good like that, because sometimes we go through hardship. Life is an obstacle. We try to overcome, try to find a way to go under it, over it, or whichever ways it's possible for us."

"So a ceremony or drumming is one way to navigate that?"

"Yep. If you really want something, you have to go for it like that, you know? You always think good thoughts and maybe you have a prayer. Everybody has a prayer. You just think about it, and the Creator can take it. That's how it is, for me. And I think when you're walking alone like that on the road, the Spirit is with you, the Holy Spirit. And for one thing that I know, your shadow, it follows you around everywhere. That's your best friend, and that's your protection. You can talk to your shadow, too, you know. Your shadow is your number one thing. Even though you say, 'No!' and you try to out-move it, it's still there. That's the Spirit, to me."

Chapter Twenty-Five

"I hope you find what you're looking for."

It turns out heaven and hell aren't so far apart. They're within walking distance of each other, in fact. Death Valley, burning and barren, was eighty miles or so from the cool alpine caress of the Sierra Nevada. It would've been even closer if I'd left Highway 190 and started walking off the road, but that was a terrible idea, wandering into the Mojave Desert just to spare myself some miles. I'd learned that the almost-hard way.

Planning my route into California, I saw that there were two other options besides passing through Death Valley. The first was I-15 toward Los Angeles, but I didn't want to walk on the interstate anymore: too dangerous, too illegal. The second was 95 north to 266, but that would take me deeper into Nevada, where the towns were so far apart that I'd have to spend the daytime frying in the sun in the middle of nowhere.

Looking at my map, the answer seemed obvious: Highway 190. It ran right through an innocuous green blob—a national park—and there were two little resort settlements within one day's walk of each other. I could travel at night from Beatty to Stovepipe Wells, find shelter there for the day, and then get to Panamint Springs the next night, and then Keeler. The map made it look easy, but it wasn't, because the map didn't convey the reality of that innocuous green blob: Death Valley's August inferno. I had a choice: suffer 120-degree temperatures in close proximity to other human beings, or suffer 110-degree temperatures alone in the emptiness, possibly without shade. I chose the former, Death Valley. It was terrible timing, it being August and all, but I preferred to get it over with rather than hang out in Las Vegas for a month or two.

I'd spent a week in Vegas. A few days before reaching town, I was on the highway when I got a call from an unknown number. A woman named Kimberly Schaefer introduced herself and said she'd heard about me through the social media grapevine. She worked for an urban revitalization program in Vegas—the Downtown Project, founded by Tony Hsieh, also the founder of Zappos.com. They owned a building of luxury condos downtown, she said, and I could stay in one of their units for a week if I wanted, for free. When I stepped inside my little kingdom on the twenty-first floor I could hardly believe it. There was air-conditioning! And a massive bed! And a leather couch! And a kitchenette! And a TV! There was a pool on the rooftop and the city was neon at night! With Death Valley just ahead, it was like a big breath before a deep dive down.

My college friend Sam Harrison flew out to meet up with me, thinking we'd tear up the town, but I just wanted to rest, stay in. It was hard to get excited about Sin City with Death Valley so close. One night we did go out to the Strip, though. In Caesars Palace, we got overpriced drinks at the Shadow Bar, where women danced slowly behind a screen. Men in suits ogled the silhouettes or ignored them completely. I felt very out of place and we did not stay for a second round. Outside, I was spanked by a policewoman who was definitely not a policewoman. Hundreds of people flowed around Sam and me, rushing out of one casino and into the next. Did they realize they were walking through the desert? Did they know they were surrounded by a vast and flaming emptiness? In the Bellagio, the drinks were free as long as we kept gambling. Sam lost all his money in about five minutes, but somehow I made almost two hundred bucks at the roulette table. I saw no windows. I saw no clocks. Back outside, a bomb of electric light washed out the night, obscuring the desert truth that lay just beyond its reach.

Northwest of Vegas, I walked forty-three miles from Indian Springs to Amargosa Valley in the daytime, the farthest I'd ever gone in one shot. After thirteen hours I saw a red light blinking in the dark, beckoning me into the village like a homing beacon. My entire body ached, and something was wrong with my bladder—dehydration, or a UTI from the cow-shit creek under the bridge. Probably both. There was a medical clinic down the road. I'd go there in the morning.

I hobbled into Amargosa Valley, chafed and burned, a robot, mindless, somehow still walking. I found a bar next to a boarded-up brothel. I stumbled into the bar on autopilot. I collapsed on a stool. I ordered a cheeseburger. I drank a cold beer. The bartender told me about aliens. His name was Justice.

"Why Justice?" I asked.

"My dad was arrested the day I was born," he said.

I told Justice about my bladder issues.

"Maybe it's kidney stones," he said. "They're not that bad. Just like pissing razor blades out your dickhole, that's all. I got 'em once. I had to go to the doctor because I passed out from the pain. They tried to give me some pills to break 'em up inside, but I said, 'I don't want none of your medicine.' I drank three gallons of cranberry juice and passed them all that night. There were six of those little bastards in there, about that big," and he made a dime-size okay-sign with his right hand. "They were pretty-lookin'. Kind of like turquoise."

My problem was dehydration, thank God, not kidney stones. At the medical clinic the next day, the nurse hooked me up to an IV and I lay there for a long time, swelling like a sponge. It crossed my mind that maybe I was in over my head. My body was breaking down. But getting broken, I'd come to believe, was an important part of the experience—the radical humbling of it. *I'm weak. I need help. I can't do this anymore.* The daily breakdowns were like little ego deaths, freeing me, for a moment, from the delusion that I was something more than just a little speck of dirt in a big desert. I wanted these breakdowns because they often shattered my pride, the sneaky arrogance that said I was somehow exempt from my humanness, or above it—the frailty of my body, the vulnerability of my mind and heart, the inevitable pain. Sometimes, these breakdowns were so thorough they seemed to kill off, for just a shining moment or two, a given day's incarnation of this false self, that sneaky arrogance, so I welcomed them. But then again, I didn't want them to kill me off altogether.

Before I left the medical clinic, a young woman walked into the waiting room, about my age. She was from Texas, she told me, and she worked at one of the nearby brothels, legal in Nye County.

"How is that?" I asked.

"I love it," she said. I wanted to take out the recorder, because I wanted to understand, but she didn't seem interested in chatting, and I was too exhausted anyway.

I made it the next day to Beatty, the portal town to Death Valley. Why a human being would ever choose to live in such a place, I have no idea. Its closest neighbor, Rhyolite, was an actual ghost town. Other nearby spots included the Yucca Mountain Nuclear Waste Repository and the Nevada Test Site. There was a sign at a seemingly random spot on the highway introducing the Test Site:

TESTING OF DEVICES FOR DEFENSE AND FOR PEACEFUL
USES OF NUCLEAR EXPLOSIVES IS CONDUCTED HERE . . .
THE LAST ABORIGINAL GROUP TO OCCUPY THE SITE WAS
THE SOUTHERN PAIUTE WHO FORAGED PLANT FOODS IN
SEASON AND OCCUPIED THE AREA UNTIL THE COMING OF
THE PIONEERS

"And until we blew it all up. Sorry," the sign failed to include at the end. When the bombs were dropping in the 1950s, the mushroom clouds were visible from downtown Las Vegas. Apparently the tourists loved it.

It was a bleak and burned land, furious and forever, and ramshackle Beatty was right in the middle of it. Kim Schaefer in Las Vegas had passed me along to a guy in Beatty named Richard Stephens, the vice president of the art museum. The museum had a house for visiting artists, which happened to be vacant, and Richard let me stay there. He and I got lunch at a Subway where a sweaty man with a big bag of ice over his shoulder told us they'd closed Death Valley that day.

"It got up to one twenty-seven," he said. "That's some kind of record. The cars aren't built to take that kind of heat, let alone us."

I got much more anxious after that. It seemed like someone in the park should know I was about to walk through it, so I called the Park Service. They were not reassuring.

"I can't be stronger in encouraging you not to do this," one woman said, and then she put her colleague on the line.

"I hear you're thinking about taking a stroll through our little slice of paradise," he said. "You should buy a bus ticket instead." He told me that someone had tried it just a week earlier. The guy had started walking around midday. He had a gallon of water. His plan was to take a ten-mile stroll across some salt flats. He died at mile six.

"He literally cooked his insides," the ranger said. Some people had found the guy right before he died. They took him into their air-conditioned car, but the heat had already ruined the guy's brain. Through his melted vision he saw only devils, a menace where there was none. He got violent in the car, delusional, so the people let him back out into the furnace, and when he started throwing rocks at them, they drove away. He didn't live much longer after that.

"What do you expect when it's one hundred twenty degrees, there's no shade, and all you have is a gallon of water?" the ranger said.

The rangers were right. But even still, it felt wrong to skip a section after coming so far, especially this section, the final stretch of the desert. I'd planned it well, and I believed I could do it. It would take me four days. I would have Richard's help at the beginning: We'd made a plan whereby he would pick me up at the end of the first night and drive me back to Beatty to sleep during the day, then take me back to where I'd left off. After that, there'd be the two rustic resorts where I could sleep each day. Bob would carry my stuff, and my body knew what to do. I pored over my maps on the living room floor of the silent house. I did the math over and over again—the mileage between towns, the elevation gains and losses. I tried to predict what those numbers would mean for my body. I tried to sleep, and finally, I slept.

The first night up to Daylight Pass was simple. I crossed into California at sunrise, a little wooden post marking the border. I'd been imagining this moment for months. *California.* Now that I was living it, I found I hardly cared at all. I just wanted to survive the miles ahead.

I ended up hitching a ride back down into Beatty and slept most of the day. Around midnight, Richard dropped me off at Daylight Pass again, and I began the descent into Death Valley.

Highway 190 slithered down the mountains, carving curves into the rock. Bob was heavier than he'd ever been—more than one hundred pounds with all the extra water—and on the steep mountain grade he lunged with each step like a lion on a leash. My knees felt it almost immediately, the pounding. Soon, a sign materialized out of the dark: HELL'S GATE. The heat came with it, rising as I descended, suffusing my every atom. I thought of the sun. I walked faster.

My headlamp enlightened the land around me in a little circle—the saltbush, the brittlebush, the creosote. Green eyes glinted in the light, embedded inside the skull of some long, rat-like animal visible for only a second. The Perseid meteor shower blazed above me, evanescent streaks of electric white striping the firmament. I was walking in a strange dream. This was not my life.

"It's so quiet down there it's like you can hear everything from everywhere else draining out your ears," someone had said in Beatty. "All the noise, all the bullshit, it all just drains out."

"Hello?" I said. I almost didn't recognize my own voice in the vacuum. I sang quietly, to interrupt the silence: "Oompa Loompa, doom-ba-dee-doo, I've got a perfect puzzle for you. Oompa Loompa, doom-ba-dee-dee, if you are wise you will listen to me."

I couldn't see much at all. There was only the heat. It was still rising, and now the sun was, too, just barely tarnishing the night.

All of my seeking seemed so petty now, all the questions and their answers superfluous to the point of absurdity. All I wanted was to get out of Death Valley. Nothing else mattered. It seemed that nothing else ever had. There was only this. I was as present as I'd ever been, ready for anything except death.

I finally stumbled out of the mountains, my knees throbbing. The road ran straight across the valley, leading me right out into it, unshielded, exposed. In the distance, sand dunes crashed over one another in slow motion. Mountains circled me like the walls of a colossal chalice, and the wine was nowhere to be found, not a drop of water in sight. I was under the sea, a sign told me:

ELEVATION
SEA LEVEL

Stovepipe Wells was a mile away when the sun blossomed over the summits, and I made it to the ragtag resort before it could set me aflame. There were no vacant rooms, but the staff let me stay on the couch in their air-conditioned lobby. For the first time in a long time, I felt wide awake, almost high. I'd beaten the sun! I treated myself to the breakfast buffet. French toast had never tasted so good.

I spent the day trying to sleep in the lobby, pretending not to notice the constant stream of tourists. The TV was broadcasting the London summer Olympics—the marathon. Slowly, I started coming down from my high, the exhaustion permeating me all over again, and the fear. The upcoming walk to Panamint Springs that night was going to be my swansong: five thousand feet up, twenty-five hundred feet down, thirty miles across. It was very important that I sleep, but I could not.

Rose was a waitress at the resort, a grandmother in her fifties or sixties. She was tattooed and tanned like leather, with a smoker's voice. She took me under her wing for the day. It was her last shift of the season. Whenever she was free, she'd come to the lobby and keep me company. She called me "sweetheart" a lot, and she told me about her grandson, how much she loved him, how he was such a good engineer, how he'd already pimped out his car and he was only twelve. I listened with all of myself, grateful for the chance to forget what lay ahead of me.

That afternoon, Rose introduced me to one of the staff members, an Iranian guy named Reza Baluchi. He was a world-class runner. He was working at the resort so he could train in the heat. Rose thought we'd get along. "One Man, One Mission to UNITE," his website declares. "The first man to run through every country in the world." He was a small, lithe man with dark hair. He spoke unemotionally in choppy English. I interviewed him in his trailer, hoping he'd offer a bit of inspirational advice for that night's walk. It was cramped inside, and cluttered with packaged health foods and running gear.

"I am start in ninety-six," he said. "Travel around the world. Fifty-five country. Seven continent. Forty-nine thousand seven hundred mile pedaling and running for peace. In two thousand three run Los Angeles to New York, one hundred twenty-four day, three thousand seven hundred twenty mile. In two thousand seven running around the entire perimeter of U.S., eleven thousand seven hundred twenty mile, two hundred two day. Now I try running, start in Jerusalem, Dead Sea, running nine country, go all the way to Mount Everest, and climb, go up. So, this next."

I felt like a clown, suddenly. I'd walked almost four thousand miles, and until that moment I'd thought that was pretty impressive. Reza's numbers were beyond my comprehension.

"In these long journeys that you take, I'm sure there are the highs and the lows. How do you deal with the hardship?"

"Everybody can do it. Your mind is strong? You can do what you want. Everybody can do it. Everything is your mind."

"It's pretty cool that I met you today, because before I came into Death Valley I was really nervous about it. I talked to the rangers and they're telling me people are dying out here. Tonight will probably be the hardest walk of the whole trip. So, what advice can you give me for tonight's walk to Panamint?"

"I don't know, which way you go?"

"I'm gonna go on Highway 190."

"Highway 190 all the way up?"

"Yeah, all the way up."

"Oh, my heart, you can't take a baby stroller! Road too small, car cannot see you. I don't think National Park let you go. You need a lot of water."

It wasn't quite the inspirational advice I'd been hoping for. I left Reza's trailer deflated, and even more nervous.

By nightfall, I'd given up trying to sleep. A ranger came to the lobby to deliver a lecture on Death Valley. A German couple joined me on the couch. "Despondent people come here to end their lives," the ranger said at one point. He told us about the accidental deaths, too, going into detail about the guy who'd died the previous week out on the salt flats. After the presentation, the Germans noticed Bob parked in the corner and asked me about the WALKING TO LISTEN sign. I told them what I was doing, and what I was about to do, and they started muttering to each other in German.

"You are so crazy," the guy said to me in English. Under different circumstances, I would've taken that as a compliment.

I waited until nine o'clock or so, hoping the darkness would cut the heat. It didn't. Rose treated me to a cheeseburger before I left, and a beer.

"Be careful, sweetheart," she said, hugging me good-bye.

The wind blew the burn into my skin, obliterating. At the outskirts of the resort, right before the road started up the mountains, I passed a man and a woman sitting together in the heat under the stars with glasses of red wine. They saw my headlamp on the road and called out to me. I walked over and stood with them for a while, melting inside, because I wanted it all to be over. I wanted what they had, not this. Where was my beloved? I wanted to be here with her, and with our children, showing them this hellish place I'd survived so many years earlier. The children would be asleep in our room, and the two of us would sneak out here, exactly here, and we'd sit together in the heat under the stars with glasses of red wine, and then, the next morning, the children would wake us, whispering in our ears, and we'd all eat French toast at the breakfast buffet and then drive home. Home. I wanted to be home.

"I hope you find what you're looking for!" the woman shouted to me over the wind after I'd already said good-bye. I couldn't see her in the dark.

"I already did!" I shouted back right away, without thinking. The words did not echo, but I heard them in my head as I kept walking. They just came out. I realized they were mostly true. Over the course of ten months, I'd been given so much, and I didn't want anything more from this walk. Well, I did want to get out of Death Valley alive. That'd be nice.

Pushing Bob up the Panamints on the empty highway, I felt like a sleepy Sisyphus. My eyelids kept closing involuntarily. About halfway up I couldn't take it anymore. I pulled into a campground and fell asleep on a picnic table, knowing full well that the sun would not wait for me. I don't know how long I was out—one hour, maybe two. I dreamt that I'd forgotten to lock Bob's back wheels, so he started rolling down the mountain. I gasped and jerked awake. Bob was still there. It was still dark. I still had to walk.

All I had to do was stay awake and just keep walking. Maybe that was the answer to every question. *Stay awake and just keep walking.* The sun rose over the summits, and I saw Panamint Springs down in the valley. I was going to make it. As I descended toward the little settlement, I broke one of my rules and plugged in my earbuds, blasting some more dubstep into me—I needed the adrenaline boost. A voice sang, "You don't need to hide, my friend, for I am just like you," and I dance-walked all the way down the mountainside, alive, alive, alive.

There's a legend about how Death Valley got its name. I thought of it the next night as I climbed out of the park once and for all. A party of pioneers decided to take a shortcut off the Old Spanish Trail. The shortcut, it turned out, ran straight through Earth's closest approximation of hell. The pioneers wandered through the desert for months, trying in vain to find a way up and out of the Panamints. They had to slaughter their oxen for food. They had to destroy their wagons for fire. God knows where they found water. Finally, two scouts discovered a way out. As the party finally stumbled from the flames, someone looked back and said it, the same words that I now whispered walking out of the park's western gates: "Good-bye, Death Valley."

I didn't have to imagine their euphoria. The sun was rising at my back, noticeably cooler, and the glowing granite heaven of the High Sierra was right there, lunging thousands of feet into the sky. I'd never seen mountains burst from the earth like that. There were no foothills, just a sudden wall of rock shining silver, and the desert below it blushing red and gold, varnished with the shine of manganese and iron. I couldn't stop smiling. The mountains were more than just beautiful. They signaled the end of the Mojave Desert. I skipped a clumsy do-si-do on the road to celebrate. From here on out, the heat would subside, and the invisible giant who'd been chasing me with his magnifying glass would finally go torture somebody else. There'd be no more sleep deprivation. There'd be no more dehydration. And soon, there'd be no more walking.

DYLAN TAYLOR, musician, canyoneering guide
ZION NATIONAL PARK, UTAH, sitting around the fire outside his
trailer home
JULY

"I ran away from home when I was sixteen. Just playing music, making twelve dollars an hour playing guitar. When I was in Denver, this guy, one of the most amazing sax players I've ever seen, just this old guy, dreadlocks, sitting on the side of the road, and I sat down with him and he always told me, 'Man, if you feel the music you just gotta let it take ahold of you.' More or less, just be the channel for what good music has to flow through, because you know it's out there, but to harness it takes something else, and to be able to grasp on to it, and basically hang on for the ride, you know? Just let those fingers do the work. Just being in that moment, and being able to clear your head is one of the most beautiful things. That perfect moment of pure in-the-moment. People look their entire lives to find that, and you can find it in a guitar, or a mandolin, or everywhere around you. You just have to open your eyes enough to see it. And everything you can learn from anybody else that you play with, it just adds that much more. Like jamming with you was sick. Speaking of which, come on, man, let's play a song."

Chapter Twenty-Six

"You forget."

I walked alongside the Sierras for a week, the mountains growing with each mile on the road, ragged sabers cutting the sky. By the second day I could only see them fully if I tilted my head back. Fighter jets buzzed the dry valleys, tracing the contours of the tectonically wrinkled land. Their sonic bursts caromed off the hallways of rock. Some of this rock had seen oceans come and go. It was so ancient as to have metamorphosed, its origins lost in the crucible of pressure and heat. What had it been millions of years ago? What was it now? I couldn't see any of these transformations, all that had been made new by the passage of time—just a narrow glance, what these myopic human eyes could perceive. The fighter jets flew over the palette of gray and tan, mud brown and mustard yellow, so low I could almost touch them. I assumed they were from the Air Force base I'd passed a week earlier outside Vegas. The trip probably took them a few minutes.

The clouds changed like the rock, only faster, sprouting out of nowhere in the high blue fields above. Perfectly white, they blossomed beyond reach, extravagantly, effortlessly, flexing into magnificence and then churning inward again, constantly discovering new versions of themselves. It struck me that we weren't so different, we humans. Just slower, and a bit more solid. Then the clouds would fade, their misty filaments drifting back into the blue.

*　*　*

I'd begun planning for the end, although I could hardly believe the end was so near. I'd decided to meet the ocean at Half Moon Bay, just south of San Francisco. Mom was going to be there, and some other people, too: Herb and Marian Furman were going to fly out from Alabama, and the Paisanos would drive out from the Navajo reservation. We were going to have a potluck to celebrate. I wasn't sure if Dad would be there; I didn't really know, for a while, if I wanted him to be.

He called me a few days before I started climbing the Sierras and said, "I was thinking about it, and I want to buy you a plane ticket back home. To help you finish your journey." Money was tight, he told me, so he wouldn't be able to fly out for the final day of my walk after buying my ticket home. At that moment it became clear that his absence on that day just wouldn't feel right. There'd already been so much distance between us. Odds were I was only going to walk across America once. There'd only be one day in all of my life like the final day at Half Moon Bay, one chance to experience the fullness of it, and it wouldn't be full if he wasn't with me at the water.

"I don't know," I said. "I'd kind of like you to be there at the end. You could spend the money on a plane ticket for yourself out to San Francisco instead. Think about it."

"Sure, yeah," he said. "I'll look into it."

Finally I began climbing the mountains up Highway 120 into Yosemite National Park. Bob was thrilled about this. The desert had not treated him well. The heavy UV rays had bleached his carrot orange to a pale peach. He'd developed a whimpering creak from all the water weight. He'd blown more flats than I could count, thanks to the goat-heads and the metal threads in shredded truck tires. But all that was over, climbing up the steep switchbacks into the heights of the Sierra Nevada. Bob was relieved. Euphoric, even. I was, too, at first.

At the top of the mountain pass after a three-hour climb on 120, sunlight glanced off a lake, casting brilliant white jewels into my eyes. An emerald meadow surrounded me, soft as merino, beckoning bare feet. Deeper into the mountains, evergreens leaned in close. Everything was aching with its own aliveness, so different from the desert, and as I walked through it all, just as alive as the rest, a wave of emotion hit me out of nowhere. I pulled down my sunhat so the cars couldn't see, so I could continue.

Next to beauty-walking, this was the best of them all: weep-walking, when I was feeling more than my thoughts could take and all I could do was cry. I'd never experienced anything like it before the walk, this unexpected, uncontrollable sobbing. Men weren't supposed to do that, but the more it happened to me on the road, the more I realized how much I needed it, and how much I always had. Its source was unknown, but its medium was certain: my body. It would heave me, like a spring river swollen with snowmelt. I always tried to understand it, but I never quite could. It had something to do with walking alone in an unknown place far from home, especially after mile twenty, with a screaming body and a heart left quaking by solitude. There's vulnerability in that pain. The opening is there, and with the right thought or image, the weep-walking enters. Often it felt like sorrow at first, but as it ran its course through my body, a surprising sense of astonishment often flooded in: everything had its place and purpose, everything its beauty, and what a wonder to be in it all, and to actually see it for a moment, feel it. Sometimes it got so good my throat hurt. This was when I pulled the sunhat down. It was a rare kind of walking, and I could never force it, so whenever it came I'd do what I could to let it stay.

It was as close to anything rapturous as I've ever experienced, a divine lightning bolt if there ever was one.

But something was a little different about the weep-walking in Yosemite. The road ahead that had always seemed endless was about to end. For so long, the ocean had been nothing more than an idea. It was so laughably far away it didn't even exist. Now, it was just a ten-day walk away. I'd been expecting to feel some kind of euphoria at this point in the trek, but it wasn't that at all, especially when I realized there was no avoiding the end.

Suddenly, I didn't want it to end, even though I knew it must. The walk had been so consuming and drawn out that its life trajectory had become my own, and in some way there was no comfortable distance between them. I had a sense, a certainty even, that something besides just the walk was going to end that day at the ocean—an old self, an expired way of being. The sensation was so powerful that I actually got confused, and began to conflate the end of the walk with death; I became a bit of a hypochondriac, a bit paranoid even. Maybe a truck was finally going to hit me, or maybe I'd get Hantavirus in Yosemite, which had already killed a few people that summer.

I'd always known I was going to die someday, like everybody did, but it was only in the Sierras—ten days left to walk—that I really believed it, beyond my intellect. On the road in those last two weeks, there was nothing at all to distract me from these thoughts, and the occasional delusions, so I went deep into them, contemplating and visualizing my death such that it became very real for me, and not the forgettable fairy tale it had been up to that point. It wasn't some abstract, far-off idea anymore. It was as much a part of me as my own breath—ever-present, unavoidable, and even necessary in a way that I couldn't yet accept. I hadn't felt that kind of dread before, a dumbfounding panic I'd never known I had in me.

At the same time, I knew, in my more rational mind, that I was only getting the tiniest glimpse of mortal fear. I wasn't in a war zone, or living on the street without options; I wasn't terminally ill, or watching a loved one slowly pass away. My fear was overblown, maybe even absurd. But what doesn't seem absurd in retrospect is the realization of how terribly unprepared I am for death, and how vulnerable, and inexperienced. I no longer felt invincible in the Sierras, like I had when I left home. I felt humbled. Afraid.

"I think a big part of facing death, when you know it's right here, leads one to fear less." Georgette Endicott had said this to me back in Albuquerque. She'd taken me in for a few days, and told me about her experience with cancer. "Death doesn't scare me anymore. It took walking through that process and learning to be quiet, to just sit in the silence. I think a part of what's scary for many of us is that quiet place. We keep our minds busy or numb them."

"But what about the sadness of good-bye?" I'd said. "Isn't there a sadness to that?"

"Well, what if it's sadness, but there's not judgment about it. Sadness is just as good as gladness. That's what it seems like to me these days. Yeah, it's sadness! Isn't it great that you can feel that? What if you didn't feel sadness? Then you probably couldn't even feel joy, either. There is no good or bad. As soon as you have one thing you have the opposite of it, and in those contradictions is where Spirit lives. Because that's what life is. As soon as you have hello you have good-bye. Isn't that beautiful? Get it? Even when somebody leaves us permanently. We just have the judgment that life is better than death.

"Expect the best. That's my mama. Every morning she'd just shuffle to the kitchen and she'd open the curtains and look outside. It was Washington State, so it was always a gray, cloudy damn day, but she'd always open the curtains and say, '*Che bella giornata!*'

What a beautiful day! At first it was like, 'Mom, it's gray and rainy, what are you seeing out there?' *Che bella giornata.* She'd say that every day. You might as well expect the best, and be satisfied. Be grateful. It might as well be a beautiful day. I might as well be satisfied."

I remembered her words as I weep-walked through the Sierras, trying to be satisfied and grateful. *Che bella giornata,* I'd say in the mornings, even if I didn't mean it. *Che bella giornata.*

"It's too much blood. I can't lose all this blood." The guy was still strapped into his seat. His face was pale. He'd survived the plane crash somehow, but I could tell he wasn't going to live for long. Liam Neeson walked over to him, and the guy grabbed his arm. "Help me, okay? Something's wrong. Something's really, really wrong. I don't feel right."

Liam Neeson didn't look hopeful. He never does. "Listen," he said. "Shh, listen. You're going to die. That's what's happening."

The movie was hitting a little too close to home. I half-wondered if the Gleasons were messing with me. We were sitting in their dark living room together, Bil, Gelyn, and I. The two of them had stopped on the road earlier to say hello just as I was walking out of Yosemite. They invited me to stay with them at their house for the night. The cottage was tucked away in the pine forests of the Sierra Nevada. Just west, the mountains fell into the foothills that began the Central Valley and the last leg of my walk. Bil was an old-school, Deadhead hippie with curly blond hair and a big, easy laugh. Gelyn was a native of the Philippines, as quiet as her husband was ebullient.

"I just like talking to people," Bil had said over a dinner of shrimp and rice before the movie. It was my last recorded interview.

"I go up to strangers all the time. In fact, I got a T-shirt made that says, 'I Talk to Strangers.' I might as well warn people. I'll get in an elevator and look at everybody instead of looking up at the lights, and everybody else is looking away thinking, 'Why the fuck are you looking at me?'"

He chuckled. Bil was an excellent laugher. It had been obvious from the moment he pulled over on the roadside. He'd let out a guffaw when I told him I was pushing a baby in my stroller up and down the mountains. The sound of it made the rest of the miles a little easier.

"I like putting people off ease. Everybody's too comfortable. Everybody walks through life asleep. We forget how amazing it is. I know I almost died hiking one time in winter. We went out and got stuck on the side of a mountain. It was supposed to be three hours, but it was thirteen in the end. We were out there, two in the morning in the snow, it was dark, no flashlight. I was throwing up from dehydration, but when I'd eat snow I'd start shaking from hypothermia. And then I'd keep walking. Dehydrate. Eat some snow. Start shaking. Start walking. Dehydrate. It looked grim for a little while. But we survived, and after that I was like, 'Oh, God, I'm alive! I will never forget! I'm going to be so joyful every day for the rest of my life!' And that lasted about a month or so, you know? You forget. I can think back on it and refresh it a little, but it's so easy to forget how blessed we are just waking up in the morning and seeing stuff."

After the movie ended (everybody died) I said good night to Bil and Gelyn and went out to my tent. It was my last night in the Sierras, and I wanted to be outside for it, or I'd wanted that before the movie, at least. Now, I zipped my tent shut the same way I used to run up the stairs at night when I was a little boy, convinced a hand was going to grab my ankle at any moment and pull me down.

I had less than ten days to walk. What if I had less than ten days to live?

Whimpering and weeping, sighing and sniveling, I walked. I knew it was all a bit melodramatic, but I couldn't help it. Whitman would have scoffed, told me to stop being so self-absorbed in my own sorrow, missing the big, beautiful picture. "All has been gentle with me," he wrote, but he could have said "you." "I keep no account with lamentation. / What have I to do with lamentation?"

I was glad I'd asked Dad to be there at the end. The past didn't matter anymore. If I was going to die I wanted to do it right, goddammit, and that meant having him there. After almost a year on the road, I was far too tired to be angry at him, and far too grateful, even for the divorce. The pain of it had been my first coming-of-age, an entrance into the harsher realities of the human experience, and it was now a way for me to connect with other people, a way into empathy. Without it, without Dad, I might not have discovered my own frailty until much later. I might have gone on for years living in a fantasy, not understanding that at any moment everything could shatter. I might not have felt such a strong desire to seek and listen and learn. I might not have walked.

The next day it was hot again, stumbling down into the Central Valley. Not hot like Death Valley, but still. The summits had fallen to foothills and the land rolled like sound waves. Knee-high straw grass waved in hues of ochre and amber, and a gnarled scrub oak stood alone against the golden wash. The earth was fertile here. Almond groves lined the narrow country highway ahead. Peaches and strawberries stippled the soil green and pink and red, sweetening the breeze. A brilliant blue winked above, the sky's response to the eloquence below.

The sun was burning a dry heat, and I was thirsty. At the outskirts of a tiny village called Catheys Valley, a general store wavered into sight like a mirage. It was called the Oasis, appropriately. I bought an iced tea inside, chugged it, and then did it all over again immediately. It was bliss, but it didn't last. It couldn't. Nothing did. I was just on my way out when a man walked into the store with an impressive watermelon cradled in his arms like a newborn child. The man was narrow-waisted and stick-legged, and an imposing salt-and-pepper mustache seemed to make him top heavy. He could barely hold the mammoth watermelon.

"You won't believe it," he said, addressing the cashier and me. He was shaking his head solemnly. "You just won't believe it. I was out there in the park with my buddy Darren and I saw this sucker sitting over there in the vines on the side of the road, out where I cut weeds. I said, 'Hey, Darren, look at that! That's a watermelon!' So I went over there, snip snip, and here we go!"

The watermelon was perfectly spherical. Alternating stripes ran down its smooth face, pine green and lime green—the subalpine forests of Yosemite and the Mormon lawns of the southern Utah desert. It was the size of a basketball.

"Can you put it in the fridge to cool it for me, Pam?" the man asked.

"As long as I can have a slice," Pam said, taking the trophy fruit. "I'm just surprised the rabbits didn't get it. I can't grow nothing in my garden 'cause of those rabbits."

"Nice one, man," I said, feeling strangely jubilant and wanting to share in the celebration. Sure it was just a watermelon, but it was a big watermelon, and it had been growing right there on the highway under the guy's nose all along. The odds of that watermelon becoming what it had become were so slim—the rabbits, the traffic, the untended dirt of the highway shoulder. And yet, it had become. And the guy had found it, on a hot day no less.

"Can you believe it?" the man said to me. "A watermelon, just sitting right there. I thought it fell out of a turnip truck or something, but sure enough it was growing on the vine."

"That's awesome," I said. "It's gonna taste great on a hot day like today."

"You should come sit out in the park with us. Get a drink and enjoy the shade. If you hang out long enough for the watermelon to cool off you can have a slice."

I bought a third iced tea right away.

It was a scraggly park, more of a lot than anything else. A wall of brambles buffered the park from the road. A few shade trees stitched a canopy above, and a gazebo stood in the center with a picnic table underneath. We took a seat at the table, joining a man with thin tawny hair that tickled his shoulders. He had yellowed teeth and wore a beat-up cowboy hat with a falcon feather stuck in it.

"This is my buddy Darren," the watermelon man said to me. "They call him the Mayor, because he's pretty much the mayor of the park. And I'm Jeff. They call me the Groundskeeper. I take care of the park."

"You see that watermelon?" the Mayor asked me.

"I sure did," I said.

"Some watermelon, huh?" He shook his head in disbelief. "Some damn watermelon. Jeff saw it over there sitting in the vines and said, 'Look, there's a watermelon,' and I said, 'No way,' and then he brought it over here and sure as shit it was a watermelon. I mean, that doesn't happen every fuckin' day. Goddamn."

We all reveled in it together, and the two of them told me a few more renditions of the watermelon story in awed tones. I'd had some practice in the discipline of astonishment walking across the continent, but the Mayor and the Groundskeeper appeared to be sage gurus in it, so easily recognizing the wondrousness disguised in the seemingly simple. I admired them this. Whitman would have, too:

> To walk up my stoop is unaccountable . . . I pause to consider
>   if it really be,
> That I eat and drink is spectacle enough for the great
>   authors and schools,
> A morning-glory at my window satisfies me more than the
>   metaphysics of books.

Whitman might've sounded high to someone who didn't know how to recognize the wondrousness in its many disguises, just as the Mayor and the Groundskeeper might've seemed a bit slow to someone who didn't know how to slow down themselves.

"You hear two more people died in the river yesterday?" the Groundskeeper asked the Mayor, the watermelon forgotten for a moment.

"Yeah, I heard," the Mayor said. "River's claiming a lot of lives this season."

"I was out there fishing all last night," the Groundskeeper said, turning to me. "I like fishing out there at night. I like the quiet. It's peaceful. But it's kind of a scary place, too. My dad used to fish that river, and it's where he shot himself in the head. Right in that same river that took those two people yesterday, where I was fishing last night."

"Oh, man, I'm sorry about that," I said.

"It's all right. It was a long time ago. I ain't like my old man. I'm fifty-three and still climbing trees. I normally sleep right up there." He pointed above us to the eaves of the gazebo. There was a plywood board lying over the wooden crossbeams: his bed.

"It's perfect here at night. Not too warm, not too cool, just perfect. I climb right up there almost every night and sleep like a baby. My old man never used to climb like that."

"I love climbing trees," I said, trying to change the subject. "I haven't climbed a tree in too long."

"I just climbed a thirty-foot cross yesterday," the Groundskeeper said.

"Like, a Jesus cross?"

"Yeah. It had a hundred lights on it and I had to replace thirty-five of them, so I climbed right up there. My mom says, 'Don't do that, I worry about you,' and I just say, 'Mom, I'm okay. If I stop doing that, I'm finished.' It keeps me alive. Like I said, I ain't like my old man."

"That must have been hard. Did you," I paused, "you know, see him?"

"No, but I seen plenty other dead people. I used to fight forest fires. We'd kite parachute right in there. Once, we were flying into a fire—or that's what they told me—but it was actually a plane crash and we were the cleanup. We got there and the plane was scattered in different parts everywhere for seven miles. The bodies were, too. I couldn't do it. Putting it all in a big pile and stuffing the bags full. I just couldn't do it. It was so disgusting. No, it wasn't disgusting. It was terrible disgusting. They didn't know about my dad. They didn't know about me finding a prostitute hanging, or finding another man hanging from a tree. I've seen a lot of dead people in my life. I'm okay now, though. I think I'd be all right if I saw one today. I don't know."

It had shown up quite uninvited, this talk of death. I almost wasn't surprised. I'd been thinking about it so much I must've magnetized myself for it. We all sat in silence for a while, enjoying the shade and sipping our drinks, letting the dead dissipate once more into the background, waiting for the watermelon to cool.

"So what's your mission?" the Mayor asked me. I told him about the walk, that I was listening to people's stories as I went— the elevator speech.

"No, man," he said, "what's your mission in life? You walked this whole way, you must've figured something out by now."

I said I wasn't sure. The Mayor waited.

"I guess it's something like spread love and be happy. Be at peace. I don't know."

"That ain't bad," he said.

"How about you?" I asked. "What's your mission?"

"To go pick up my codeine pills in Merced. I can't get a new script 'cause I ate all the old ones too fast and they won't give me any more. Goddamn bastards."

The watermelon wasn't cool yet, but I wanted to get to Merced by nightfall. I shook the Mayor's hand good-bye. The Groundskeeper stood up to give me a stiff hug and a pat on the back.

"I'm proud of you," he said. "You're almost there."

CATHY BROOKS, LGBTQIA activist and business consultant
LAS VEGAS, NEVADA, on the rooftop of a condo building on a hot afternoon
AUGUST

"It was around seven thirty in the morning and I went to take the dog for a walk. I took him out to the way eastern end of the downtown area, and it's desolate down there. It's just vacant lots pockmarked with weeds, chain-link fences around them. There are people out there who are living kind of on the fringe. There was one guy walking down the sidewalk and he had this scowl on his face, and I'm walking along. I could've reacted in a couple different ways. I could've reacted with fear. You know, big guy walking toward me, looked like he might be a little inebriated, and here's me, alone, there's nobody around to help me if I scream. I could've referred to him with some sort of disdain or judgment. Or I could remember that he's just a human being, probably hasn't had anybody look him in the eye and smile in a while. So I did. And after a moment of brief shock, he smiled back, and said, 'Good morning.' Then he said, 'Nice dog,' which I appreciated, because I do have a nice dog.

"When you start realizing that everyone around you has something. We've all got something we're carrying. We're all scared of something. We're angry at something. We're all wanting something. Everybody. And when you share on that level with people, it takes away the Other, and when you remove the Other, you remove so many things. You can start discourse."

Chapter Twenty-Seven

"Your walk will continue."

I was pushing Bob up the mountains again, the final undulations of land before the sea. Highway 84 swooped up the slopes. There was no shoulder, and soon the night would whisper everything into darkness. The end of the climb was still a few miles away, but I'd come far enough. The beach was close; I'd be able to get there the following day. Down the mountainside to my left, I saw a flat spot nestled in one of the road's curves, big enough for the tent. I parked Bob and began ferrying everything down, hoping no one would see me.

The redwoods were young, and in the canopy they reached out to one another other, their arms interlacing. Broken constellations of sunset glimmered on the floor of fallen needles. I sat down before setting up camp. *This is it*, I kept hearing in my head. *This is it*. I let in the silence and the stillness; they felt like old friends now. I turned to Rilke one last time: "What is necessary, after all, is only this: solitude, vast inner solitude. To walk inside yourself and meet no one for hours—that is what you must be able to attain." For at least a moment, this moment, I could do it. I could rest there, here, in this vast inner space that could be filled by nothing but my own presence. I read more, and it felt like a dear teacher was saying good-bye to me, wishing me well, pushing me out of the nest: "Believe in a love that is being stored up for you like an inheritance, and have faith that in this love there is a strength and a blessing so large that you can travel as far as you wish without having to step outside it."

The chill of the air tickled my skin, a blessed contrast to the desert. Cars drove by me through the forest and the fading day, blind to me. I began to feel that inexplicable satisfaction rising, born of a long day's walk. There had been so many. My body remembered the tension of every mile, and lying on the pine needles at dusk, it could relax at last.

I set up my tent for the last time, and I ate my last dinner from the food bag. The chores didn't feel mundane like they normally had, because I would never do them again. I'd been floating along in this extraordinary sensation all day. That morning, I'd gone into a gas station for breakfast, and it had hit me that I would never experience this particular kind of delight ever again, the delight of drinking a coffee and eating a Honey Bun on a walk across America. The coffee and the Honey Bun became monumentally important in that moment. I ate and drank with something like reverence. And it made me wonder: If the little things could take on such significance at the end of a long walk, how much more would they take on in the final moments of life? How sweet and strange and sad it would be to eat my last Honey Bun someday. And what about the not-so-little things? How unspeakably good to feel the final touch of someone else's hand on my own, and how hard to let go.

Far above me, misty contrails dashed across the sky. I traced them forward, searching for the airplane, and then there it was, framed for a split instant by a window in the branches, its metal body reflecting all the colors of the soon-to-be-slumbering sky. And then it was gone.

I'd slogged through Silicon Valley that day. Throngs of techies had pretended not to see me as we passed one another on the sidewalk. I'd never felt so much a stranger. I didn't want to be there. I wanted to be in the trees, alone, roots growing from my feet, moss growing on my face, taken back into the earth. Instead, I got lost in

Apple's lunch-hour rush. No one spoke to me, and I didn't start up any conversations, either. I was in no mood to talk. Chitchat was impossible with the ocean so close—the speechlessness of deep gratitude, the silence of a sorrow that no one else could understand.

Before it got too dark in the woods, I took out Kahlil Gibran for the first time in almost eleven months on the road. *The Prophet* was full of ruminations on different subjects, and I felt certain death was one of them. I opened the book at random, and the words stared back at me as if they'd known exactly what I was looking for:

> Your fear of death is but the trembling of the shepherd
> when he stands before the king whose hand is to be laid
> upon him in honor.
> Is the shepherd not joyful beneath his trembling, that he
> shall wear the mark of the king?

What was it, anyway, this ambiguous fear of the end? Was it not, in fact, a trembling joy at all that I'd been given, a wonder at all that I was? Was it not gratitude disguised? Because the king had already marked me. To deny that was to deny everyone I'd met on the road. The king had so many faces and voices. I could feel them with me, four thousand miles of them, in their great and baffling complexity, their beauty, each one their own inimitable version of existence, never seen before, never to be seen again. Their longings. Their triumphs. Their brokenness. All the ways they'd chosen to be themselves, to be here. And my God, their kindness, all the stories of their lives so freely given. They'd marked me as worthy, even when I felt I wasn't. They'd believed in me more than I'd believed in myself. They'd shown me that I was enough, that there was nothing more I had to become, nothing else.

I heard Whitman's farewell words, as I lay on the forest floor: "I have perceived that to be with those I like is enough, / To stop in company with the rest at evening is enough, / To be surrounded by beautiful curious breathing laughing flesh is enough."

Cars rolled by me on the road, the luminous paths of their head-lights broken by the trees, and I had this thought: that if I were in one of those cars right now, looking into the dark forest outside, I'd probably think it was a scary place, but because I was *in* the forest, I knew it wasn't a scary place. It was actually quite lovely in here. And the fears of death I'd been carrying with me, in that moment, they lifted. They were, after all, just fears—creations of my own mind that were powerless beyond my belief in them. It didn't have to be scary. It could be whatever I wanted it to be. "Expect the best," Georgette had said. Why had I ever chosen to expect anything else?

But I could also see how the experience of imagining and then incorporating the presence of death into the living of my life—how walking with it close, hand in hand, and watching my reactions to this new companion—how all of that fear was a necessary part of the path toward peace, toward the letting-go of fear that Georgette had attained, a letting-go that I hoped to settle into myself one day. I knew, sitting there in the woods, that this might just be a momentary respite from that fear, but I also knew that if I could feel free now, then I'd probably be able to again someday. Right then, my fear of death seemed like a guide into the next phase after the walk, an introduction to the lessons I still had to learn, a whole new set of questions. But that night in the forest, my last night, I didn't feel so afraid of the end.

There wasn't a shoulder on the highway into Half Moon Bay, so I had to walk in the lane of oncoming traffic. Someone called the police. Two officers were waiting for me on the outskirts of town in their squad car. When I reached them, one got out and approached me, arms across her chest.

"We got a call about a guy pushing a baby stroller on the highway?"

"Yeah, that's me," I said. "Sorry about that. But everything's fine. I don't have a baby in here. You might not believe this, but I've been walking across America for about a year now, and I'm almost there. I'm literally finishing at the beach just ahead."

"Are you serious?" she said.

"I swear to God."

She looked at her partner, and he shrugged his shoulders.

"Well get going, man!" she said. "We're not gonna stop you now!"

I invited them to the potluck. As I got into town, I started recognizing people on the sidewalk, the ones who couldn't stand to wait for me at the beach. There was Willy Grey, who'd put me up in Alabama, and Mark and Ivonne Hancock, who'd taken me in just a week earlier in the Central Valley. Kathy Sermas, the wife of Gus the Greek taskmaster from my landscaping days, had flown out, too. And then I saw Dad. He wasn't quite running toward me, but almost, waving and shouting hooray goofily. Watching him come, I saw a man who loved his son the best way he knew how, and for the first time in a long time, I didn't need him to be any different. He was here, now. We embraced, and he squeezed me in quick staccato bursts, the same way he used to when I saw him for the holidays, like he'd either forgotten how to give a normal hug or just couldn't contain himself. As he walked with me at my back, I felt something like acceptance. I knew it would be an ongoing project, and that it probably wouldn't always flow freely, but I also felt that this moment of clarity would be enough to last us both a long time.

Chris and James Paisano had driven all the way out from the Navajo Nation. They'd called me the previous week and asked if they could perform a ceremony at the very end.

"It's to recognize that you are now a changed person," Chris said, "and that your mind is someplace else, and we want to help you with this last part, and honor the moment. Our people used to do this, this kind of pilgrimage, but we don't really do that anymore. You can take our prayers and good wishes with you and give them to the ocean. The ceremony is supposed to mark this special event, and to continue that. Because your walk will continue, even after you get to the ocean."

Chris was waiting for me near the parking lot by the beach with his brother, Michael, who happened to live nearby. They were both dressed in colorful ceremonial garb. Michael began drumming and chanting in Navajo, and Chris sprinkled a path of cornmeal in front of me. I couldn't believe it was all happening. We turned a corner and then I saw them, a group of forty or fifty people waiting for me. One of them broke away, giving an almost animal-like shout. My mother. The sand slowed her a little, and it jumbled up her gait, but she didn't stop until she reached me. She was sobbing.

"My son," she kept saying as we hugged, "my son, my son, my son."

She'd spent the whole morning decorating the beach with streamers and balloons. She'd spent the whole year letting me go. I couldn't really imagine her sacrifice, what it was like to surrender her own child to the highway, but I could see how hard it had been on her, and how relieved she was now that it was finally finished. She joined my dad behind me, and we all walked together toward the group.

The drumming and the chanting took me into a surreal other-world, and the sand gave against my weight, and the surf roared like a highway. So many people had come—friends from high school and college, people I'd met on the road, perfect strangers who just happened to be there at the beach that day. They all formed a circle. Chris led me into the middle and then left me there on my own. I didn't know what to do, and so I just stood there and wept. After a few seconds my friend Lucy ran out and hugged me, and then I went around the circle, embracing each of them. It didn't matter if I'd never met them before. It only mattered that they were here, and that we were here together, and that none of us had to walk alone that day.

However much I knew that I wasn't actually dying, and however much less afraid I'd been in the last fifteen hours or so, at this moment, it really did feel like I was entering some kind of heaven, far more spectacular than anything I'd ever imagined—so many people waiting there for me, a long-held sigh of relief, no more walking to do, just floating. As the moment worked its way through my brain, my heart, I could feel it changing me—how it would be much harder from here on out to forget that this life would all be over someday, how it would be a little easier to remember the sheer wonder of it, the cosmic improbability. I'd never felt the urge to bow like I did now, to prostrate myself in reverence, in gratitude for the miracle of simply being here.

Everyone drew close around me. Each of them took a pinch of cornmeal from Chris, as he'd instructed, and dropped it into my cupped hands—their blessings for me, their own prayers for themselves, their hope and their hurt—and then we went down to the water, where James was waiting. I'd walked all the way across the continent to get to him, this elder standing at the edge of the ocean. A vision flashed in my mind of the grandfather I might be someday, the old man at the end where the land met the water at last. This elder was smiling very slightly, as James was smiling now, and standing patiently before me, me, this young man who still had so many miles to walk. "You know exactly what to do," I imagined him saying. "There's no need to be afraid. Keep walking."

When I reached James, he put his hands on my shoulders and welcomed me as his own son. "When you first walked through our home, I called you *Ashkíí Nagháhí*, which means Boy Who Walks. Now, you have a new name. You are *Hastíín Níha Nagháhí*, which means Man Who Walks for Us. You carried all of us with you on your walk, and now you can take our prayers with you into the water."

I didn't know what to do with that at the time, and just felt overwhelmed, but I see now, four years later, that the name is quite fitting, because it carries the crux of the whole thing in that last word. Us. The people were like my footsteps: Every one of them was necessary. Each contributed to the movement. We were inextricably bound together, giving and receiving, speaking and listening, seeing and being seen. We were all walking, side by side. We were the walk itself, all of us, every one. What a way to walk, for us. What a way to live, to live *for* others, experiencing light and dark and every shade in between so that the experiences might be an offering for someone else someday, so that my life might serve something greater than just myself. It was quite a name. I'd have to earn it anew each day, or else I wouldn't be able to call it my own.

The ocean couldn't wait any longer. It sent out a wave and took me by my feet, the final welcoming. I followed it, offering the cornmeal in my hands to the cold blue, remembering everyone who was with me even as I walked out into the water alone, whispering thank you, thank you, thank you, thank you.

Acknowledgments

There's an old hymn I'm hearing in my head as I sit down to begin offering my thanks: "Forgive the song that falls so low, beneath the gratitude I owe." These acknowledgments are a song like that one, sure to fall far below the heights of gratitude that I'll probably spend the rest of my life trying to live up to—but of course I sing the song anyway.

Thank you, Jay Allison, for welcoming me home, for believing in this book at a time when I'd forgotten how, and for offering key suggestions on the manuscript. Without your encouragement and collaboration, this story wouldn't be here. And thank you, Melissa Allison, for what you've created in that little golden kitchen of yours, and I'm not talking about the food, you know.

Thank you, Viki Merrick, for taking me under your guardian angel wing. Your reflections on the manuscript were critical, and your friendship throughout the process has been precious to me.

Thank you to Transom.org and the rest of my friends in Woods Hole, Massachusetts, especially Sydney Lewis, Sam Broun, Rob Rosenthal, Sarah Reynolds, Holly North, Matthias Bossi, Carla Kihlstedt, Connor Ahearn, Megan Zottoli, Tara DiGiovanni, Andrew Hicks, Elise Hugus, Daniel Cojanu, Serena Kabat-Zinn, and Hugh Birmingham of Coffee Obsession.

Thank you, Daniel Greenberg, for guiding me through the wilderness of the publishing industry. Thank you also to the whole team at the Levine Greenberg Rostan Literary Agency, especially Timothy Wojcik.

It took three editors to get this book written. Thank you, Courtney Young, for your instructive notes at the beginning. Thank you, Wylie O'Sullivan, for your essential eyes—this book needed you, and I am humbled by the mystery of how it found you. And thank you, Anton Mueller, for your passion from the very start, for your feedback on the manuscript, and for sharing the vision here at the end, as we begin again. Thank you also to my copy editor, Janet McDonald; my proofreader, Michael Lisk; Gleni Bartels; Jenna Dutton; Sarah New; and the entire team at Bloomsbury.

Thank you, Moriel Rothman-Zecher, for your grounding kindred spirit; Jacob Udell, for your deep brotherhood; and Rhiya Trivedi, for your fierce sisterhood, and thanks to all three of you for your comments on the first draft. Thank you, Roberto Ellis, for your *habibi* heart. Thank you, Penn Daniel, for getting my back like a maniac, and Chris Speers, for the home you've shared with me, inside and out. And thank you to all of my friends, without whom I'd be lost in some desert or swamp, especially to Tolly Taylor, Jim McNinch, Rob Bryan, Shantanu Tata, Lark Mason, Henry Toothman, Nicola Fleischer, Sean Gerstley, Josh Speers, Graeme Daubert, Alex Kennedy, Andrew Powers, Danny Metzger-Traber, Abe Katz, Bianca Giaever, Ellie Moore, Aliza Persing, Shaina Cantino, Susan Pincus, Ryan Richards, Martin Legg, Colette Garrigues, Erin Ferrentino, Greg Disterhoft, Andrew DiMola, Jannie Dziadzio, Nick Maione, Nate Kraus-Malett, Mariel Lugosch-Ecker, Maria Darrow, Omar Baena, and Nicholas Tuff.

Thank you, Will Speers, for teaching me at your round table, and for a critical pep talk when this book's future hung in the balance. Thank you, Sue Halpern, Dan Brayton, and Chris Shaw, for your close mentorship at Middlebury, and to all of the teachers who have touched my life in important ways, especially Barbara Patterson, Ginny Rogers, John Austin, Wes Goldsberry, Nigel Furlonge, Gretchen Hurtt, Peter McLean, Marc Cheban, Al Wood, David Miller, Ana Ramirez, Pam Brownlee, Donald Duffy, Michael Geisler, Carrie Wiebe, Tom Moran, John Bertolini, David Bain, Jeff Howarth, Mark Lapin, Steve Trombulak, and Rebecca Bradshaw. Thank you Nigel and Nicole Furlonge, for helping to craft such penetrating study questions for the paperback.

I wrote this book on the road over the course of several years. Thank you to everyone who put me up during the process, often for months at a time, providing me with everything I needed to write: Marian and Herb Furman in Camden, Alabama; Joan and Don Kinney in Ripton, Vermont; Quinn Kerrane and Dan O'Connell in Boulder, Colorado, with Liam, Finn, and Rowan; Joni Glazebrook in Woods Hole, Massachusetts; and Brian Pardini and Patty Baldwin in Erie, Pennsylvania. I probably should have paid rent for the amount of time I spent at the Mushrooms Café in Chadds Ford, Pennsylvania—thank you, Meryle Voytilla and Jen Tillman.

The Jentel Artist Residency Program in Banner, Wyoming, gave me a month of perfect conditions in which to write. Thank you to Neltje, Mary Jane Edwards, Lynn Reeves, and Melissa Albrecht, and to my fellow residents: John Radtke, Jean Koeller, Kathleen McCloud, Barbara Marks, and especially Amelia Whitcomb, for zapping this book with the high-voltage defibrillator of your encouragement when its heart stopped—you are fantastic in all ways, my friend.

Thank you, Darryl Slim, for your beautiful garden, and for pointing me back to mine. Thank you to Ashley Gates Jansen, for being there right when I was looking for you, and even before, and now, and to Rob Jansen, for holding it down like you do. Thank you, Boyd Varty, for helping me fall apart at a critical moment in this book's unfolding, and to Todd McCormack, for advising me at several important junctures throughout the process. Thank you to Gale Flynn, for your morning prayers, and to Sharon Simmons, Jim and Nancy Bryan, Jim and Mary Murphy, Sheila and David Daskovsky, Alice Edwards and Jamie Borowicz, Gus and Kathy Sermas, Meg and Bill Maley, Willy Moton, Barbara Buchmann, Carol Burger, and Nancy Syburg, for rooting me on.

Thank you to Emma Lennon and the whole family (John, Judy, Rachel, and Grace) for taking me in as one of your own, and thank you, John Carver, for sharing your work with me, and then setting me off to sail my own seas.

Thank you, Pete McLean, for showing up big, and to the crews at Brookfield Farm and Book & Plow Farm in Amherst, Massachusetts, for welcoming me home when, once again, I had no idea where home was anymore, especially Dan Kaplan and Karen Romanowski, Tobin Porter-Brown, Zoe Abram, Leila Tunnell, Jake Mazar, and Will Van Heuvelen. Thank you to Trellis Stepter, for your song, and to Tim Eriksen and Zoë Darrow, for each of yours.

Thank you, Hannah Jacobson-Hardy, for your royal kindness and company.

To Walt Whitman, Rainer Maria Rilke, and Kahlil Gibran: thank God for each one of you. And to all of the other poets and teachers I've never met, the living and the dead, thank you for generously expressing your human processes. Lights in the dark, you lead me to my own.

Thank you to my grandparents, Francis and Mary Jornlin, Vincent Theisen, and Mark and Joan Forsthoefel; and to all of my grandmothers and grandfathers. Thank you to my godfather, Len Jornlin; to my godmother, Mary Ellen Keyes; and to all of my aunts and uncles, especially Frank Jornlin, for advising me through the turbulence.

Thank you to my dad, Tom Forsthoefel, for celebrating me the way you do, for supporting me in my walk, and for cheering me on in this book. Needless to say, none of this would have happened without you, and for that—for you—I am grateful. Thank you to my stepmother, Beth Gylys, for your encouragement and support.

Thank you, Caitlin, for being my sister. Thank you, Luke, for being my brother. It's impossible to imagine walking any of this without you. What a gift this is, what gifts you are.

And Mom, good God you are one hell of a mother. Thank you beyond thank you for everything you've lived, everything you've given, and everything you are. This has been a profound chapter in whatever book we've been writing together over the course of ages. Walk in beauty, Therese Marie.

And finally, thank you to everyone I met on my walk—far too many to count here, but you are each named on my blog—for teaching me what I was asking to learn, showing me what I needed to see, and telling me what I was open to hear, day after day after day. I'll never know who I'd be without you, but I suspect you saved my life in more ways than I can imagine. Truly, I am humbled to have walked with you for a while, and know that I am walking with you still, and will for the rest of my days.

Selected Bibliography

Gibran, Kahlil. *The Prophet*. New York: Alfred A. Knopf, 2003. Print.

Holmes, James. James Holmes 12CR1522 People's Exhibit #341. http://extras.denverpost.com/trial/docs/notebook.pdf.

Rilke, Rainer Maria. *Letters to a Young Poet*. Ed. Stephen Mitchell. New York: Vintage, 1984. Print.

Rilke, Rainer Maria. *Rilke's Book of Hours: Love Poems to God*. Translated by Anita Barrows and Joanna Macy. New York: Riverhead Books, 1997. Print.

Whitman, Walt. *Leaves of Grass*. Ed. Malcolm Cowley. 1855 ed. New York: Penguin, 1986. Print.

Study Questions for *Walking to Listen*

1. At the outset of his walk, Andrew is aware of the privileges he has in undertaking the project of walking across America to listen. He suggests these privileges are connected to his "whiteness, and how my freedom of movement was largely predicated on my skin color" (page 4). Furthermore, when he meditates on the reality of living in America for many citizens, he argues, "That's what racism and sexism looked like today, that surreptitiously yet overwhelmingly lopsided distribution of privilege" (page 5). To what extent does Andrew's experience throughout his walk confirm, but also complicate, the very notions of privilege that he outlines at the beginning of the book?

2. Andrew notes, "I didn't take a smartphone. I knew I'd just end up nose-down, following the blue dot across the entire continent. There was magic in not knowing, a transformation of the unremarkable into the sublime" (page 48). What impact does Andrew's choice not to take a smartphone have on the experience he has while on this journey, both with himself and with others? What evidence do you see in the text that suggests a "transformation of the unremarkable into the sublime"?

3. One of the rules Andrew created for himself during the walk was to see everyone as extraordinary. "I'd view everyone as a

teacher of some sort" (page 26). Imagine living with this rule for a day. How might your day look if you saw everyone as your teacher? What might be challenging about living with this rule? Identify one of Andrew's teachers on the road. Explain the nature of their teaching and why they stood out to you.

4. Andrew carries "little polished pebbles" (page 54) called vogesite stones along his journey. What do you see as the significance of his choice to carry the vogesite stones and then share them with people? In his very carrying of the vogesite stones, what do you believe Andrew is anticipating as he walks to listen?

5. There is an implicit, and sometimes explicit, discourse in the text about trust, vulnerability, and the goodness of humans (page 63). What and whom did Andrew have to trust on his walk? What are the potential consequences of trusting others? Are there consequences, too, involved with not trusting others? What does *Walking to Listen* suggest about the essential nature of humanity?

6. Andrew asks the reader to imagine, through his own journey across America, what it means to listen, to be present in the moment. How does *Walking to Listen* describe these moments of being present and attentive? How does being present allow Andrew to have an experience that he may have otherwise missed? What does Andrew learn about listening along the way? How does his sign—"Walking to Listen"—influence his interactions with the world? What are some of the invisible signs you wear, and why?

7. Andrew explores concepts of silence, listening, and the dynamic

of the inside-outside self in *Walking to Listen*—particularly in the sections of the book where he is walking in the American South. While in Selma, he references the "appalling silence of the good people," reflecting on a quote from Dr. Martin Luther King (page 79), and he grapples with staying quiet, "disgusted at my silence, stunned by the power of my fear" (page 149). Why is Andrew disgusted by his silence? Under what circumstances might you yourself decide to speak up and under what circumstances might you stay silent?

8. Andrew meditates on the power of perception as it relates to one's experiences of self, other, and the world in *Walking to Listen*. He quotes Walt Whitman on this topic: "All architecture is what you do to it when you look upon it" (page 286). What does this mean? Find an example in the text in which perception influences reality. How is this dynamic connected to what Woody Curry tells Andrew in Maryland (page 16): "You see your life as being at the whims of some power greater than you, but I want to know, what fucking power is there in the universe greater than you when you can accept or reject any damn thing coming at you?"

9. Andrew writes about the limits to listening (page 240). Here he quotes Walt Whitman again, who argues, "You shall listen to all sides and filter them from yourself." Later, Andrew meets a young man, who describes himself as the messiah, on the side of the road. After walking with "the messiah" for some time, Andrew decides to walk ahead of the young man, deciding not to listen anymore (page 292). Under what circumstances does Andrew choose not to listen? Why? What are the conditions in which you choose not to listen?

10. Andrew leaves home with the intention to come of age, or to learn about coming of age. Describe the experiences of adolescence, adulthood, and the threshold between the two. What is coming of age? In what ways does Andrew change over the course of *Walking to Listen*? What moments in the text might you point to as a catalyst for and evidence of how Andrew has changed? What primary elements of his journey may have contributed to an experience of transformation?

11. Identify moments in the text when Andrew encountered pain, in himself or in the people he met. What happened in those moments? How did he respond, or not respond? What is suffering to you? How might it be a part of coming of age?

12. What does it mean to "turn the lens on yourself" (page 260), as Andrew's college professor suggests he do? How might this lens-turning connect to the concept of *hózhó* that Andrew encounters when he connects with the Navajo community (page 284)?

13. How would you answer Jean-Sébastien's question to Andrew (page 313): "What's your idea of the perfect life? Your perfect life?"

14. Near the end of the book, Andrew quotes Rainer Maria Rilke: "What is necessary, after all, is only this: solitude, vast inner solitude. To walk inside yourself and meet no one for hours— that is what you must be able to attain" (page 358). Andrew oscillates between having moments of solitude on his journey

and connecting with people he's never met before while listening deeply. What role does solitude play in Andrew's journey? How is this solitude important to Andrew as he then encounters the people he meets? Finally, what do Rilke's words mean to you personally?

A Note on the Author

Andrew Forsthoefel is a writer and speaker based in Northampton, Massachusetts. After graduating from Middlebury College in 2011 with a degree in environmental studies, he spent eleven months walking across the United States, gathering stories along the way.

To hear the voices of some of the people who appear in this book, visit Transom.org (transom.org/2013/walking-across-america-advice-for-young-man) and Cowbird.com (cowbird.com/collection/walkingacrossamerica). To follow the author, visit Walkingtolisten.com.